BC

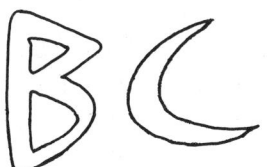

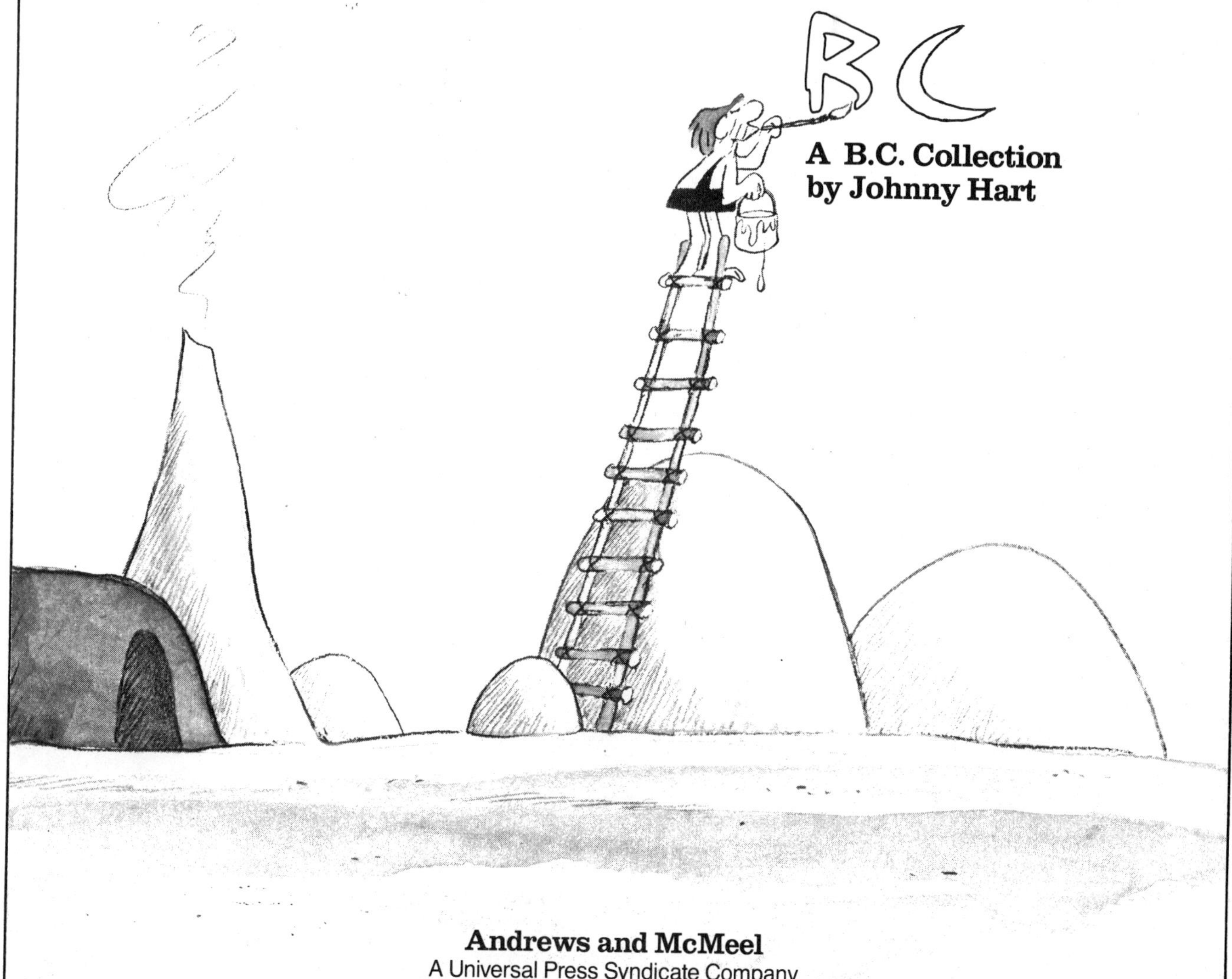
BC

A B.C. Collection
by Johnny Hart

Andrews and McMeel
A Universal Press Syndicate Company
Kansas City • New York

B.C. is syndicated internationally by Creators Syndicate, Inc.

B.C. copyright © 1990 by Creators Syndicate, Inc. All rights reserved. Printed in the United States of America. No part of this book may be used or reproduced in any manner whatsoever without written permission except in the context of reviews. For information, write Andrews and McMeel, a Universal Press Syndicate Company, 4900 Main Street, Kansas City, Missouri 64112.

ISBN: 0-8362-1818-3

Library of Congress Catalog Card Number: 89-82502

——————— ATTENTION: SCHOOLS AND BUSINESSES ———————

Andrews and McMeel books are available at quantity discounts with bulk purchase for educational, business, or sales promotional use. For information, please write to: Special Sales Department, Andrews and McMeel, 4900 Main Street, Kansas City, Missouri 64112.

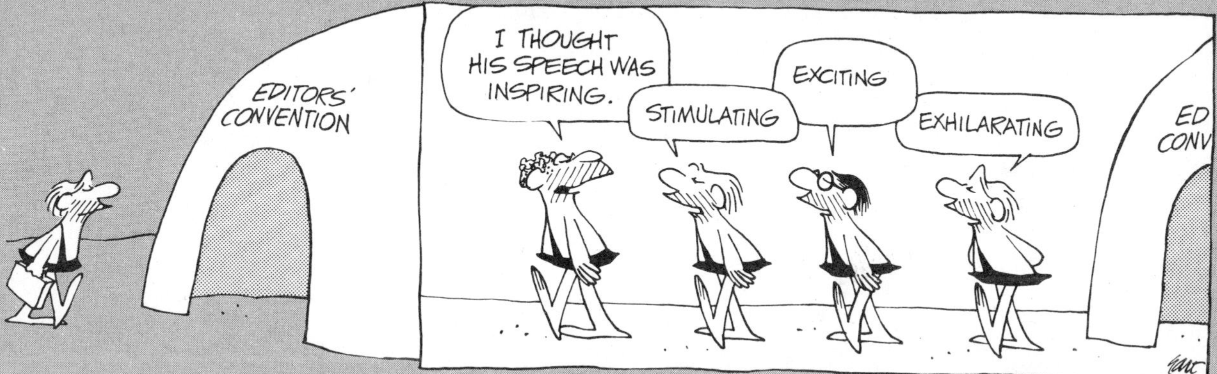
EDITORS' CONVENTION
I THOUGHT HIS SPEECH WAS INSPIRING.
STIMULATING
EXCITING
EXHILARATING
ED CONV

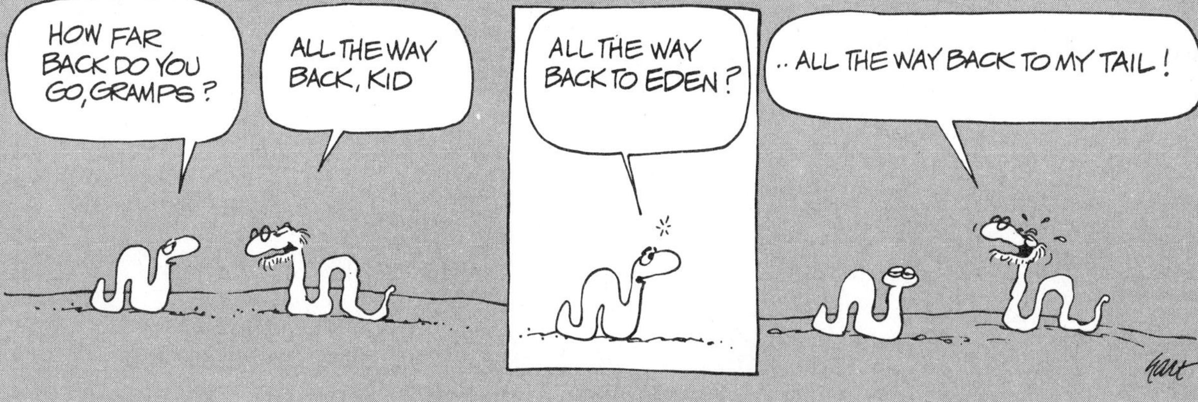
HOW FAR BACK DO YOU GO, GRAMPS ?
ALL THE WAY BACK, KID
ALL THE WAY BACK TO EDEN ?
.. ALL THE WAY BACK TO MY TAIL !

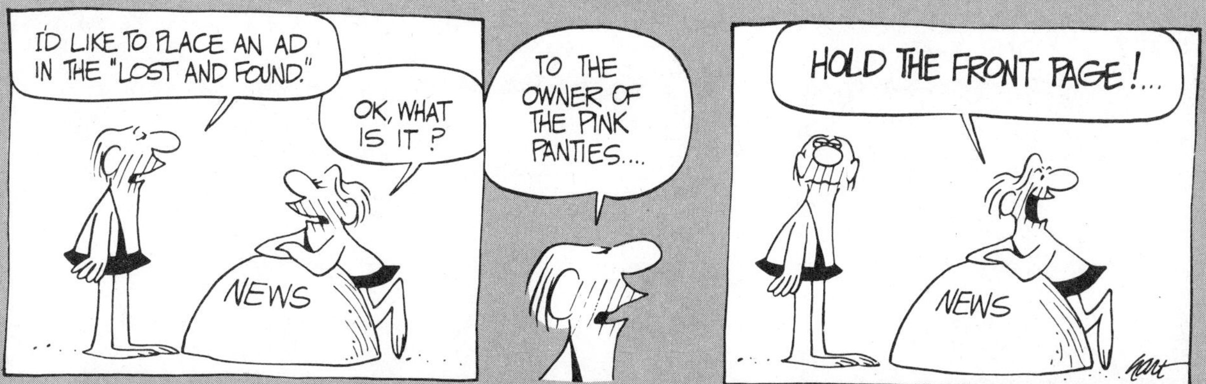
I'D LIKE TO PLACE AN AD IN THE "LOST AND FOUND."
OK, WHAT IS IT ?
NEWS
TO THE OWNER OF THE PINK PANTIES....
HOLD THE FRONT PAGE !...
NEWS

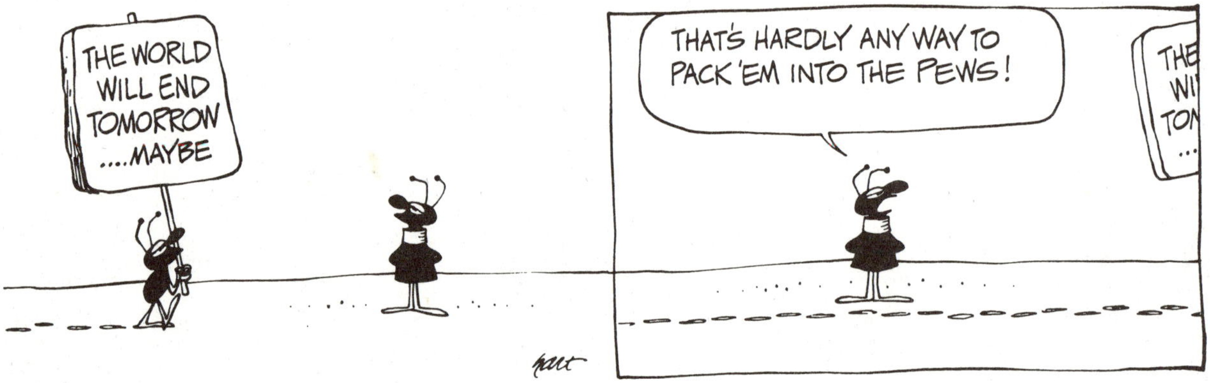
THE WORLD WILL END TOMORROW ....MAYBE
THAT'S HARDLY ANY WAY TO PACK 'EM INTO THE PEWS!

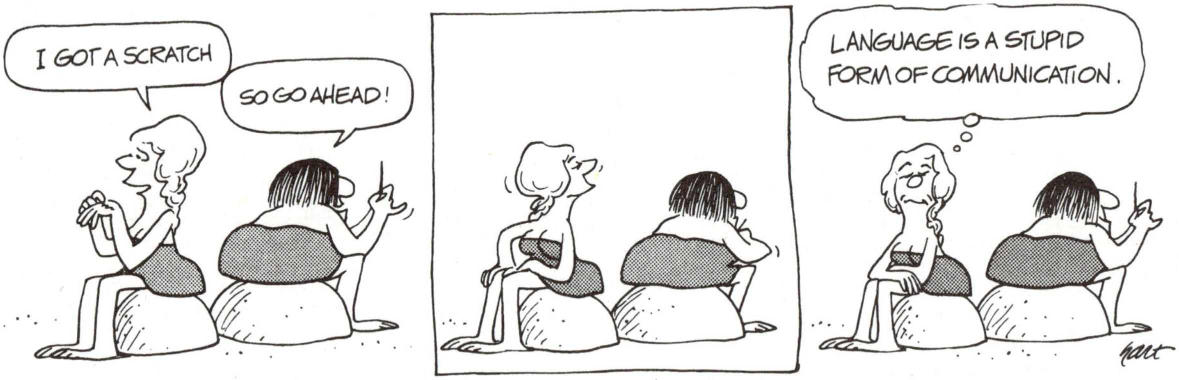
I GOT A SCRATCH
SO GO AHEAD!
LANGUAGE IS A STUPID FORM OF COMMUNICATION.

Z
GET OFF MY BACK!

I TOOK A MIDNIGHT STROLL WITH THOR LAST NIGHT.
DID HE GIVE YOU HIS 'COME HITHER' LOOK?
NOT EXACTLY...
MORE LIKE STAY THITHER.

HAS YOUR TEAM EVER HAD A GOLD GLOVE WINNER ?
NO, ...BUT WE HAD A RUNNER-UP FOR THE 'TIN MITT' !
hart

DO IT FOR GOD,
AND IT WORKS FOR GOOD.
DO IT FOR GOOD.
AND IT WORKS FOR GOD.

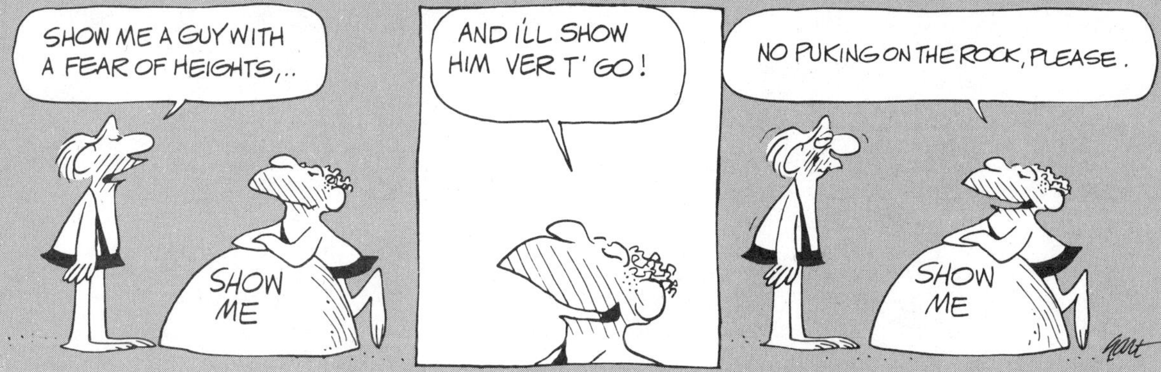
SHOW ME A GUY WITH A FEAR OF HEIGHTS, ..
SHOW ME
AND I'LL SHOW HIM VER T' GO!
NO PUKING ON THE ROCK, PLEASE.
SHOW ME

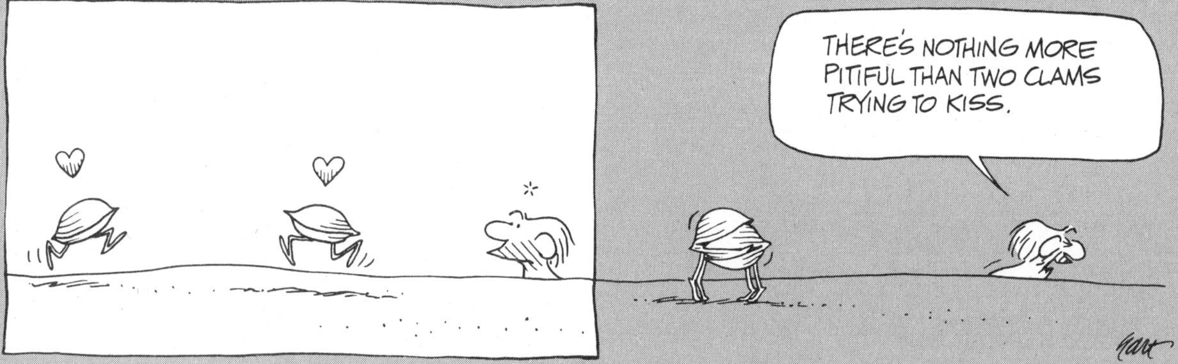
THERE'S NOTHING MORE PITIFUL THAN TWO CLAMS TRYING TO KISS.

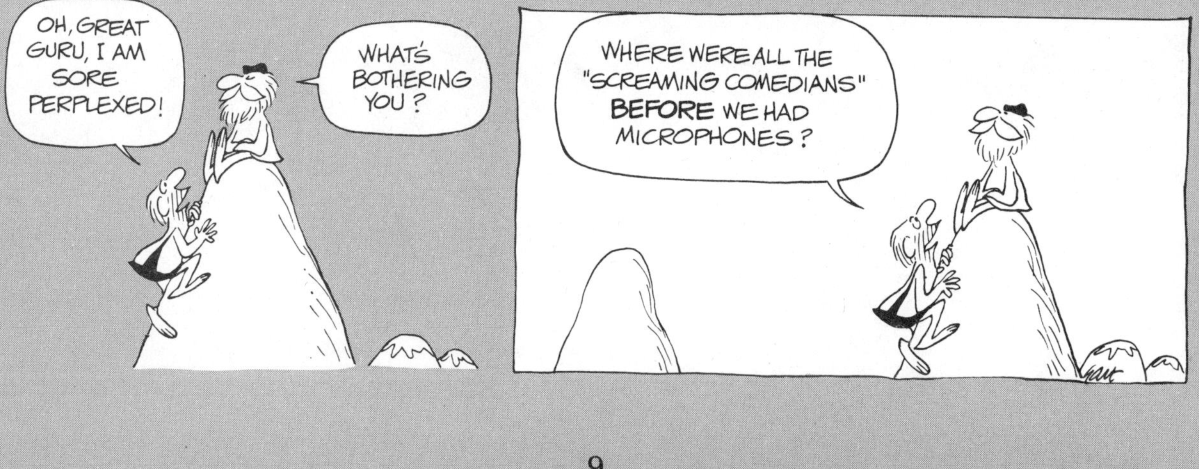
OH, GREAT GURU, I AM SORE PERPLEXED!
WHAT'S BOTHERING YOU?
WHERE WERE ALL THE "SCREAMING COMEDIANS" **BEFORE** WE HAD MICROPHONES?

HOW COME NONE OF YOUR PLAYERS KNOW HOW TO BUNT ?
BUNT ?...
hart

WHAT'S THE AQUATIC STATUS OF THE CREEK, CLUMSY ?
THE SNAIL DARTERS ARE DARTING, THE FLOUNDERS ARE FLOUNDERING BUT THE FROGS HAVE ALL CROAKED !
...YET THE MUD IS LITERALLY TEEMING WITH MUD PUPPIES..
hart

RUMBLE
RUMBLE

MY GUESS IS, IT'S A DOOR TO SOME PRIMITIVE CHAMBER FOR STORING ICE.

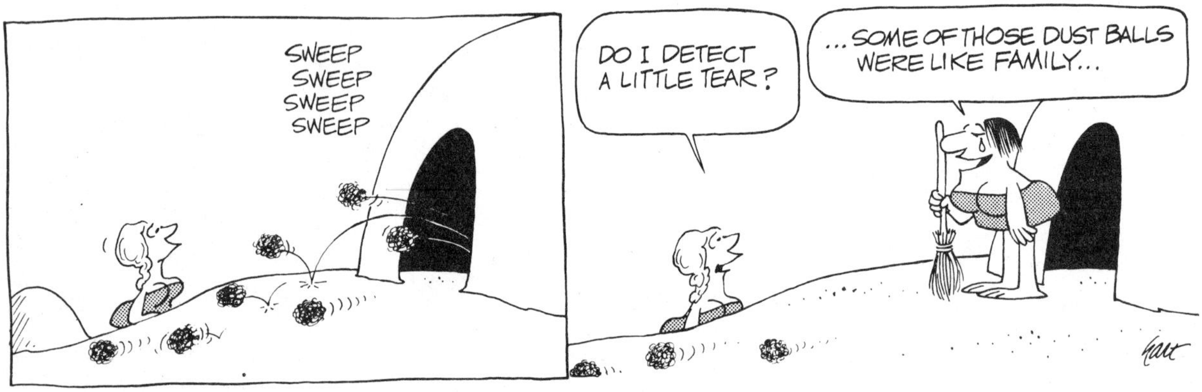
SWEEP
SWEEP
SWEEP
SWEEP
DO I DETECT A LITTLE TEAR?
...SOME OF THOSE DUST BALLS WERE LIKE FAMILY...

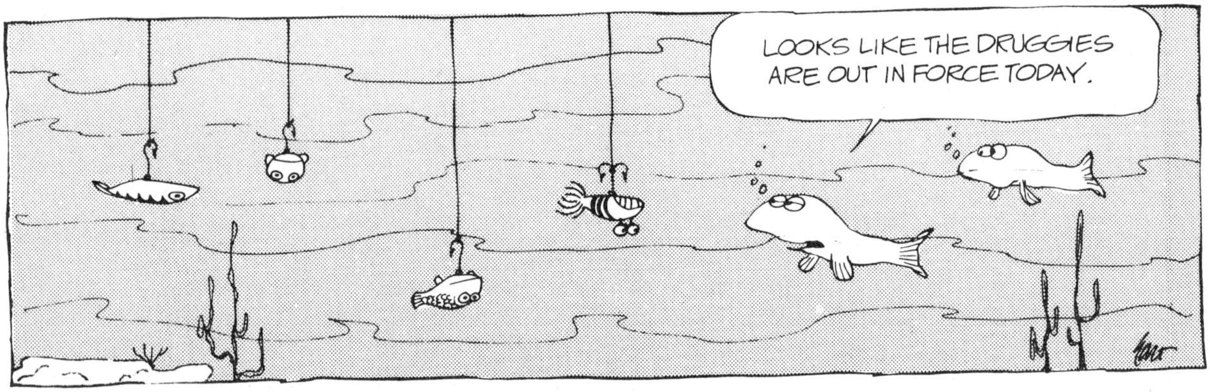
LOOKS LIKE THE DRUGGIES ARE OUT IN FORCE TODAY.

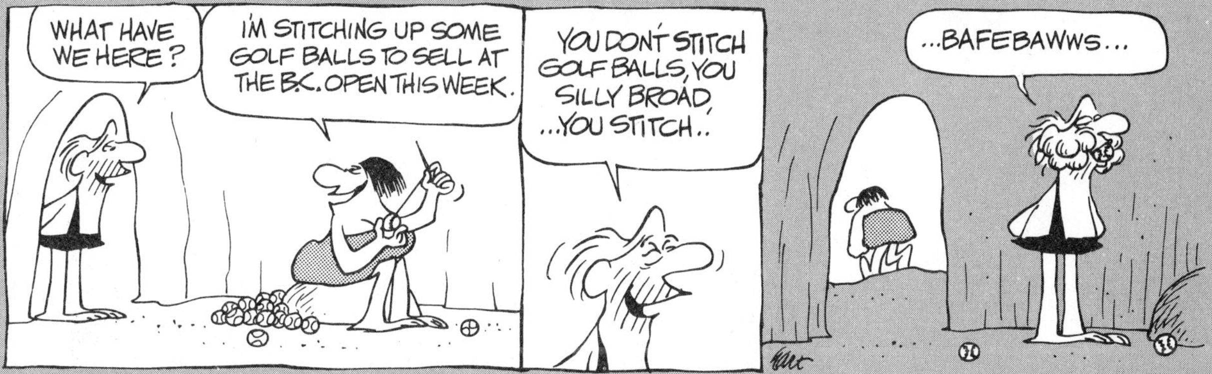
WHAT HAVE WE HERE?
I'M STITCHING UP SOME GOLF BALLS TO SELL AT THE B.C. OPEN THIS WEEK.
YOU DON'T STITCH GOLF BALLS, YOU SILLY BROAD, ...YOU STITCH..
...BAFEBAWWS...

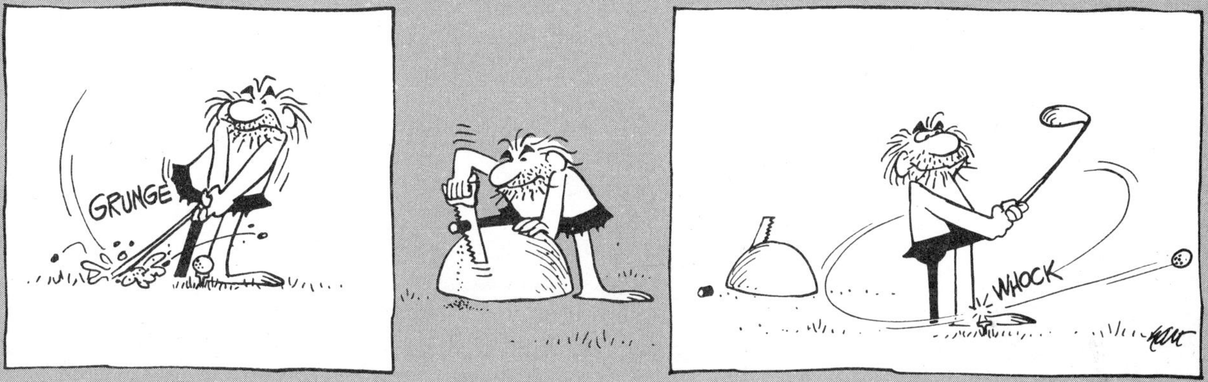
GRUNGE
WHOCK

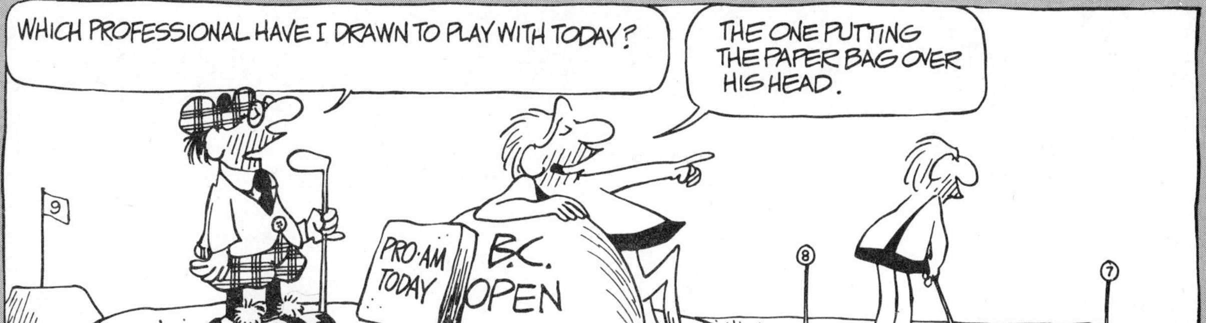
WHICH PROFESSIONAL HAVE I DRAWN TO PLAY WITH TODAY?
THE ONE PUTTING THE PAPER BAG OVER HIS HEAD.
9
PRO·AM TODAY
B.C. OPEN
8
7

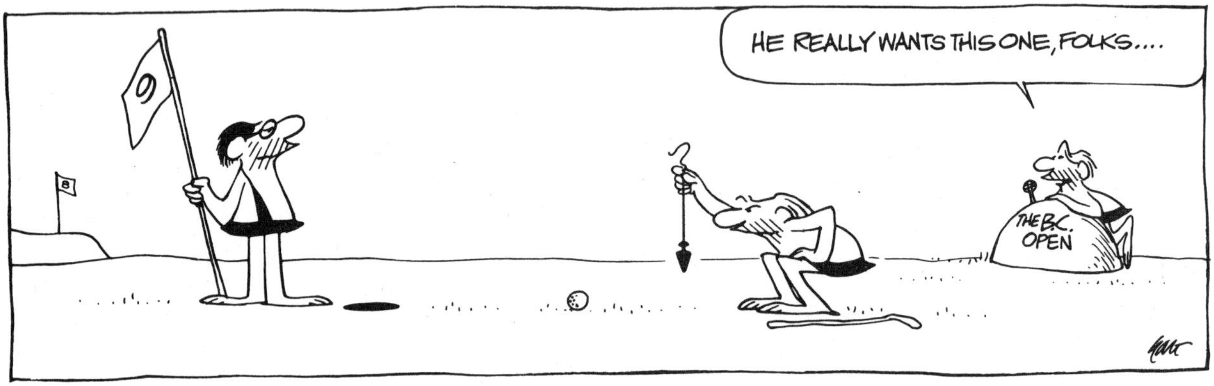
HE REALLY WANTS THIS ONE, FOLKS....
THE B.C. OPEN

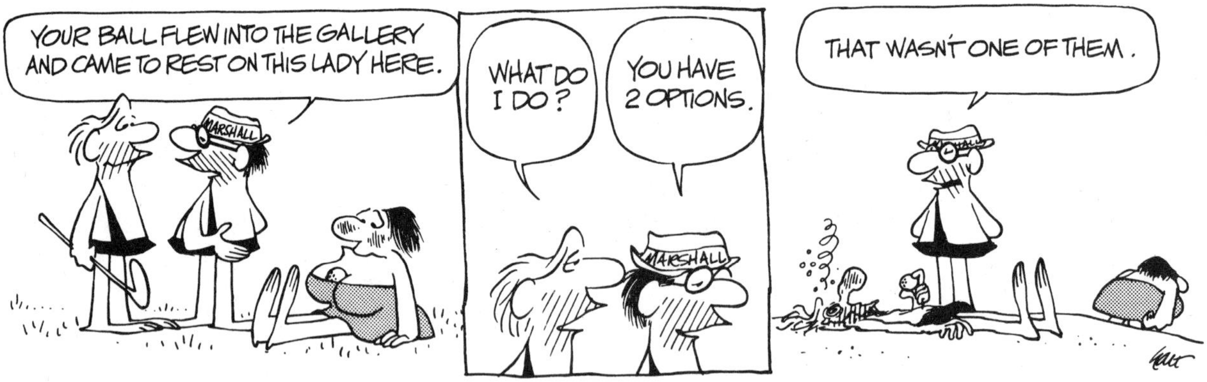
YOUR BALL FLEW INTO THE GALLERY AND CAME TO REST ON THIS LADY HERE.
MARSHALL
WHAT DO I DO?
YOU HAVE 2 OPTIONS.
MARSHALL
THAT WASN'T ONE OF THEM.

DO YOU REALIZE YOU'RE MINUS 14 GOING INTO THE FINAL ROUND ?
I KNOW.... I'M SORRY.
..SORRY...?
THE DARN THING KEEPS FALLING IN THE HOLE !

HOW'D YOU MAKE OUT IN THE 'CLOSEST TO THE PIN' CONTEST ?
NOT TOO GOOD.
WHAT'S THE TROPHY FOR ?
"FURTHEST FROM CIVILIZATION."

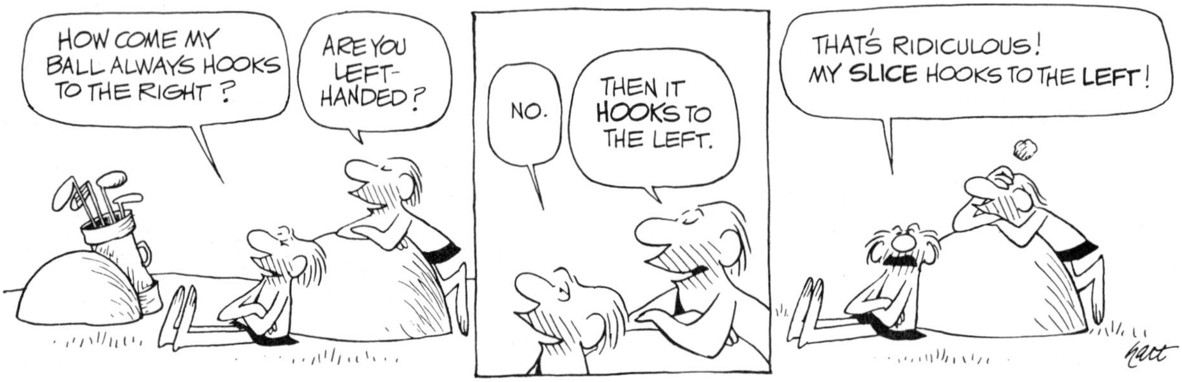
HOW COME MY BALL ALWAYS HOOKS TO THE RIGHT ?
ARE YOU LEFT-HANDED ?
NO.
THEN IT HOOKS TO THE LEFT.
THAT'S RIDICULOUS! MY SLICE HOOKS TO THE LEFT!

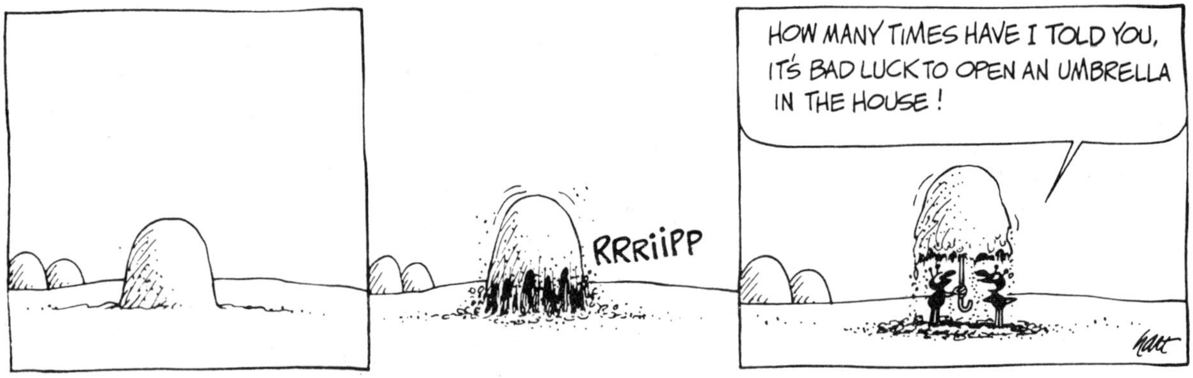
RRRiiPP
HOW MANY TIMES HAVE I TOLD YOU, IT'S BAD LUCK TO OPEN AN UMBRELLA IN THE HOUSE!

HERE'S A BEAUTY ... I CAUGHT A 20-LB. BASS ON ONE OF THESE.
CLUMSY'S BAIT SHOP
...A BASS ACTUALLY STRUCK AT A THING LIKE THAT?
JUST BETWEEN YOU AND ME... HE LAUGHED HIMSELF TO DEATH.
CLUMSY'S BAIT SHOP
hart

LET'S 'DO LUNCH' TOMORROW.
I'LL 'DO LUNCH' IF YOU 'DO CHECK'
hart

glean n.
WILEY'S DICTIONARY
COROR YOU GET WHEN YOU MIX BRUE AND YERROW
WILEY'S DICTIONARY
hart

I'VE INVENTED A PERPETUAL MOTION MACHINE.
WHERE IS IT ?
PATENT OFFICE
PARKED OUTSIDE IN A NO STOPPING ZONE.
PATENT OFFICE

Z
PUNT

YOUR FIELD GOAL KICKER'S IN QUITE A SLUMP! 0 FOR 34.
CAN'T SAY HE DIDN'T WARN ME.
COACH
HOW'S THAT?
I ASKED HIM IF HE WAS HAPPY WITH HIS SALARY AND HE SAID, "I CAN'T KICK."
COACH

NEVER ENTER A SUBWAY WHERE THE SECURITY GUARD HAS GRAFFITI ON HIS FACE
FREE ADVICE

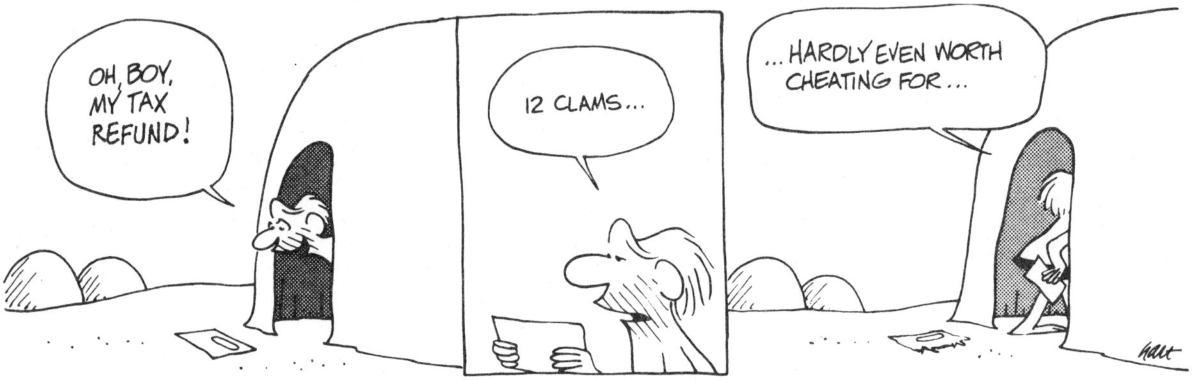
OH, BOY, MY TAX REFUND!
12 CLAMS...
...HARDLY EVEN WORTH CHEATING FOR...

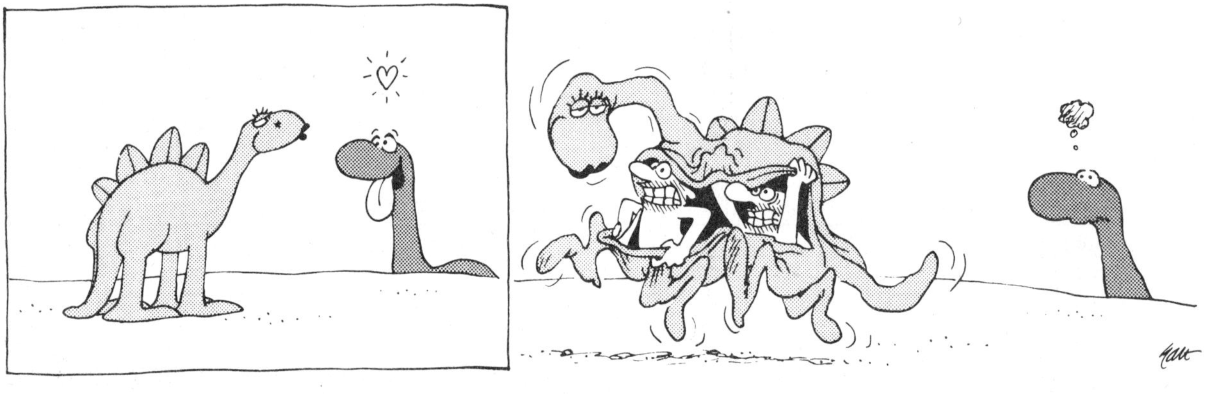

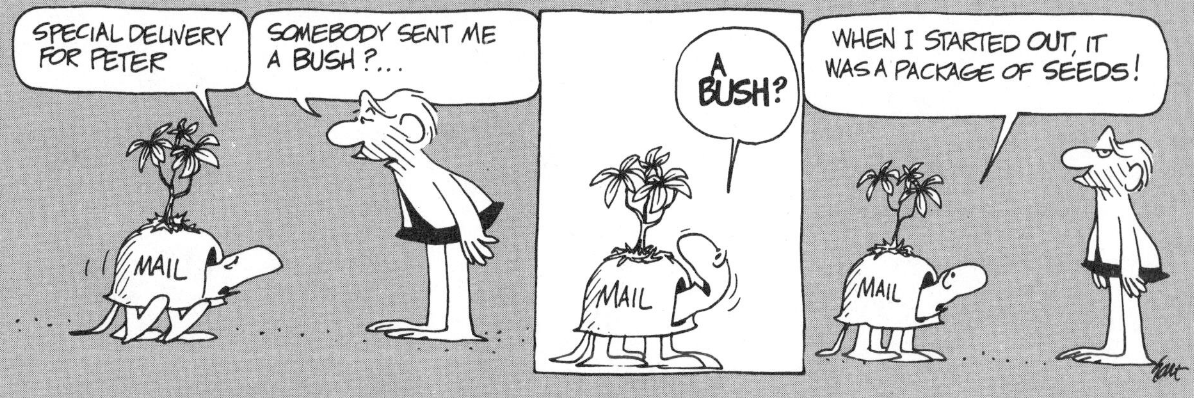
SPECIAL DELIVERY FOR PETER
SOMEBODY SENT ME A BUSH ?...
A BUSH?
WHEN I STARTED OUT, IT WAS A PACKAGE OF SEEDS!

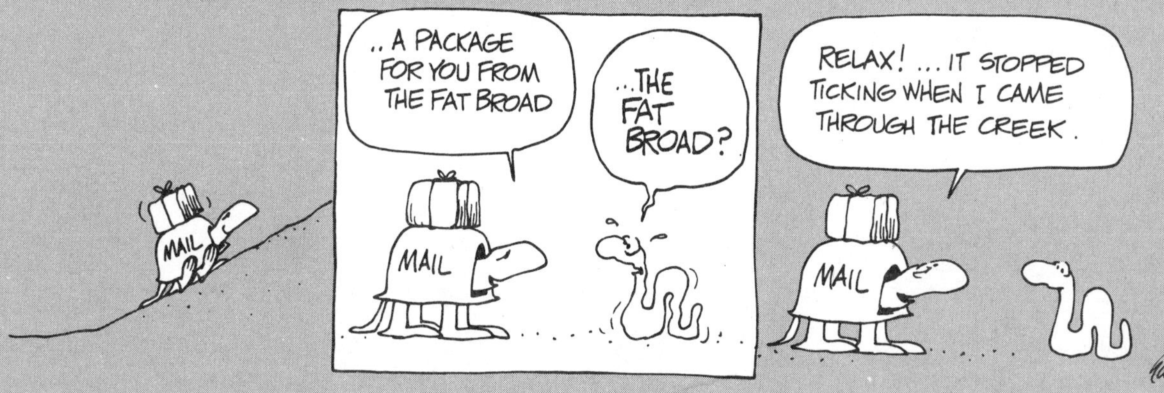
.. A PACKAGE FOR YOU FROM THE FAT BROAD
...THE FAT BROAD?
RELAX! ... IT STOPPED TICKING WHEN I CAME THROUGH THE CREEK.

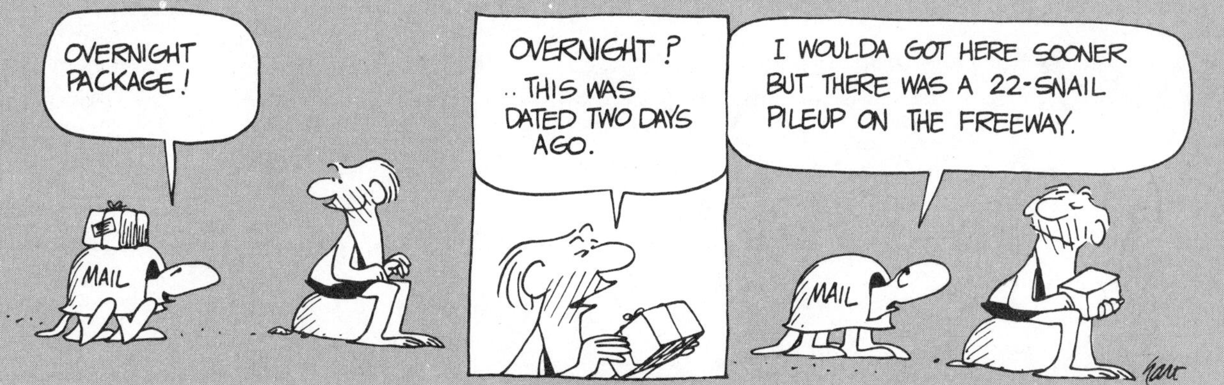
OVERNIGHT PACKAGE!
OVERNIGHT ? .. THIS WAS DATED TWO DAYS AGO.
I WOULDA GOT HERE SOONER BUT THERE WAS A 22-SNAIL PILEUP ON THE FREEWAY.

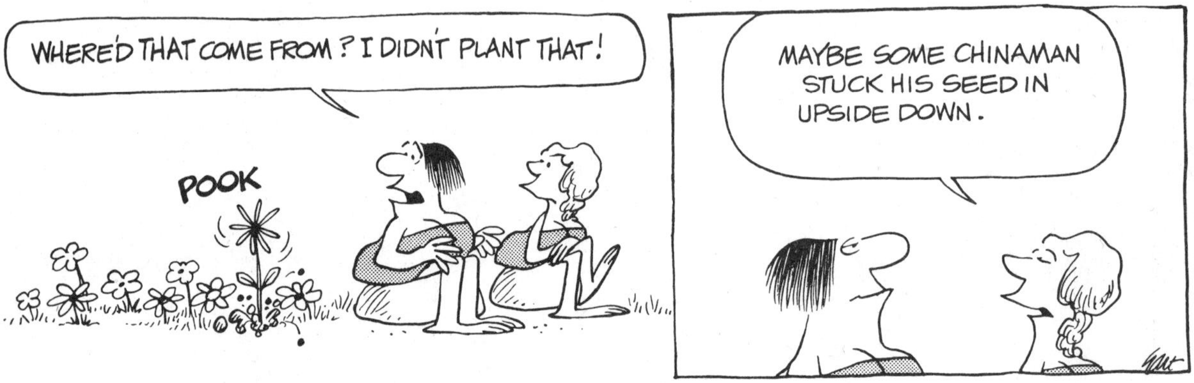
WHERE'D THAT COME FROM ? I DIDN'T PLANT THAT !
POOK
MAYBE SOME CHINAMAN STUCK HIS SEED IN UPSIDE DOWN.

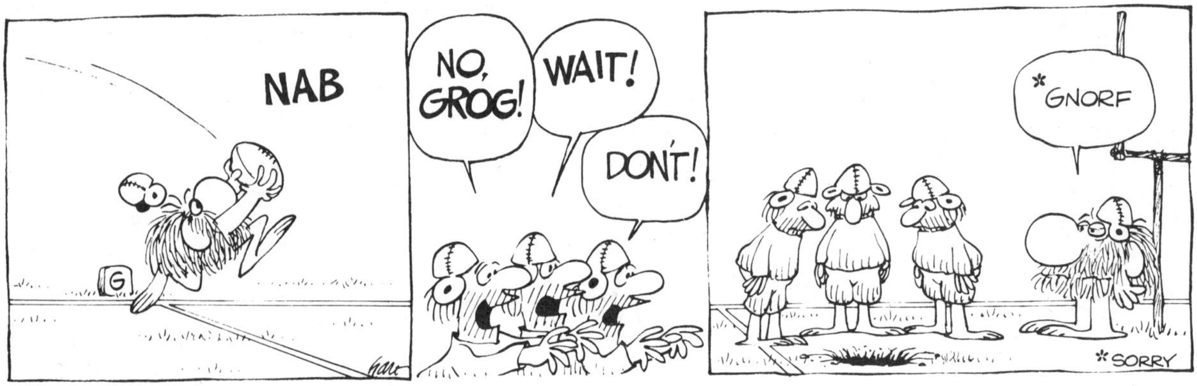
NAB
NO, GROG!
WAIT!
DON'T!
*GNORF
*SORRY

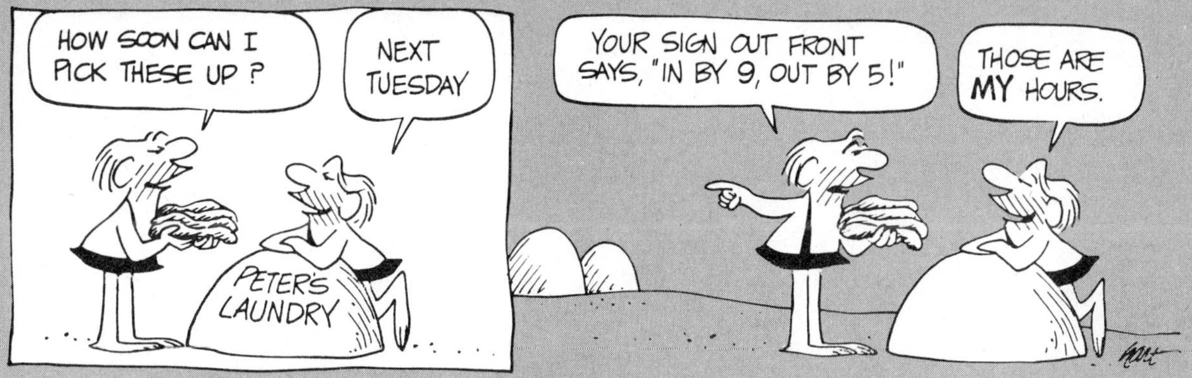
HOW SOON CAN I PICK THESE UP ?
NEXT TUESDAY
PETER'S LAUNDRY
YOUR SIGN OUT FRONT SAYS, "IN BY 9, OUT BY 5!"
THOSE ARE MY HOURS.

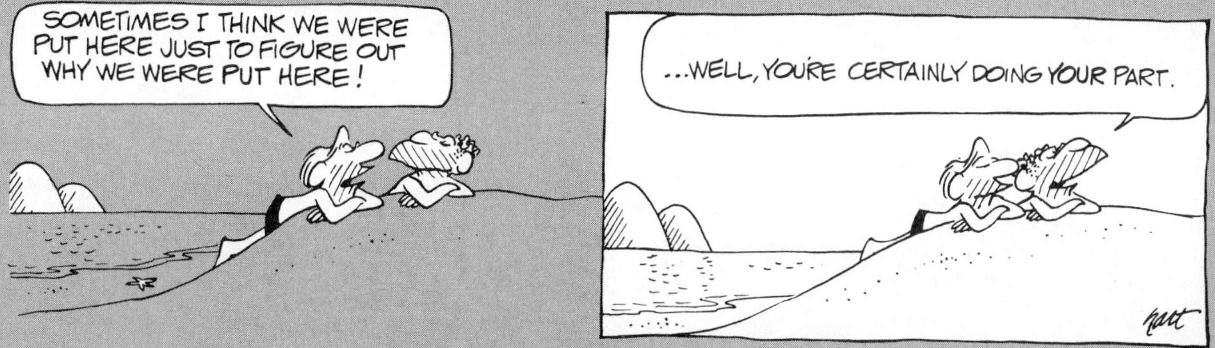
SOMETIMES I THINK WE WERE PUT HERE JUST TO FIGURE OUT WHY WE WERE PUT HERE!
...WELL, YOU'RE CERTAINLY DOING YOUR PART.

JAKE!... WHAT ARE YOU DOING WITH THAT HUSSY ?
I THOUGHT WE AGREED ON A TRYOUT SEPARATION .
THAT'S TRIAL !

WHAT'S THAT ON YOUR FACE ?
A BEAUTY MARK. IT DRIVES MEN WILD.
.. SO I TOLD HER ABOUT THIS GREAT SALVE FOR THE ZITS ... AND SUDDENLY EVERYTHING WENT BLACK .

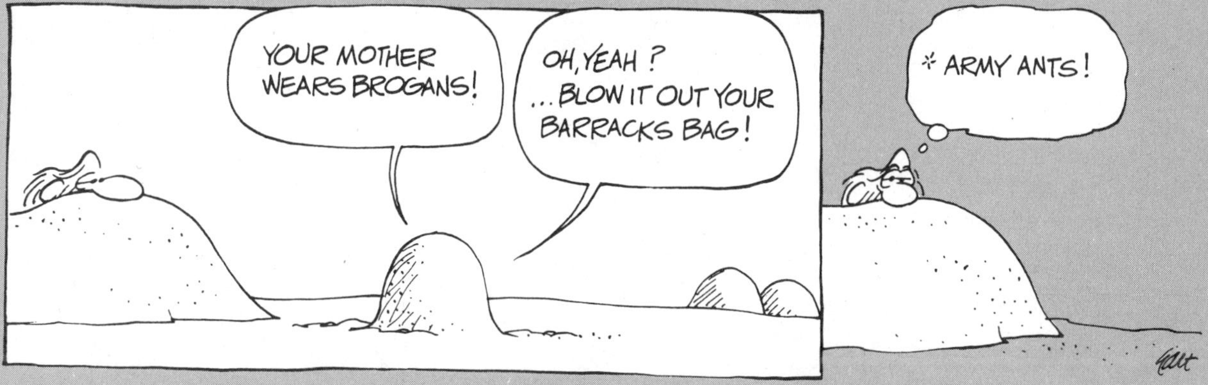
YOUR MOTHER WEARS BROGANS!
OH, YEAH ? ...BLOW IT OUT YOUR BARRACKS BAG!
* ARMY ANTS!

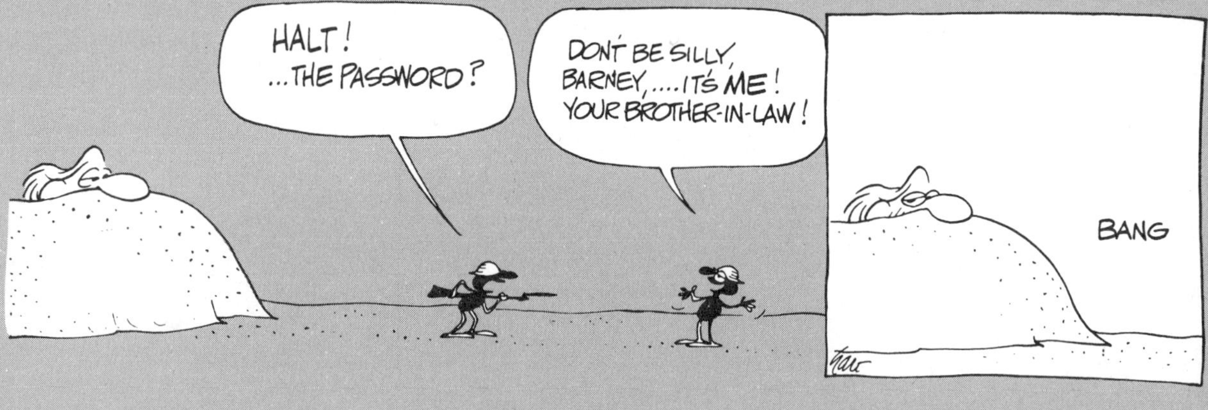
HALT! ...THE PASSWORD?
DON'T BE SILLY, BARNEY,....IT'S ME! YOUR BROTHER-IN-LAW!
BANG

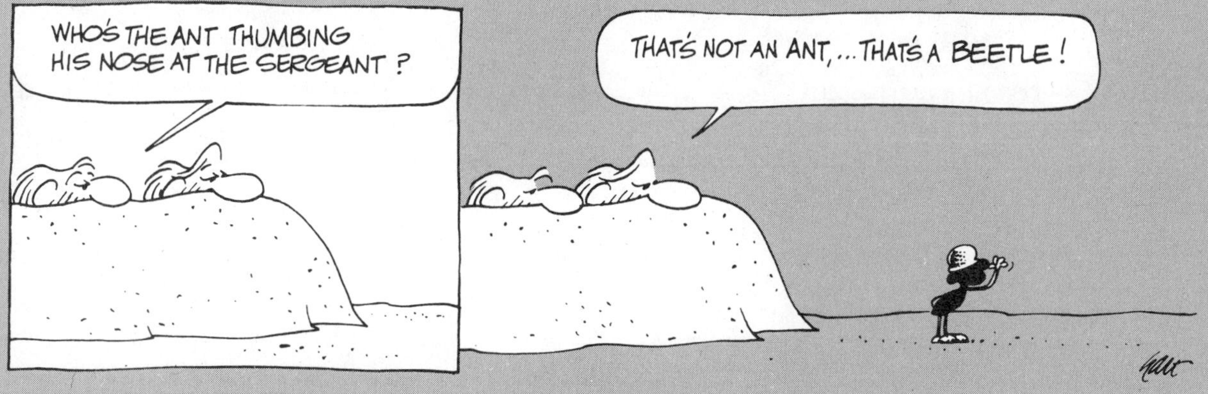
WHO'S THE ANT THUMBING HIS NOSE AT THE SERGEANT ?
THAT'S NOT AN ANT,...THAT'S A BEETLE!

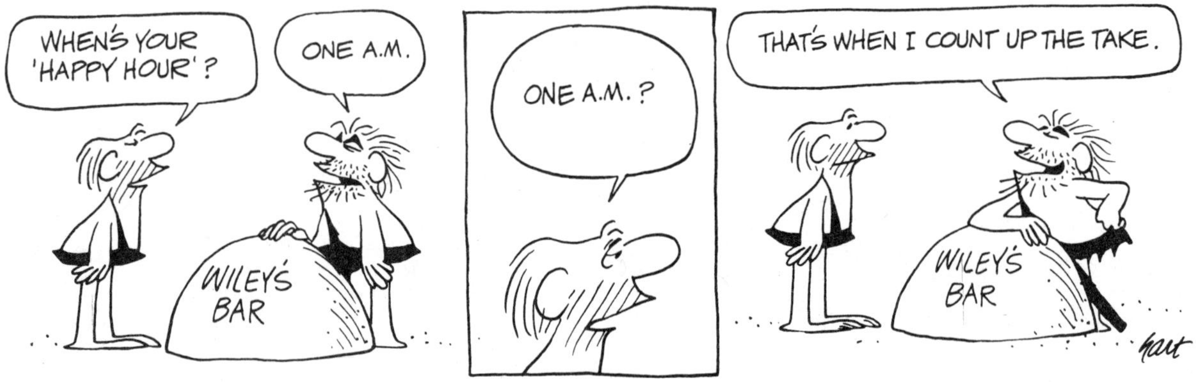
WHEN'S YOUR 'HAPPY HOUR'?
ONE A.M.
WILEY'S BAR
ONE A.M.?
THAT'S WHEN I COUNT UP THE TAKE.
WILEY'S BAR
hart

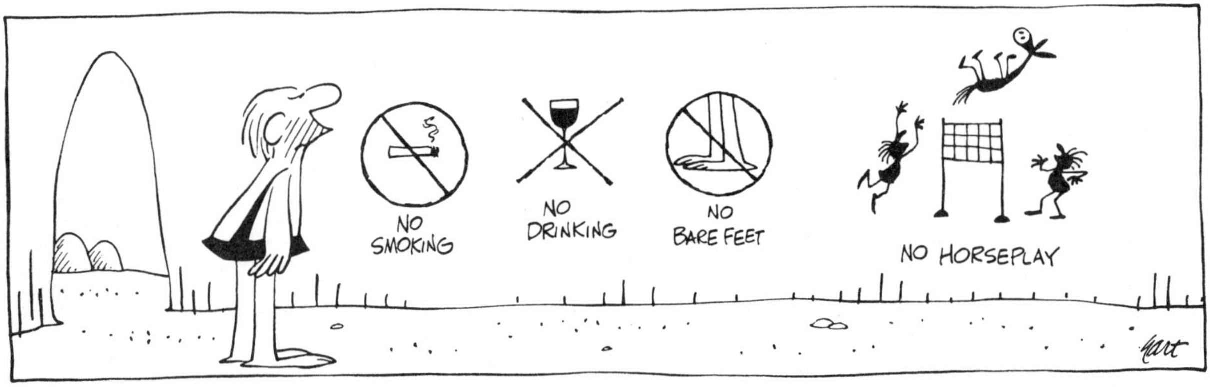
NO SMOKING
NO DRINKING
NO BARE FEET
NO HORSEPLAY
hart

IDLE-CHATTER
THE BOOK OF PHRASES
WHAT YOUR CAR MAKES AT A RED LIGHT WHEN YOUR PISTONS ARE SHOT.
THE BOOK OF PHRASES

I CAME FROM A REALLY DULL TOWN.
HOW DULL WAS IT ?
THE HIGHLIGHT OF THE YEAR WAS THE "REMEMBERING THE NAME OF THE TOWN CONTEST."

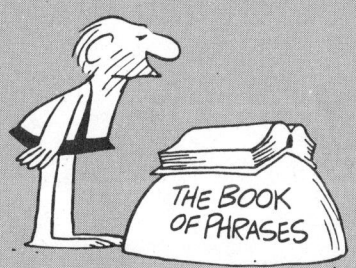

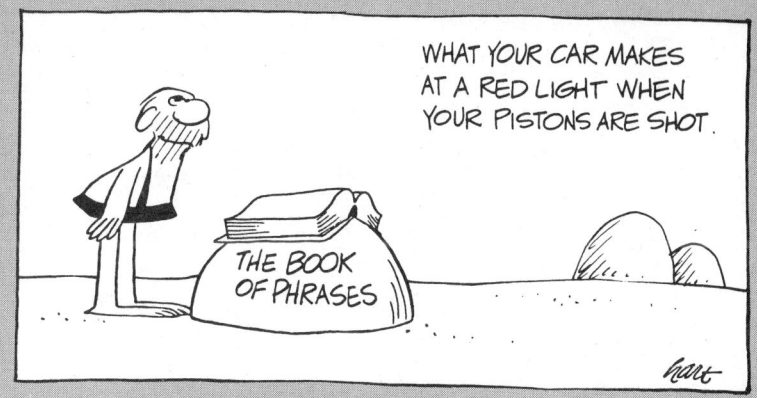

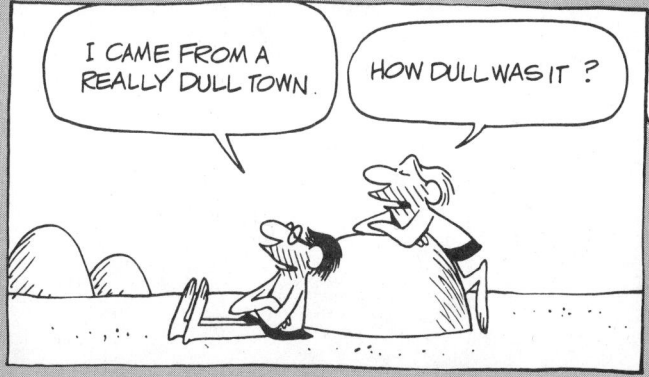

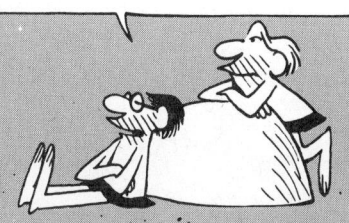

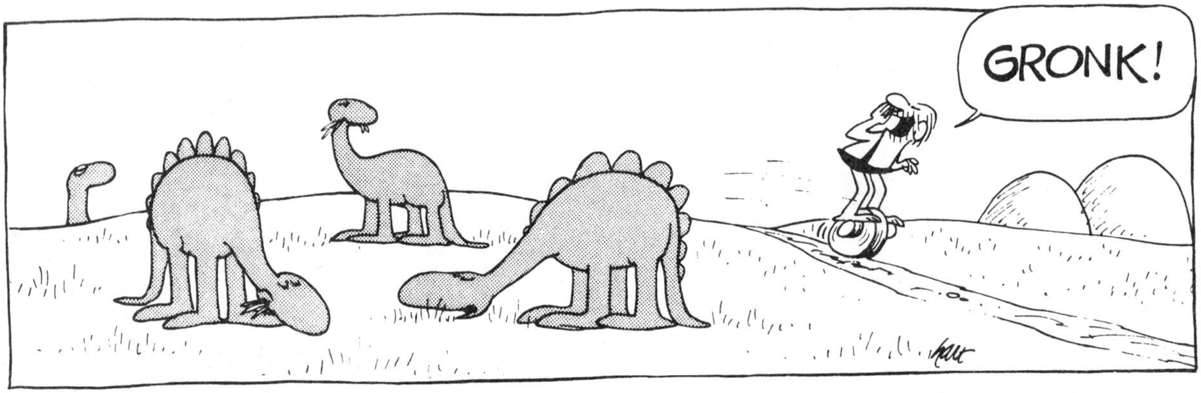
GRONK!

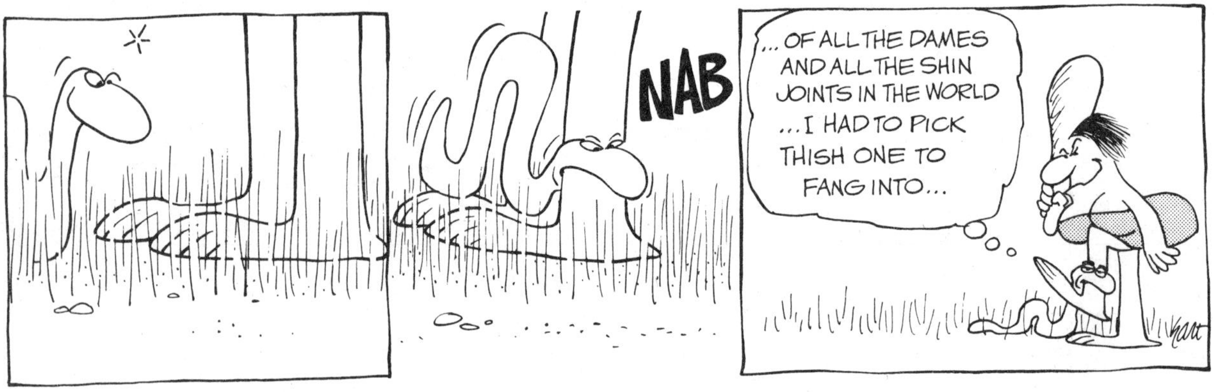
NAB
...OF ALL THE DAMES AND ALL THE SHIN JOINTS IN THE WORLD ...I HAD TO PICK THISH ONE TO FANG INTO...

YOUR QUARTERBACK BLEW 12 GAMES THIS SEASON. WHY DO YOU KEEP STARTING HIM ?
I DON'T WANT TO HURT HIS EGO.
COACH
WHAT EGO ?
I NEVER THOUGHT OF THAT....
COACH

I'M GUESTING THE 'DONAHUE SHOW' ON THURSDAY.
GREAT! WHAT'S THE THEME ?
GAG MAN
'RABBLE-ROUSING'
NOT HIS, ... YOURS!
GAG MAN

OUR TOWN WAS SO SMALL....
HOW SMALL WAS IT ?
THE GAS STATION WAS AN ANTACID DISPENSER

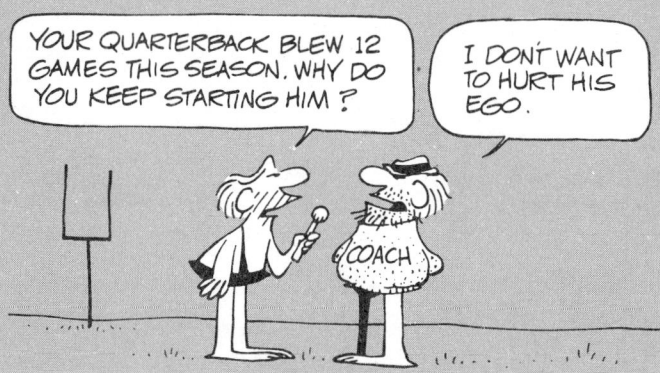

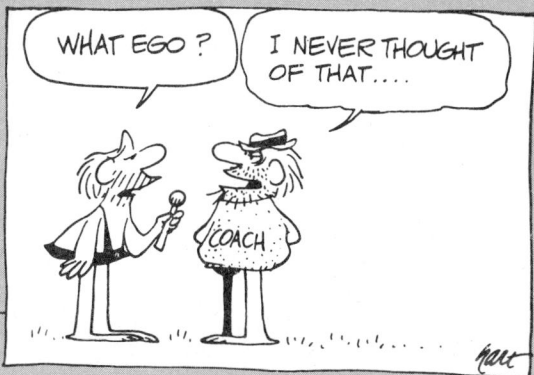

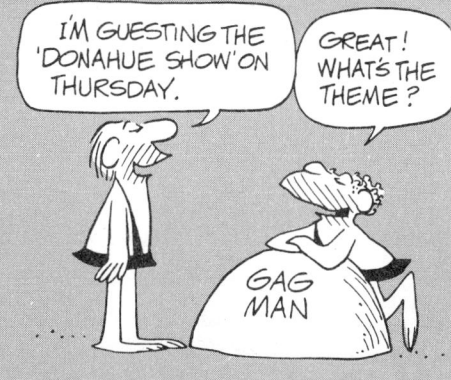

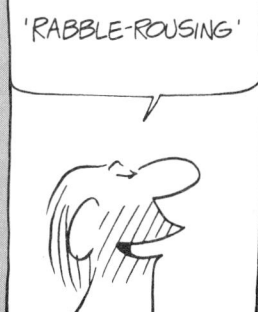

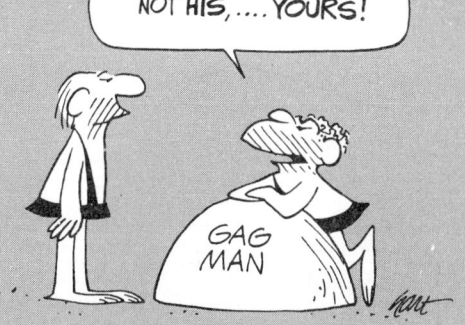

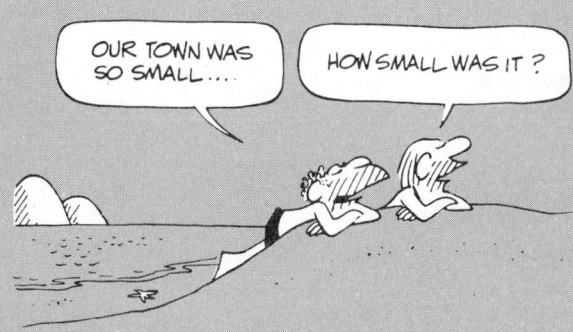

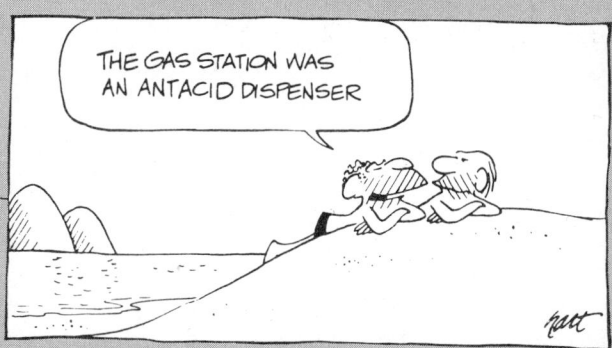

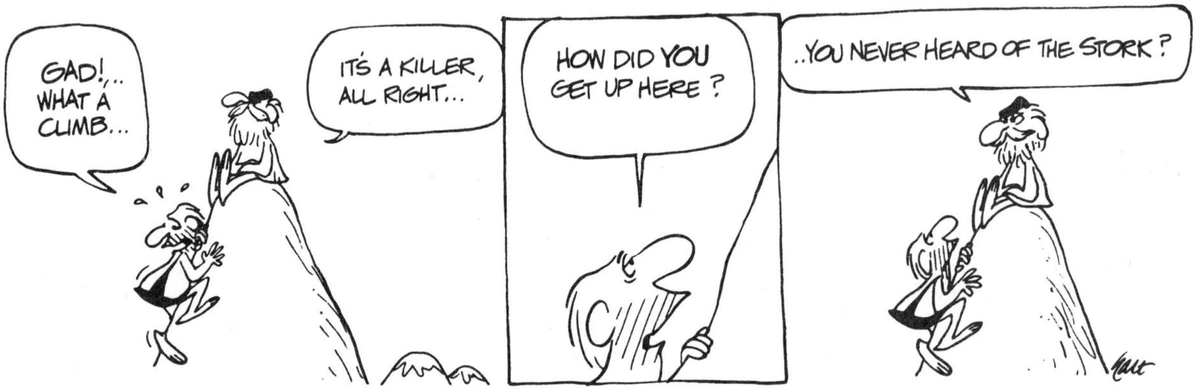
GAD!... WHAT A CLIMB...
IT'S A KILLER, ALL RIGHT...
HOW DID YOU GET UP HERE ?
..YOU NEVER HEARD OF THE STORK ?

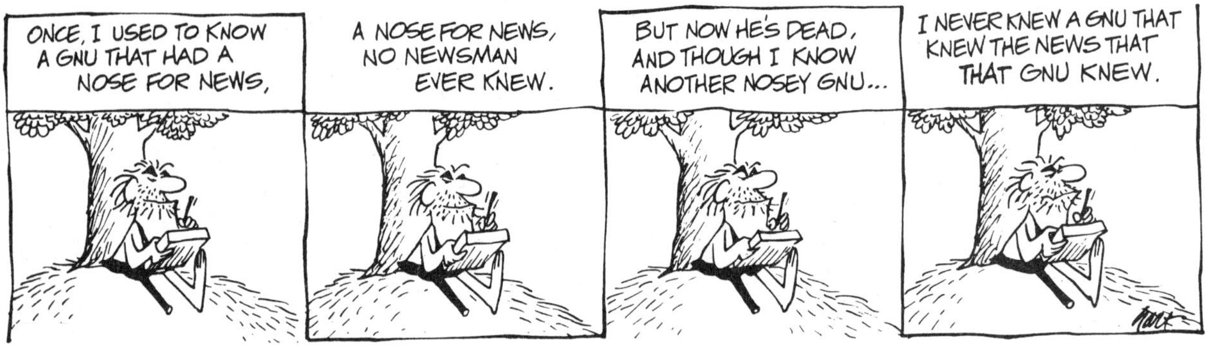
ONCE, I USED TO KNOW A GNU THAT HAD A NOSE FOR NEWS,
A NOSE FOR NEWS, NO NEWSMAN EVER KNEW.
BUT NOW HE'S DEAD, AND THOUGH I KNOW ANOTHER NOSEY GNU...
I NEVER KNEW A GNU THAT KNEW THE NEWS THAT THAT GNU KNEW.

WHAT IF I GET A HUNDRED MILES FROM HERE AND MY WHEEL BREAKS DOWN ?
JUST TAKE IT TO A LOCAL CHISELER .
THOR'S WHEELS
YOU BRANCHING OUT ?
THOR'S WHEELS

YESTERDAY'S COLLISION OF THE 3 OUTFIELDERS ON A POP FLY WAS REALLY EMBARRASSING !
FROM NOW ON, ANYTHING BEHIND HOME PLATE GOES TO THE CATCHER !

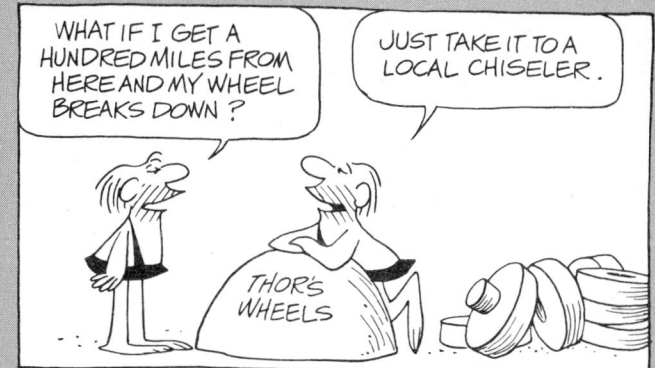

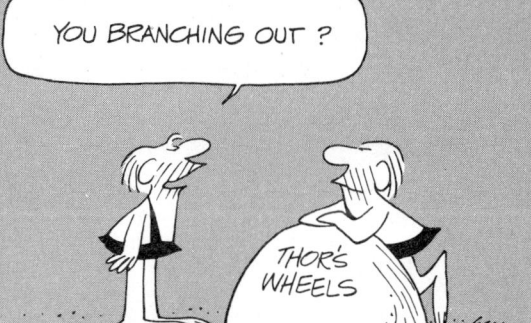

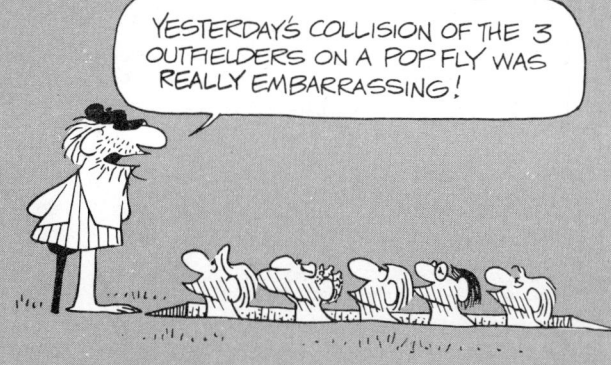

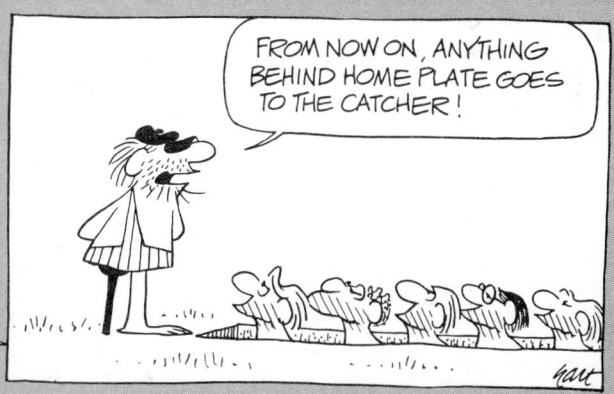

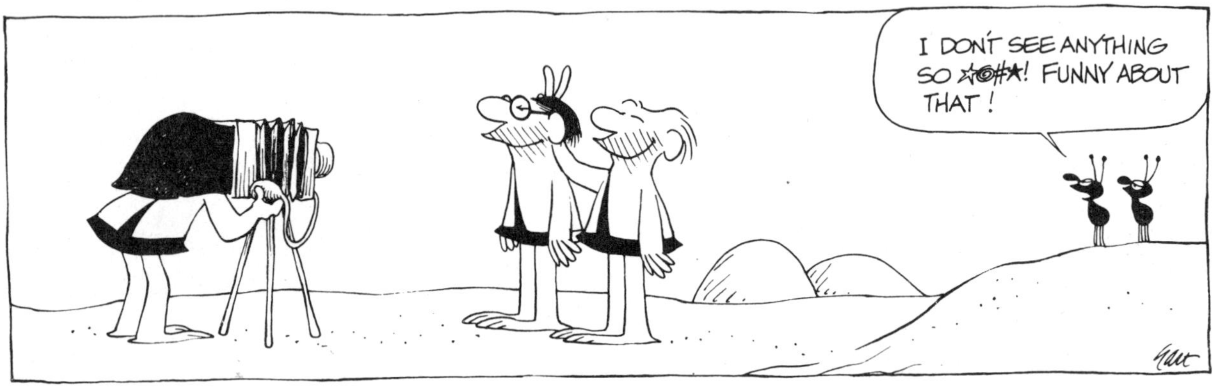
I DON'T SEE ANYTHING SO ☆@#★! FUNNY ABOUT THAT !

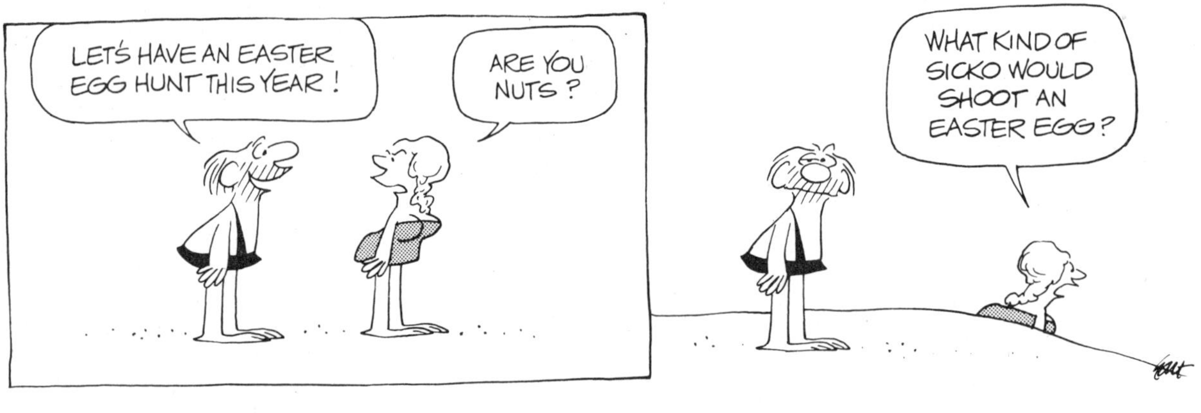
LET'S HAVE AN EASTER EGG HUNT THIS YEAR !
ARE YOU NUTS ?
WHAT KIND OF SICKO WOULD SHOOT AN EASTER EGG ?

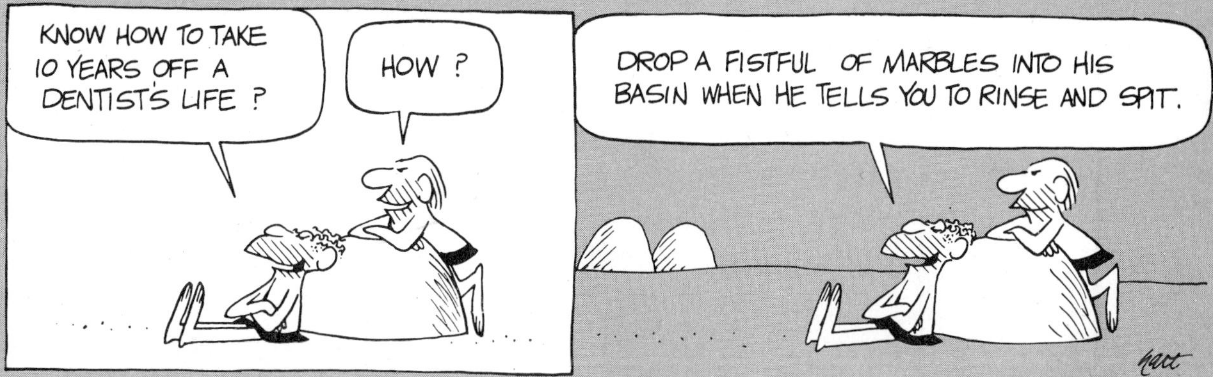
KNOW HOW TO TAKE 10 YEARS OFF A DENTIST'S LIFE ?
HOW ?
DROP A FISTFUL OF MARBLES INTO HIS BASIN WHEN HE TELLS YOU TO RINSE AND SPIT.

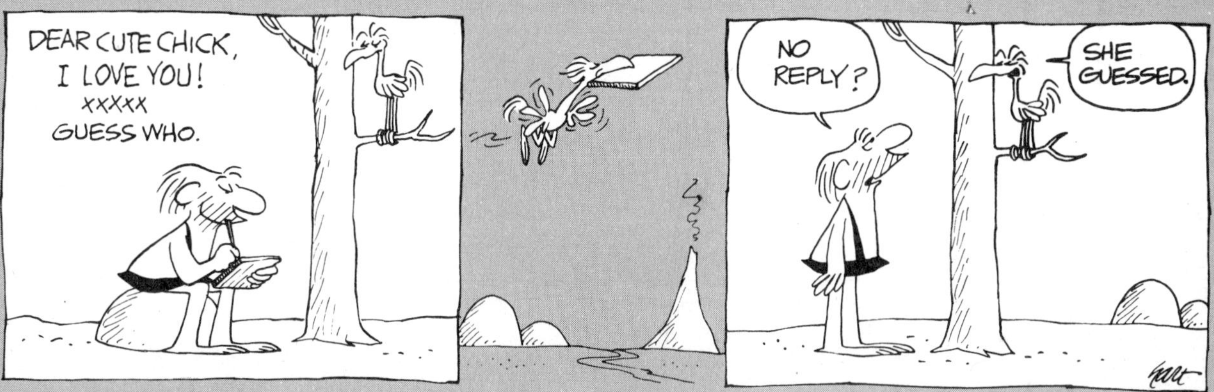
DEAR CUTE CHICK, I LOVE YOU! XXXXX GUESS WHO.
NO REPLY ?
SHE GUESSED.

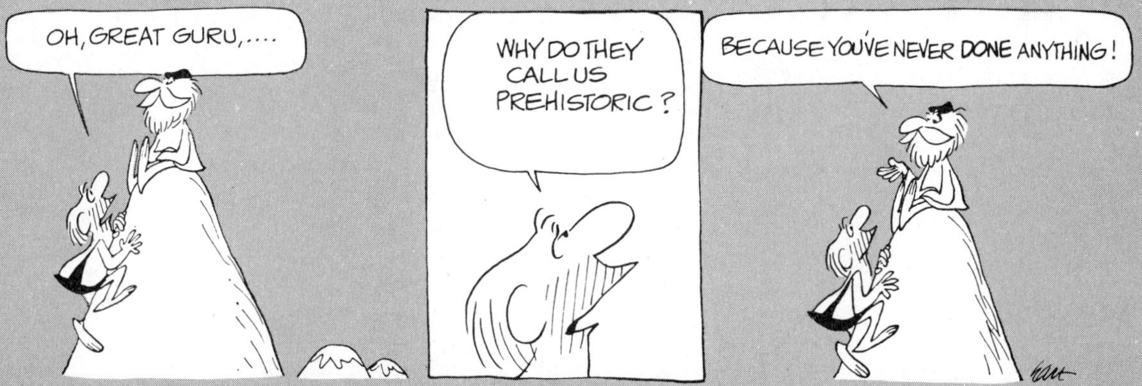
OH, GREAT GURU, ...
WHY DO THEY CALL US PREHISTORIC ?
BECAUSE YOU'VE NEVER DONE ANYTHING !

WHERE'S YOUR TRUMPET PLAYER ?
SOMEONE DROPPED IN A TWENTY-DOLLAR BILL AND HE INHALED HIS MOUTHPIECE .

AHEM.
I KNOW...IT'S TIME TO GO SOUTH......
I WAS JUST CLEARING MY THROAT.
OH.
Z
GET IT IN GEAR, SLUGGO!
RIGHT!

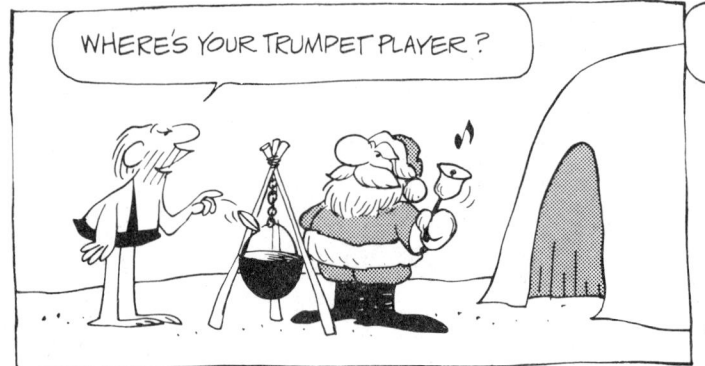

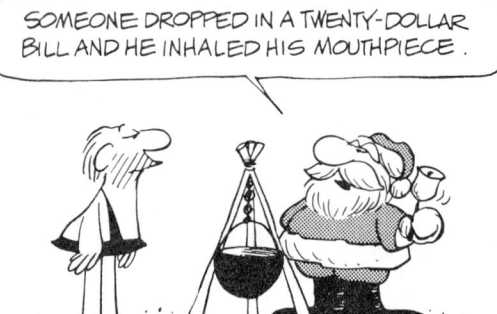

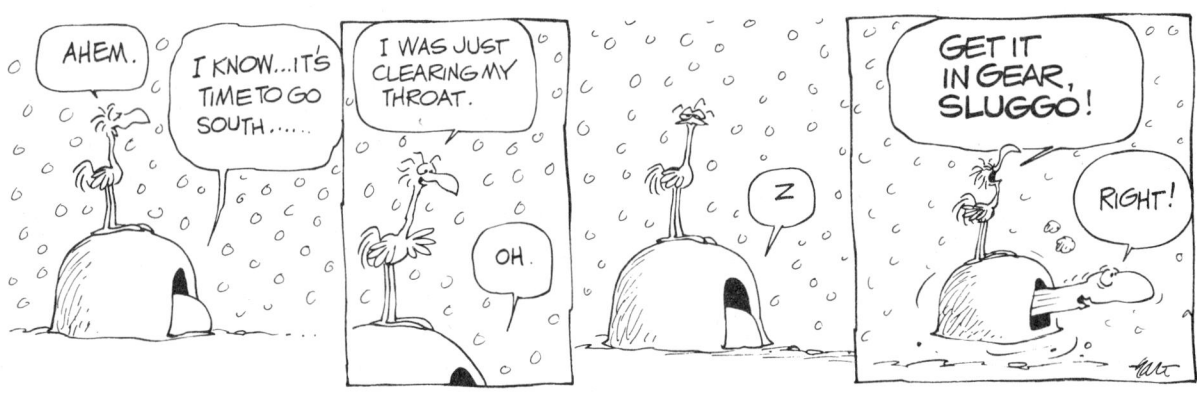

WHAT DO I NEED TO APPLY FOR A PATENT ?
PATENT OFFICE
AN INVENTION
PATENT OFFICE

NO LITTERING ON BEACH

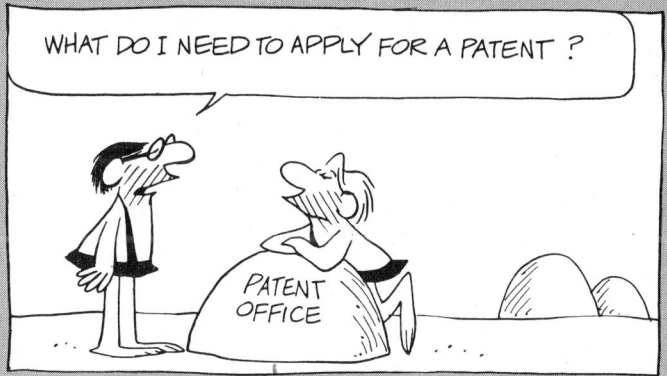

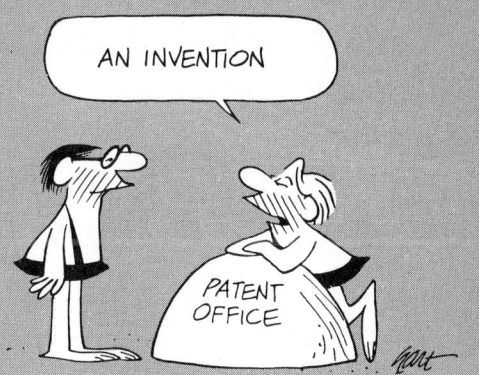

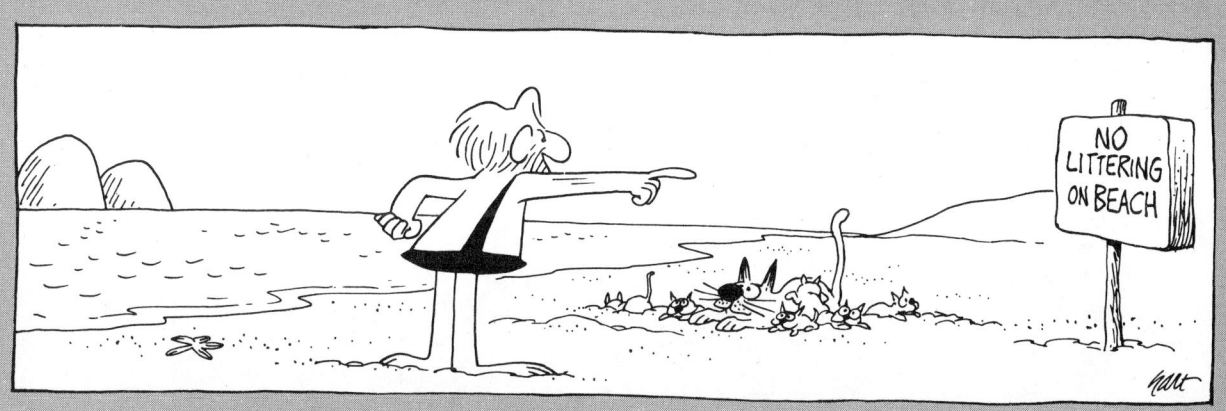

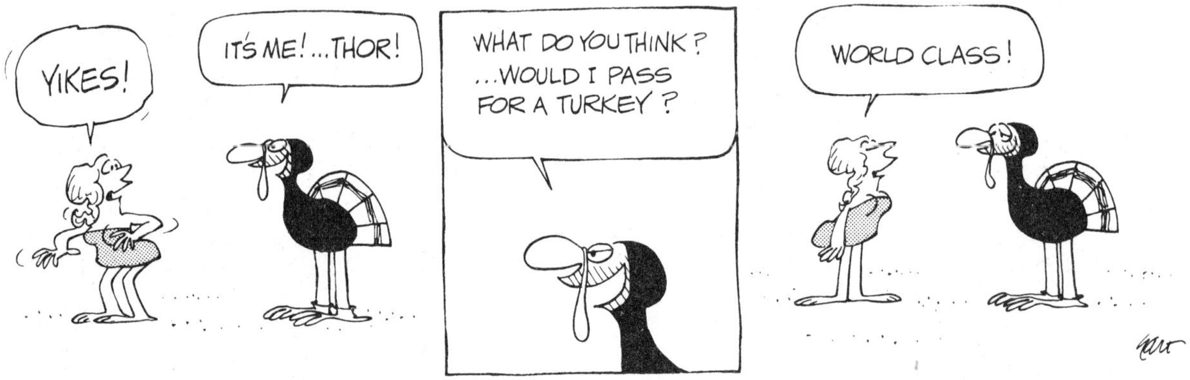
YIKES!
IT'S ME!...THOR!
WHAT DO YOU THINK? ...WOULD I PASS FOR A TURKEY?
WORLD CLASS!

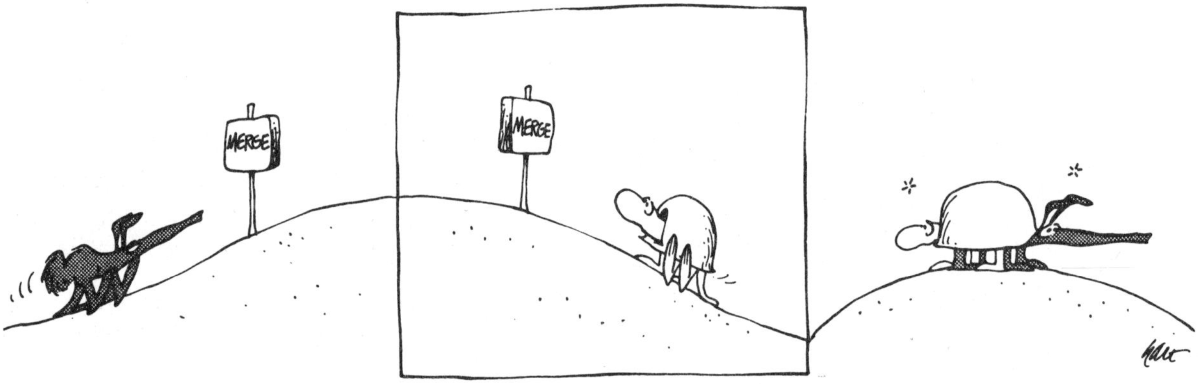
MERGE
MERGE

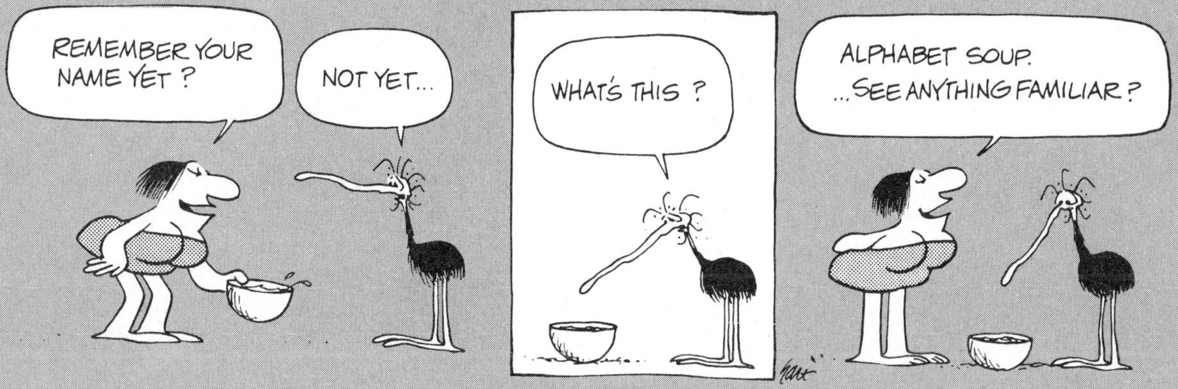
REMEMBER YOUR NAME YET ?
NOT YET...
WHAT'S THIS ?
ALPHABET SOUP. ...SEE ANYTHING FAMILIAR ?

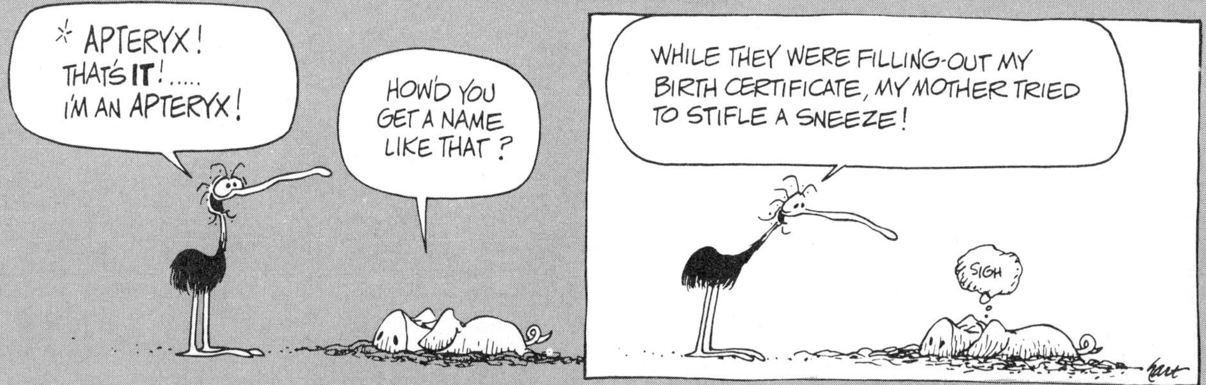
APTERYX ! THAT'S **IT** !..... I'M AN APTERYX !
HOW'D YOU GET A NAME LIKE THAT ?
WHILE THEY WERE FILLING-OUT MY BIRTH CERTIFICATE, MY MOTHER TRIED TO STIFLE A SNEEZE !
SIGH

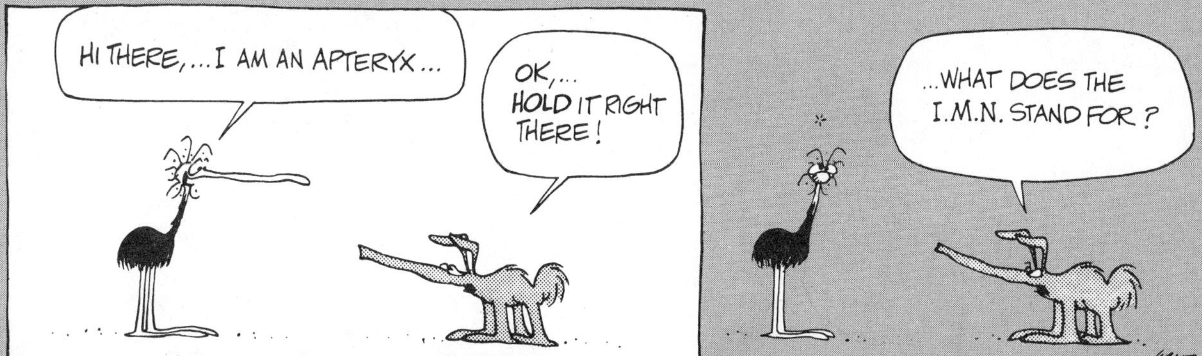
HI THERE, ... I AM AN APTERYX ...
OK, ... **HOLD** IT RIGHT THERE !
...WHAT DOES THE I.M.N. STAND FOR ?

I AIN'T TAKIN' NO FOR AN ANSWER!
OH, NO?
I AIN'T TAKIN' IT FOR A QUESTION EITHER!

WHAT THE....
TURTLE-NECK SOCKS

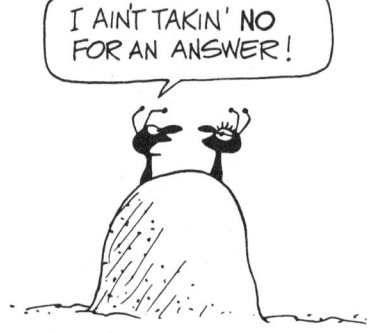

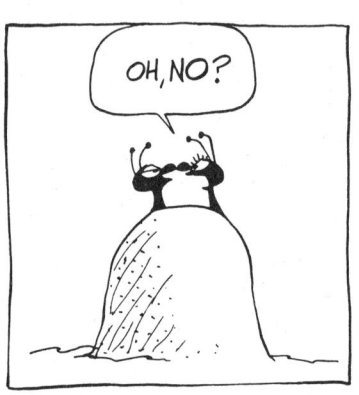

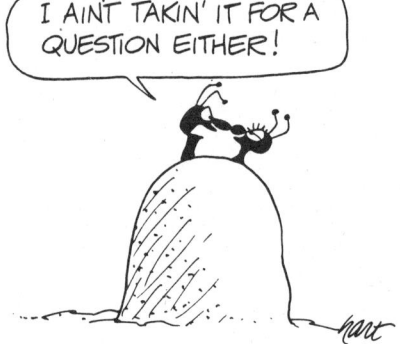

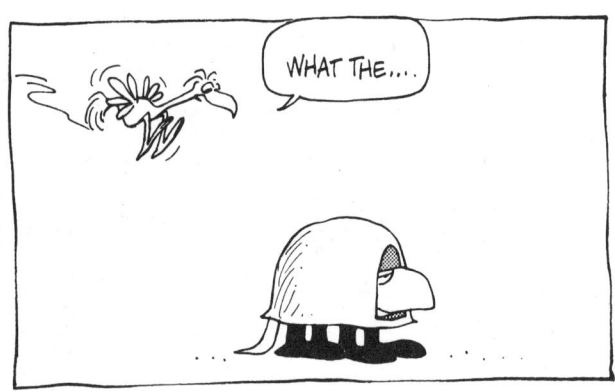

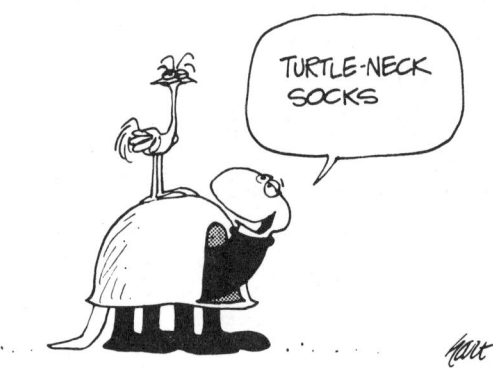

SHOW ME A MAN WHO KEEPS THE WIND TO HIS BACK
AND I'LL SHOW YOU A MAN WITH A HORIZONTAL TIE.

WHAT HAVE YOU BEEN DOING ALL THESE YEARS?
FASTING
YOU'VE BEEN FASTING FOR 67 YEARS?
DO YOU SEE ANY FOOD AROUND HERE ?

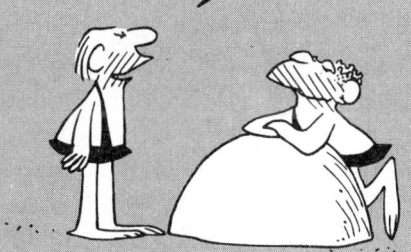

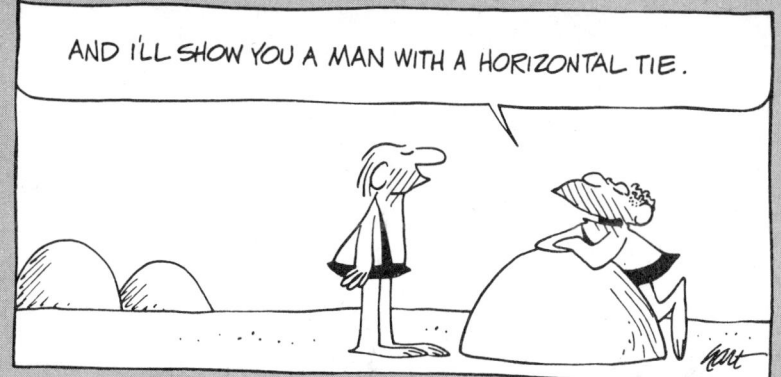

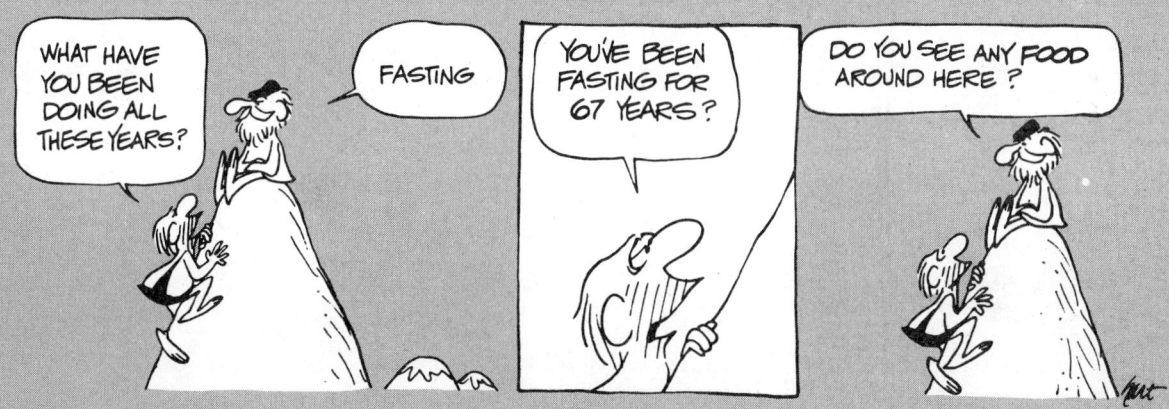

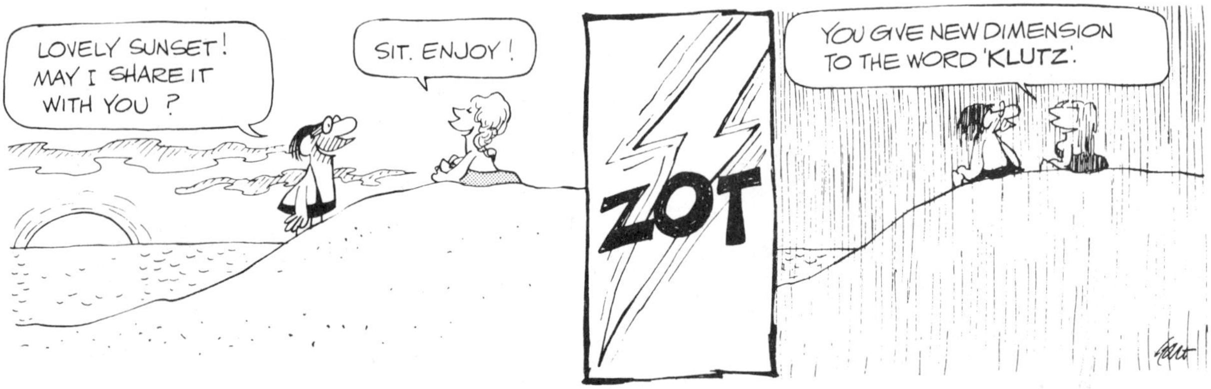
LOVELY SUNSET! MAY I SHARE IT WITH YOU ?
SIT. ENJOY!
ZOT
YOU GIVE NEW DIMENSION TO THE WORD 'KLUTZ'.

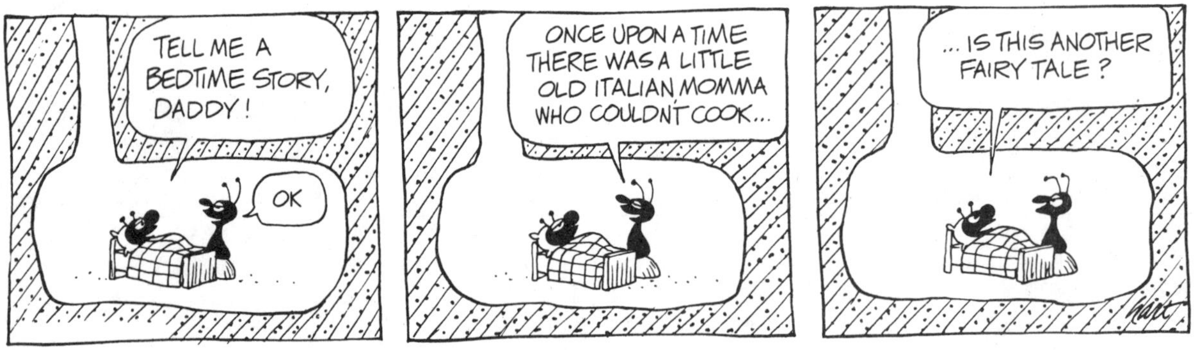
TELL ME A BEDTIME STORY, DADDY!
OK
ONCE UPON A TIME THERE WAS A LITTLE OLD ITALIAN MOMMA WHO COULDN'T COOK...
... IS THIS ANOTHER FAIRY TALE ?

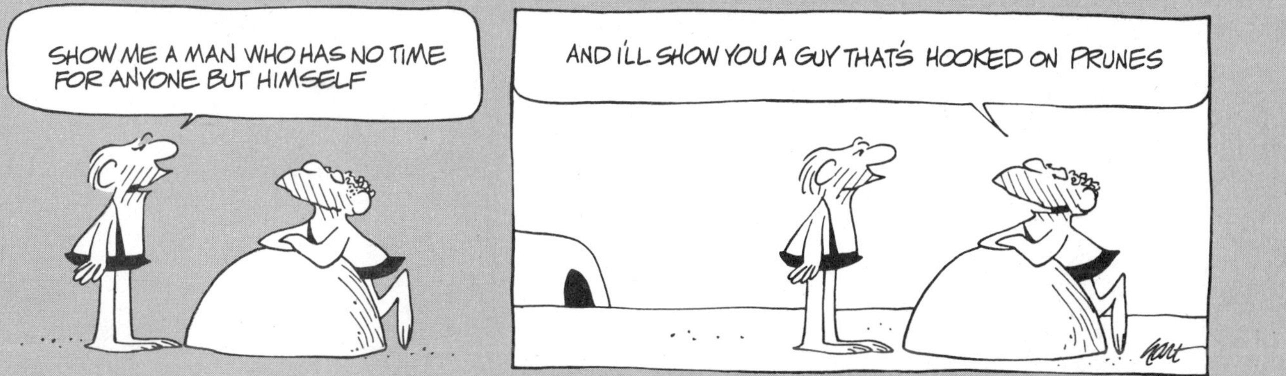
SHOW ME A MAN WHO HAS NO TIME FOR ANYONE BUT HIMSELF
AND I'LL SHOW YOU A GUY THAT'S HOOKED ON PRUNES

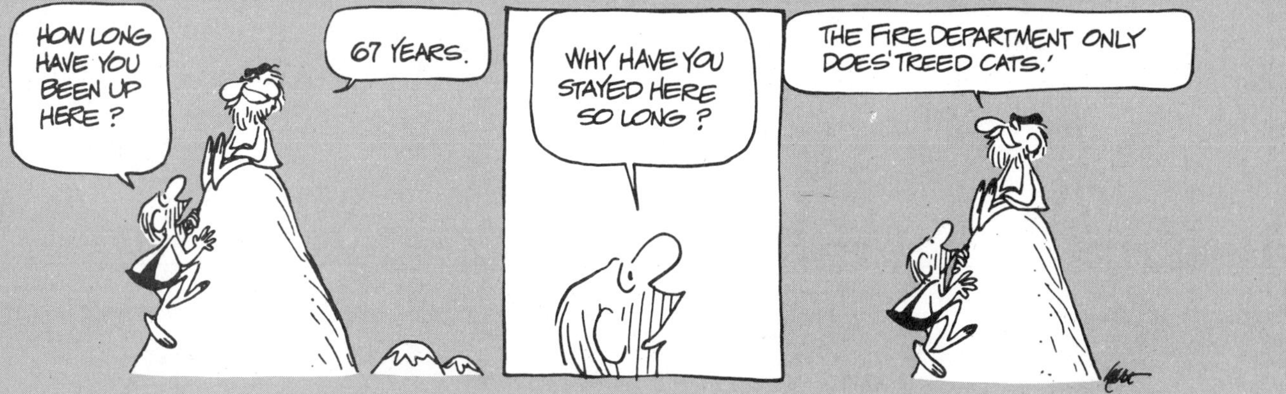
HOW LONG HAVE YOU BEEN UP HERE ?
67 YEARS.
WHY HAVE YOU STAYED HERE SO LONG ?
THE FIRE DEPARTMENT ONLY DOES 'TREED CATS.'

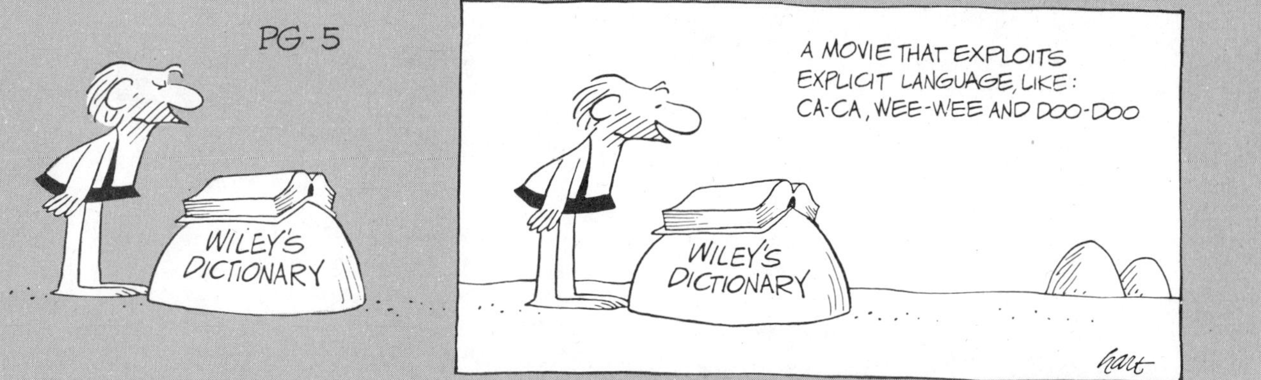
PG-5
WILEY'S DICTIONARY
A MOVIE THAT EXPLOITS EXPLICIT LANGUAGE, LIKE: CA-CA, WEE-WEE AND DOO-DOO
WILEY'S DICTIONARY

SPRIT
WHAT DO YOU CALL THAT THING?
A @#☆!! CLAM FINDER!

COULD I MAKE A FRIENDLY SUGGESTION?
CLAMFINDERS 5 CLAMS

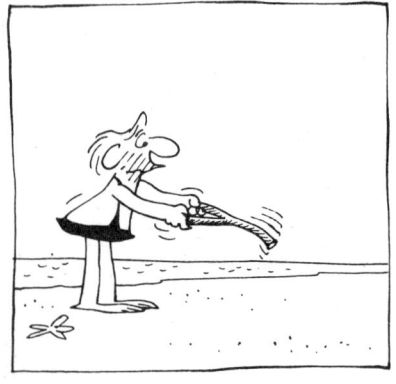

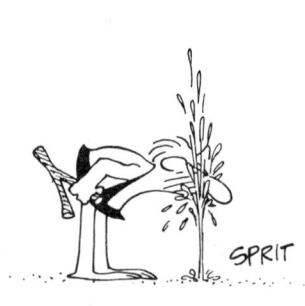

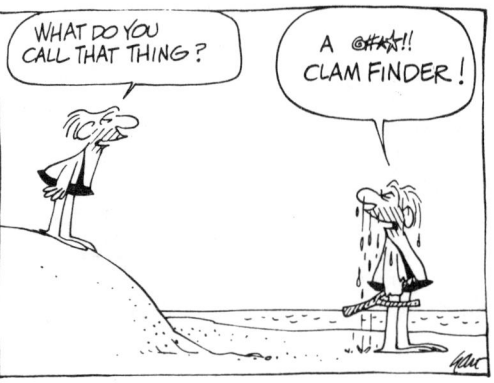

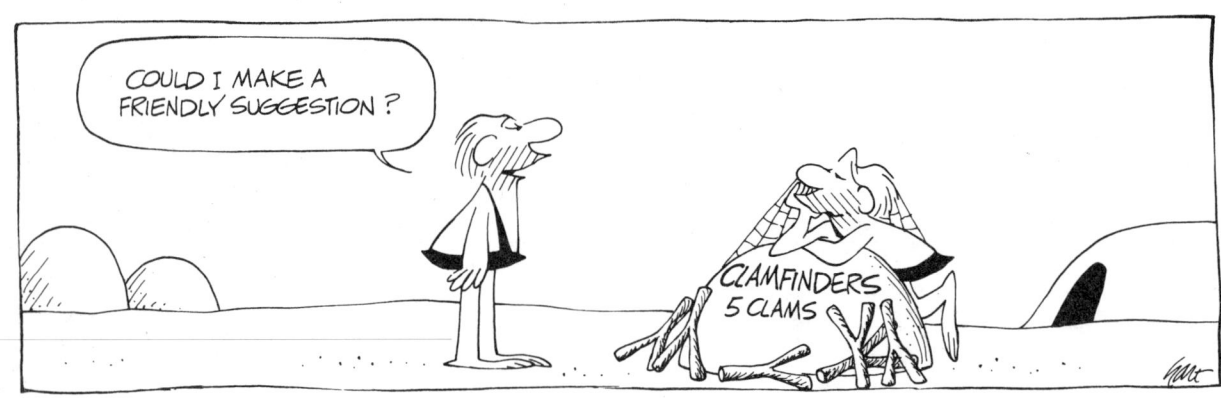

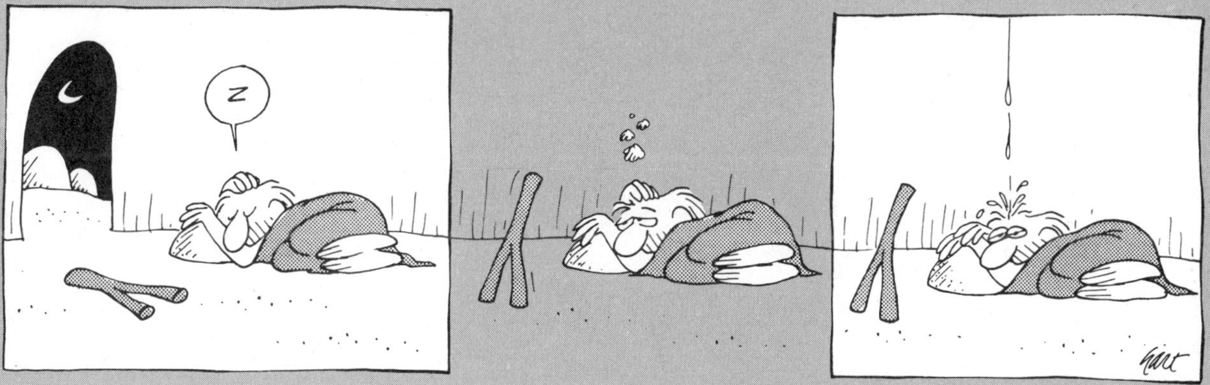
Z

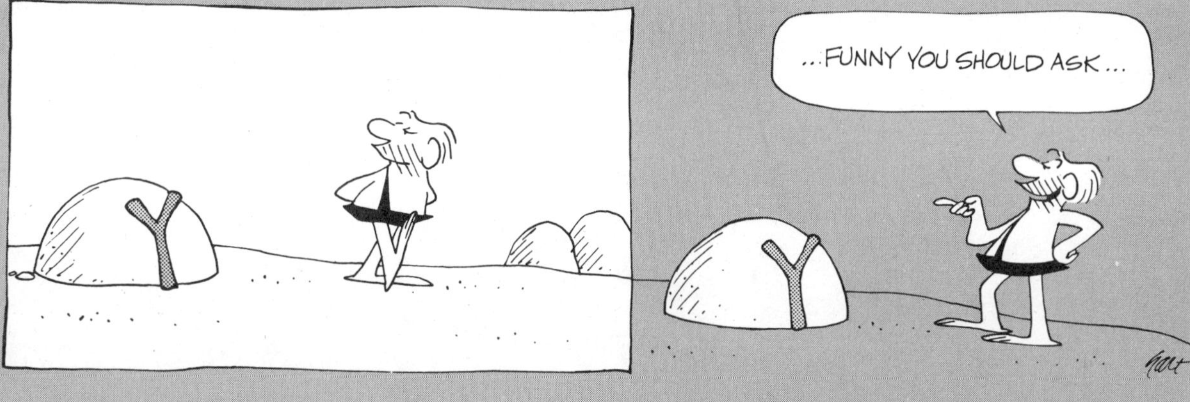
...FUNNY YOU SHOULD ASK...

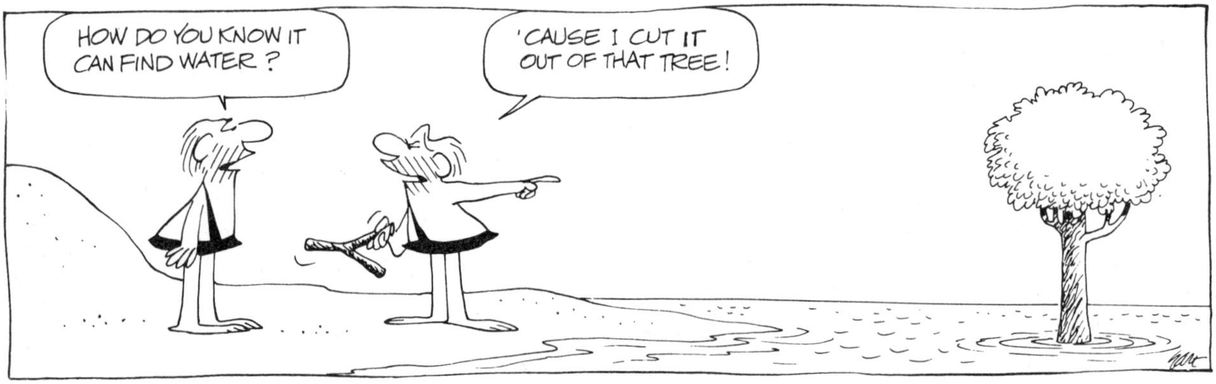
HOW DO YOU KNOW IT CAN FIND WATER ?
'CAUSE I CUT IT OUT OF THAT TREE !

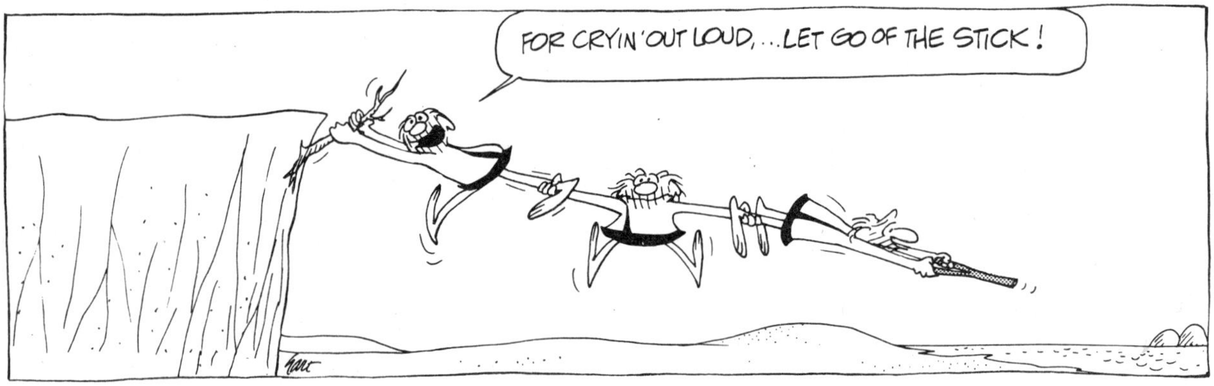
FOR CRYIN' OUT LOUD, ... LET GO OF THE STICK !

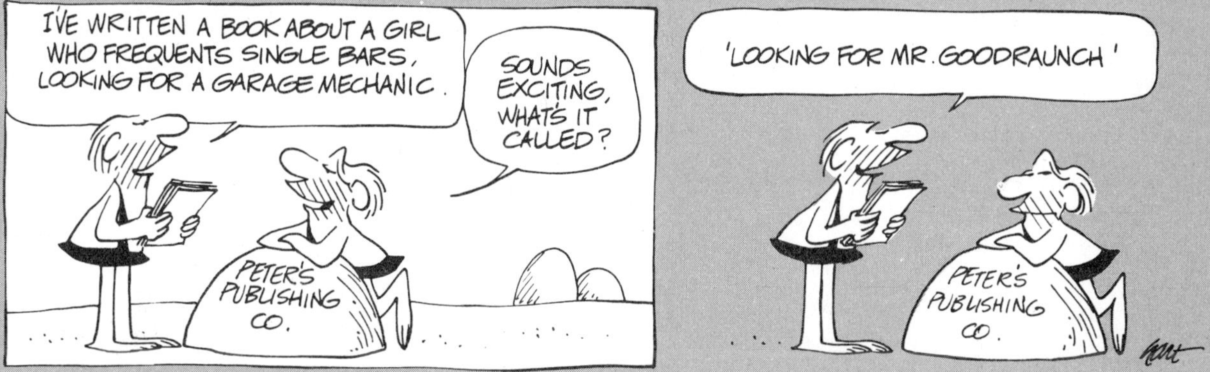
I'VE WRITTEN A BOOK ABOUT A GIRL WHO FREQUENTS SINGLE BARS, LOOKING FOR A GARAGE MECHANIC.
SOUNDS EXCITING, WHAT'S IT CALLED?
PETER'S PUBLISHING CO.
'LOOKING FOR MR. GOODRAUNCH'
PETER'S PUBLISHING CO.

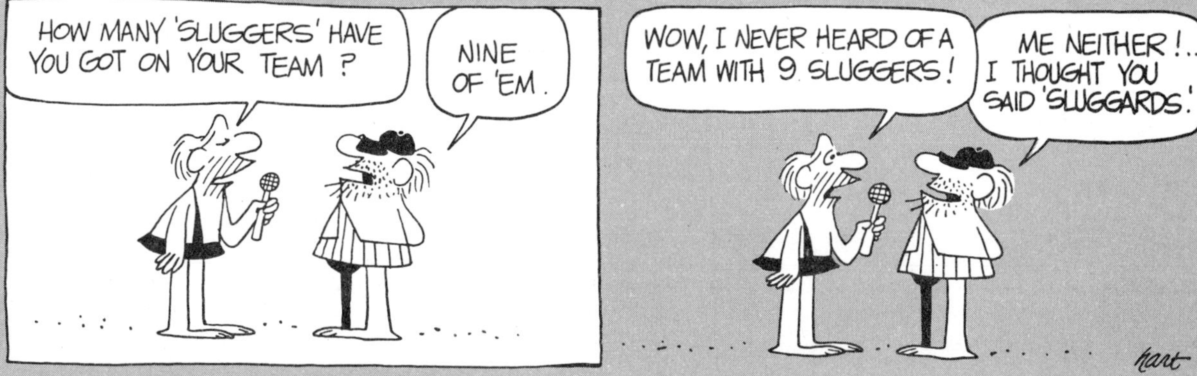
HOW MANY 'SLUGGERS' HAVE YOU GOT ON YOUR TEAM?
NINE OF 'EM.
WOW, I NEVER HEARD OF A TEAM WITH 9 SLUGGERS!
ME NEITHER!... I THOUGHT YOU SAID 'SLUGGARDS.'

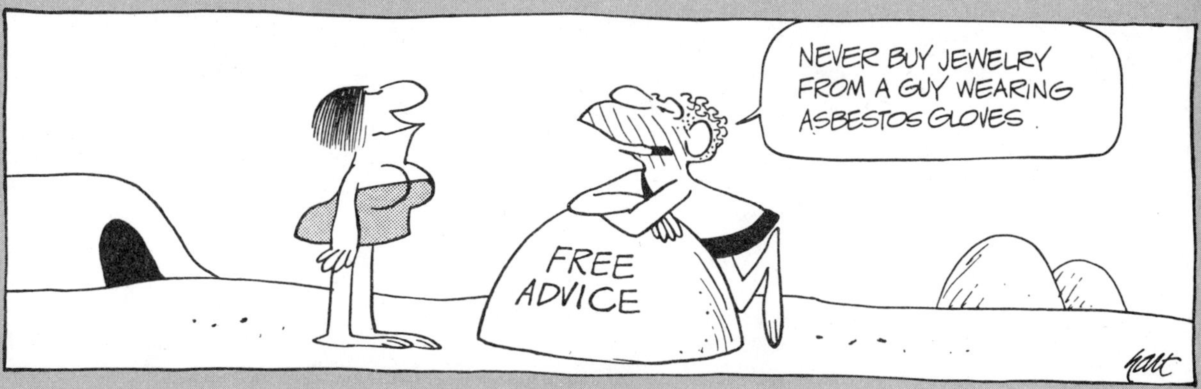
NEVER BUY JEWELRY FROM A GUY WEARING ASBESTOS GLOVES.
FREE ADVICE

DO YOU HAVE TROGLODYTE COSTUMES ?
NOPE. NOT ON THE LIST.
COSTUMES
WHAT THE HECK IS A TROGLODYTE ?
COSTUMES

I'D LIKE A CINDERELLA COSTUME FOR THE HALLOWEEN BALL!
HALLOWEEN COSTUMES
CRASH
TINKLE
TINKLE
WHAT WAS THAT ?
THE GLASS SLIPPERS JUST COMMITTED SUICIDE.
HALLOWEEN COSTUMES

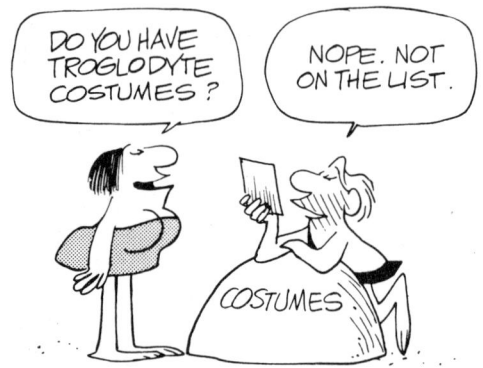

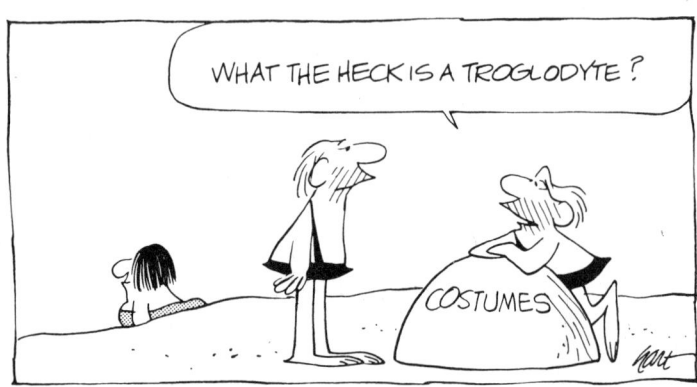

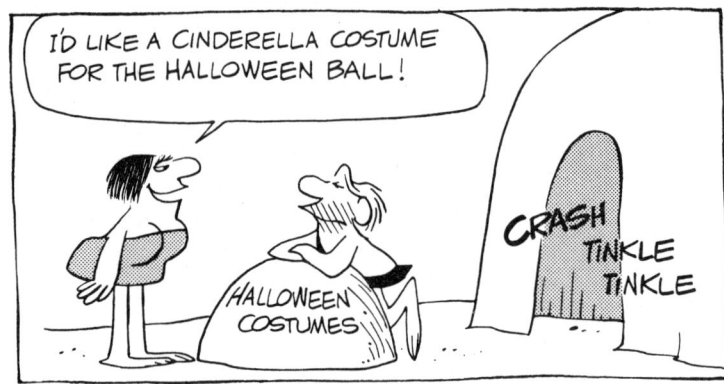

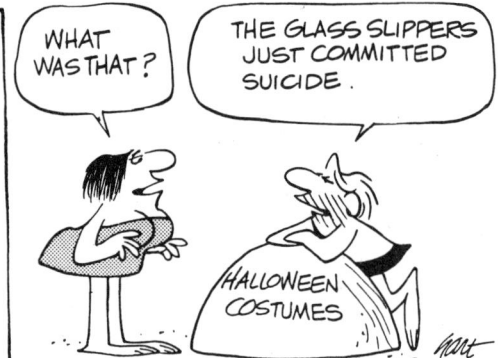

I'D LIKE THE 'PRINCE CHARMING' COSTUME
HALLOWEEN COSTUMES
HERE YOU ARE.
THERE GOES ANOTHER LEGEND DOWN THE TUBES.
HALLOWEEN COSTUMES

I'D LIKE A CLASSY COSTUME BUT NOTHING THAT COSTS AN ARM AND A LEG.
HMM.
HALLOWEEN COSTUMES
...I GUESS THAT RULES OUT THE 'CAPTAIN HOOK' OUTFIT.
HALLOWEEN COSTUMES

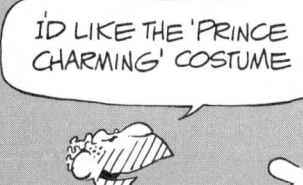

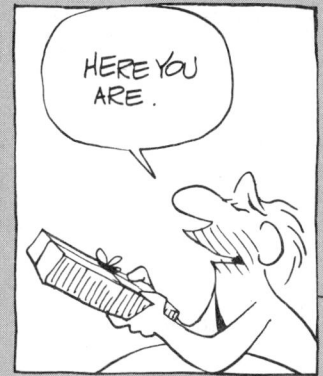

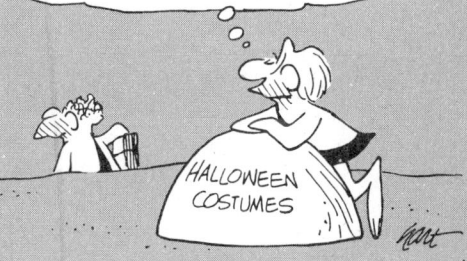

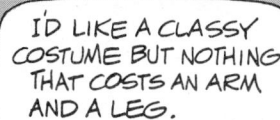

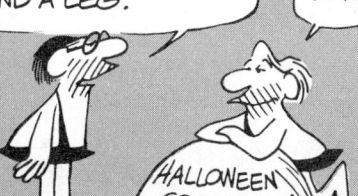

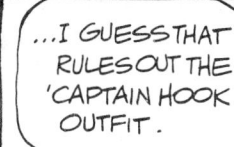

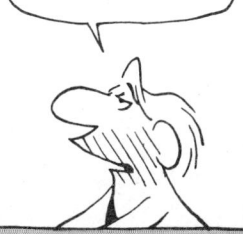

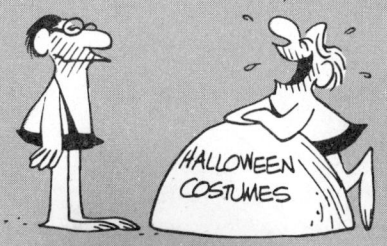

YEOW!
WHAT A GRISLY FACE!...WHERE'D YOU GET IT ?
I RIPPED IT OFF AN I.R.S. AUDITOR .

HOW 'BOUT SOMETHING DASHING, LIKE A 'ZORRO' SUIT ?
HALLOWEEN COSTUMES
NAH,... TOO TAME. WHAT HAVE YOU GOT THAT'S REALLY STUPID LOOKING ?
TRICK OR TREAT.

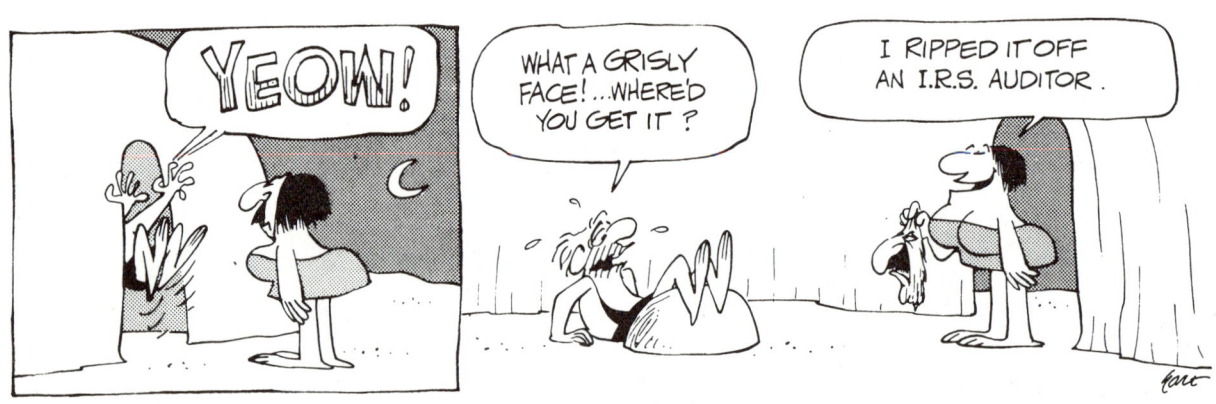

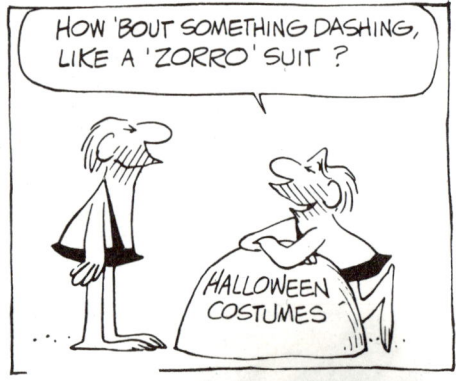

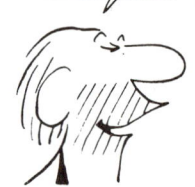

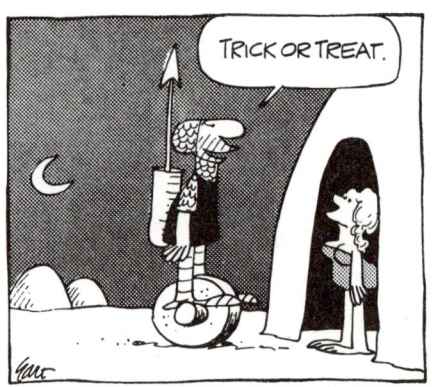

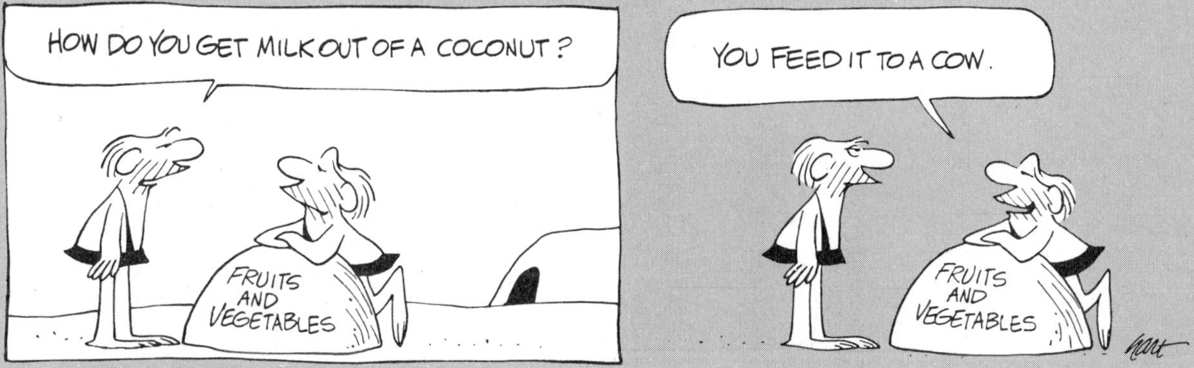
HOW DO YOU GET MILK OUT OF A COCONUT ?
FRUITS AND VEGETABLES
YOU FEED IT TO A COW.
FRUITS AND VEGETABLES

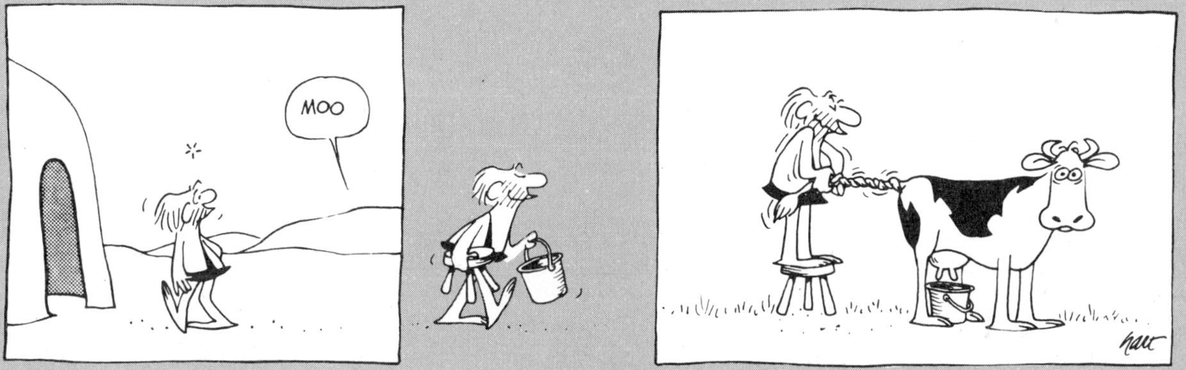
MOO

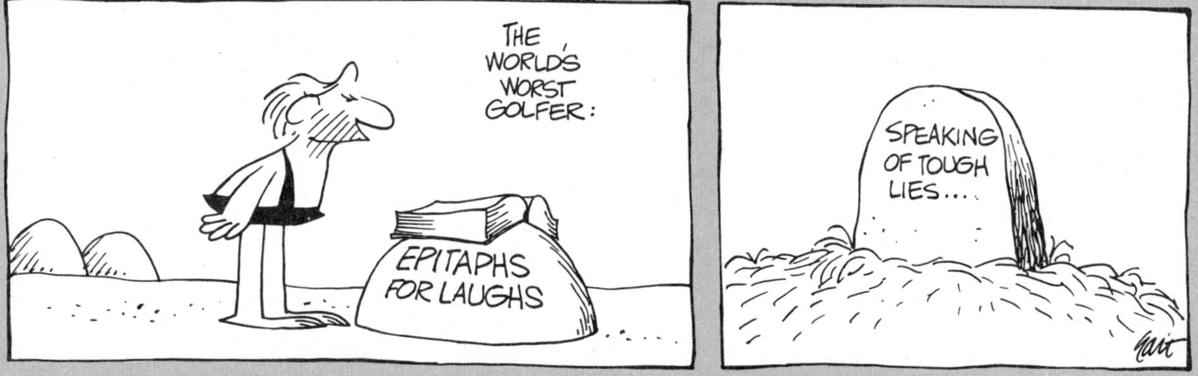
THE WORLD'S WORST GOLFER:
EPITAPHS FOR LAUGHS
SPEAKING OF TOUGH LIES....

Dear Fat Broad,
Every night my husband comes home with lipstick all over his collar.
ADVICE COLUMN
...what's a good detergent for getting out the stains? sincerely, B.B.
DEAR BIRD-BRAIN, ...
ADVICE COLUMN
hart

I RESOLVE TO RESIST THE TEMPTATION OF FLESH.
BLESS YOU, BROTHER!
ZOT
ANT FLESH IS ANOTHER THING ALTOGETHER!
hart

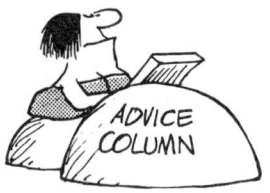

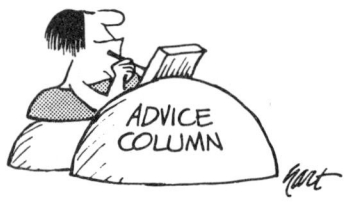

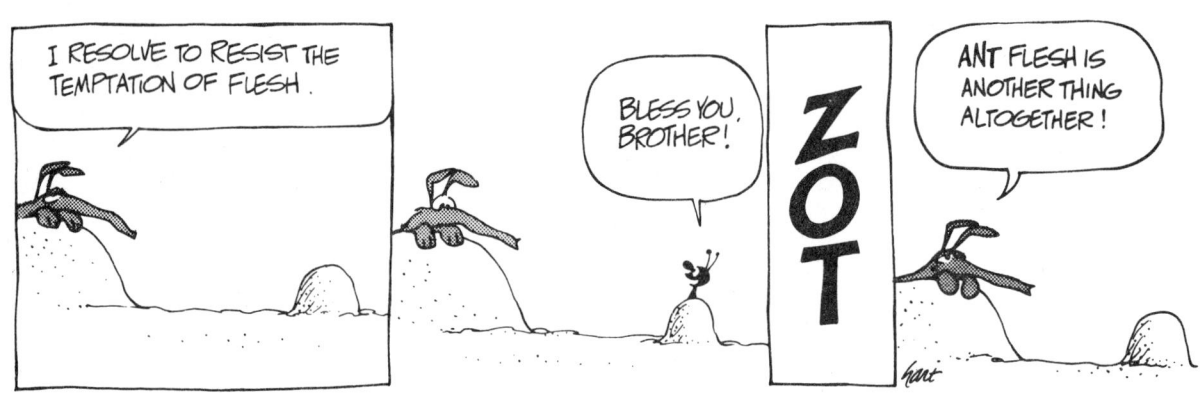

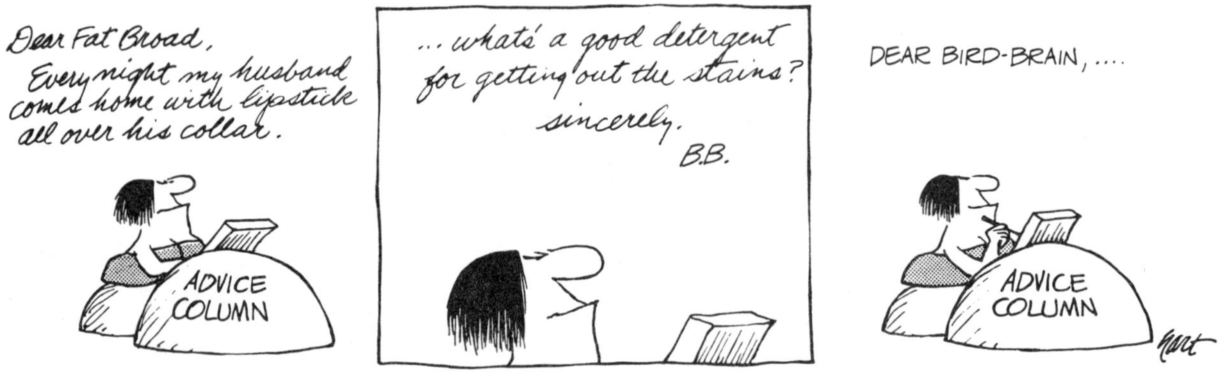

WHAT DO YOU THINK?
YOU GOT COLLISION INSURANCE?
BODY SHOP
YEP.
RUN IT OFF A CLIFF.
BODY SHOP

HARD DAY, HON?
HARD?
BZZZZZZZ
I SPENT SIX HOURS SUCKIN' MY BRAINS OUT AT A 'SILK FLOWER SHOW' ...AND YOU ASK ME IF I HAD A HARD DAY?

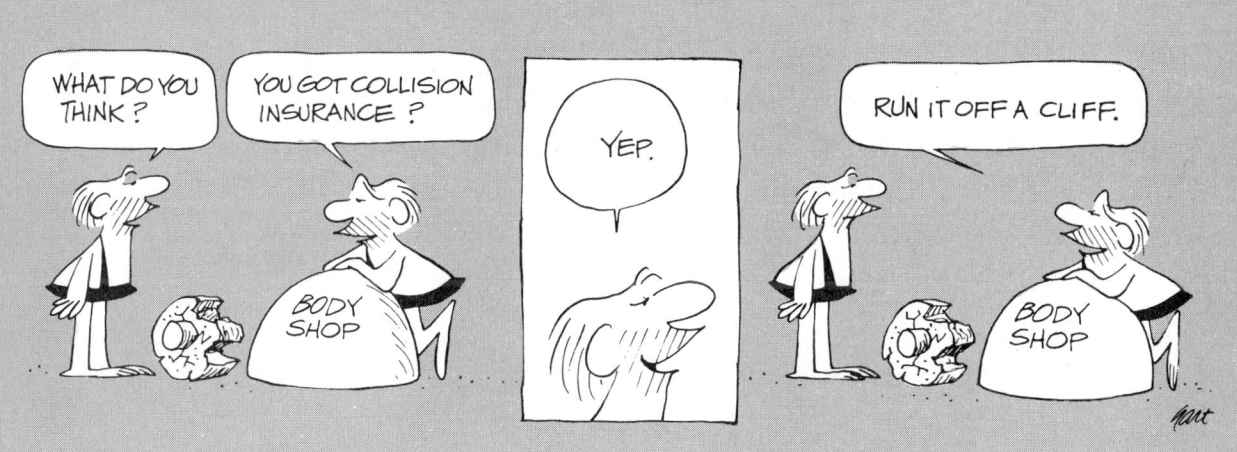

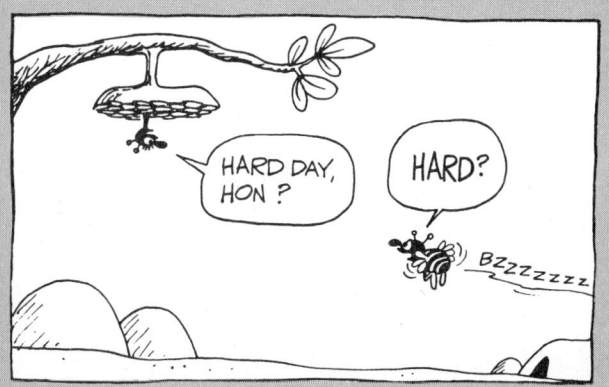

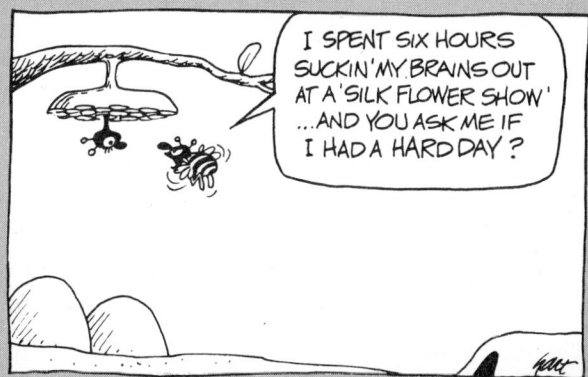

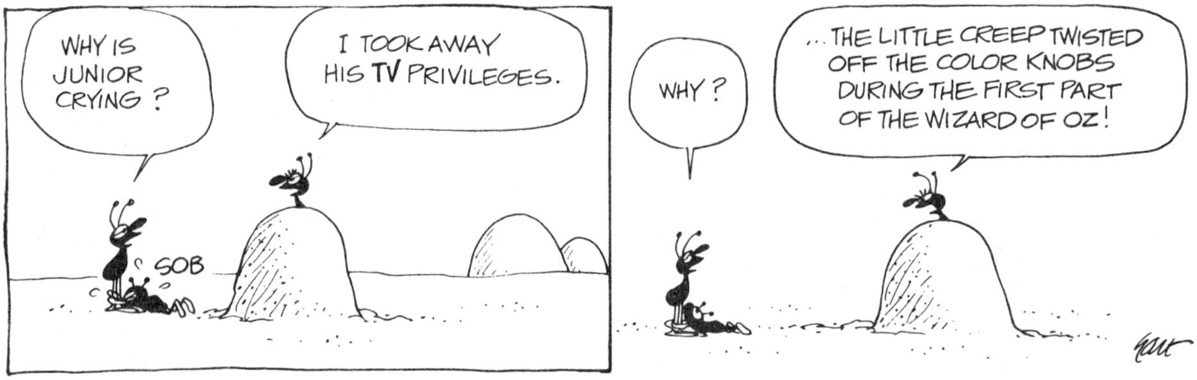
WHY IS JUNIOR CRYING ?
SOB
I TOOK AWAY HIS TV PRIVILEGES.
WHY ?
...THE LITTLE CREEP TWISTED OFF THE COLOR KNOBS DURING THE FIRST PART OF THE WIZARD OF OZ!

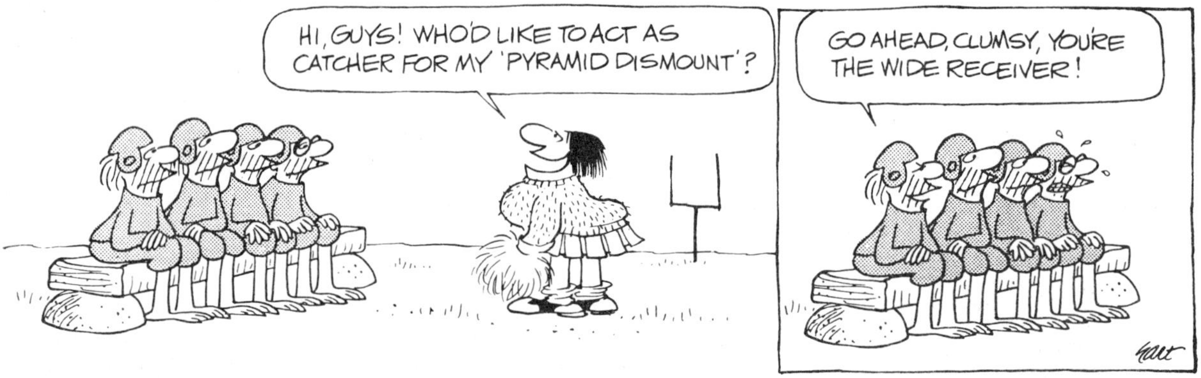
HI, GUYS! WHO'D LIKE TO ACT AS CATCHER FOR MY 'PYRAMID DISMOUNT'?
GO AHEAD, CLUMSY, YOU'RE THE WIDE RECEIVER!

I'D LIKE TO EXCHANGE THIS PEEK-A-BOO NIGHTIE MY BOYFRIEND GAVE ME FOR A LUG WRENCH.
WHAT DO YOU NEED WITH A LUG WRENCH ?
I NEED IT TO SCREW HIS EYES BACK INTO HIS HEAD.

I'D LIKE TO EXCHANGE THIS FOR SOMETHING MORE PRACTICAL.
GIFT EXCHANGE
WHAT IS IT ?
A DASHBOARD.
GIFT EXCHANGE

CAN I EXCHANGE SOMETHING SLIGHTLY USED ?
THAT DEPENDS,... WHAT IS IT ?
GIFT EXCHANGE
A FISH HOOK.
GIFT EXCHANGE

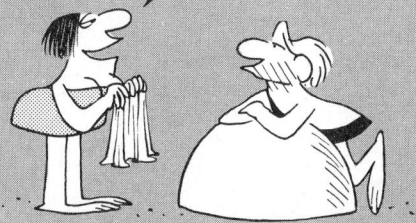

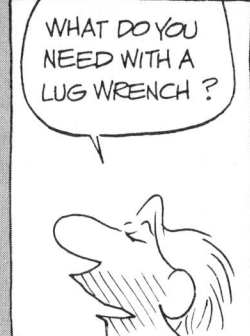

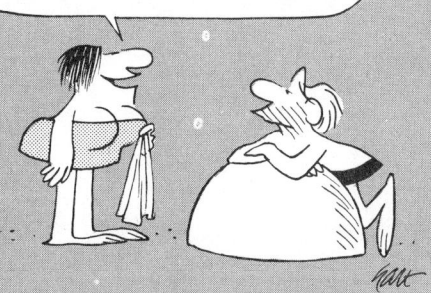

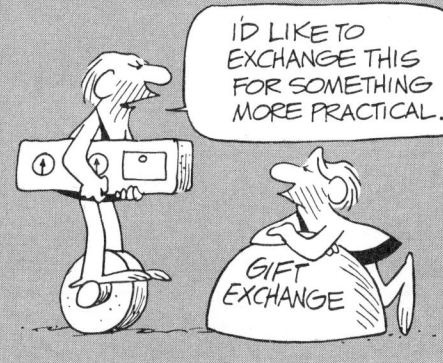

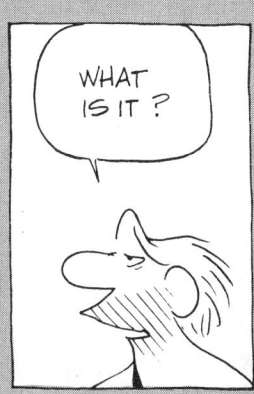

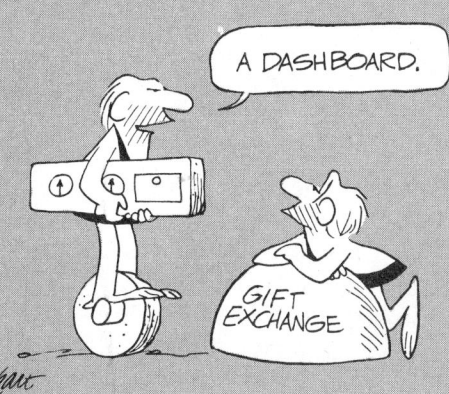

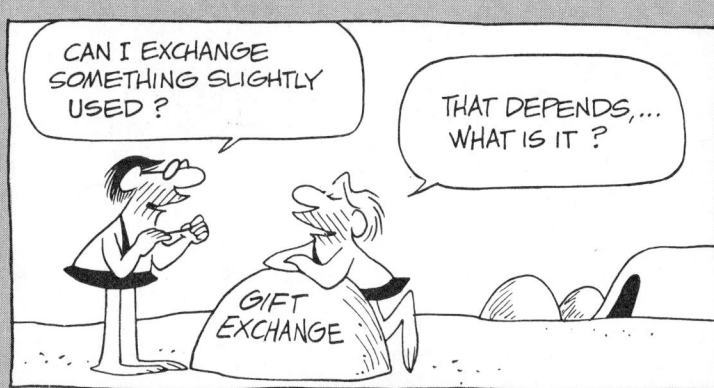

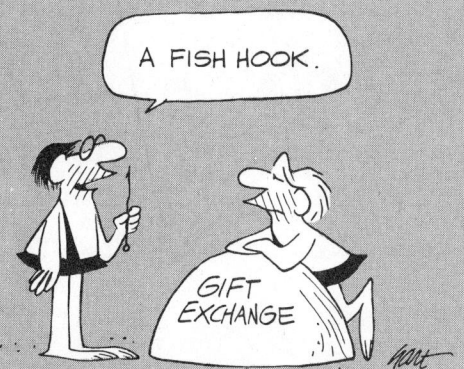

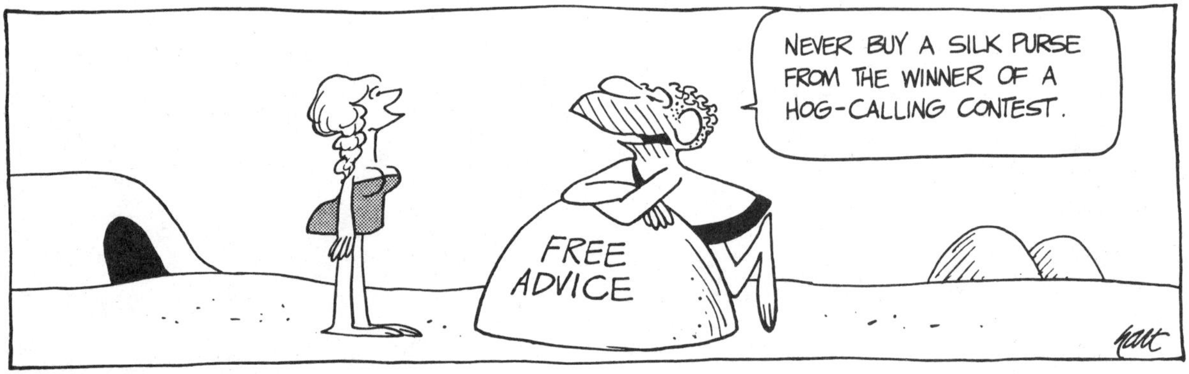
NEVER BUY A SILK PURSE FROM THE WINNER OF A HOG-CALLING CONTEST.
FREE ADVICE

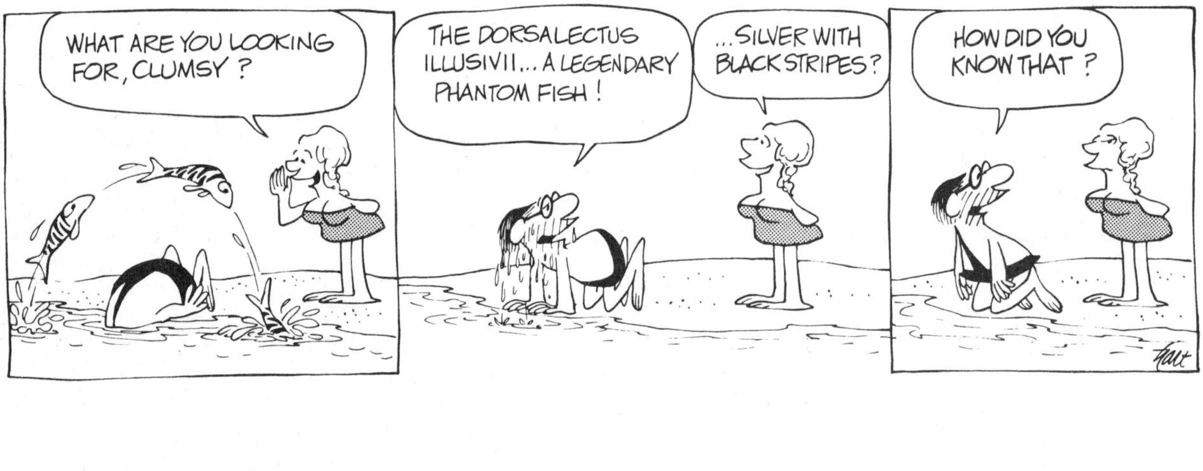
WHAT ARE YOU LOOKING FOR, CLUMSY ?
THE DORSALECTUS ILLUSIVII... A LEGENDARY PHANTOM FISH !
...SILVER WITH BLACK STRIPES ?
HOW DID YOU KNOW THAT ?

HOW DO I GET RID OF STINKWEED?
GARDEN TIPS
BAG IT UP AND SELL IT ON THE STREET.
GARDEN TIPS

WHAT IN THE...?
IT'S THE LOTUS POSITION. I'M RAISING MY LEVEL OF CONSCIOUSNESS.
I DON'T THINK IT'S WORKING.
WHY DO YOU SAY THAT?
YOU'RE SITTING ON MY FISH HOOKS.

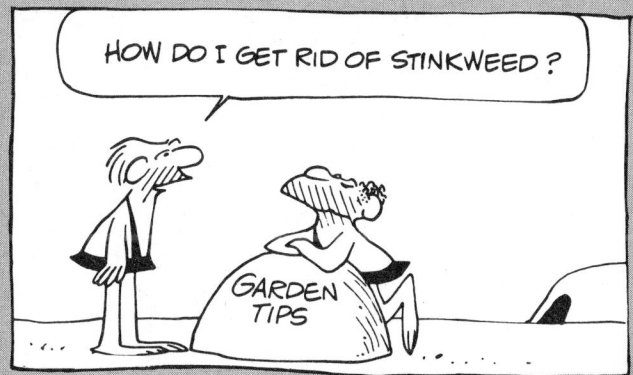

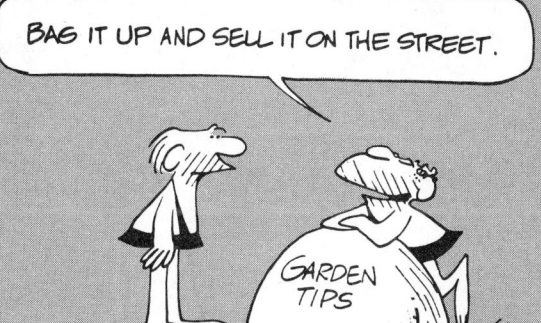

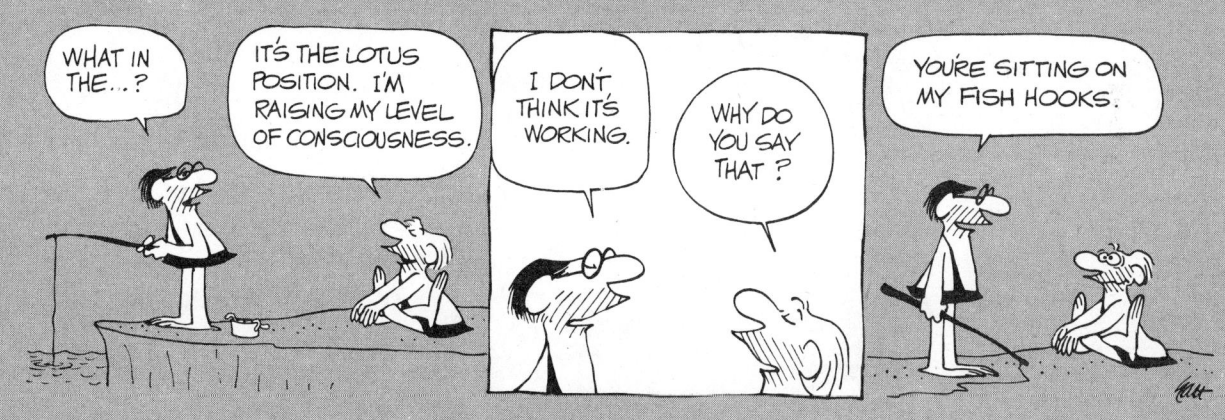

Dear Fat Broad,
ADVICE COLUMN
How can I break my dog of drinking out of the toilet?
GO TO THE BATHROOM IN HIS WATER DISH.
ADVICE COLUMN

HAVE YOU EVER SUFFERED ANY ILL EFFECTS FROM YOUR NOTICEABLY ONE-SIDED DIET?
AN OCCASIONAL NOSEBURN.
POLL TAKER
WHAT DO YOU TAKE FOR IT?
POLL TAKER
ANTACID
POLL TAKER

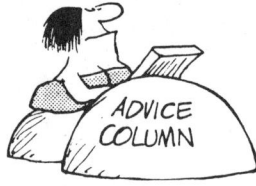

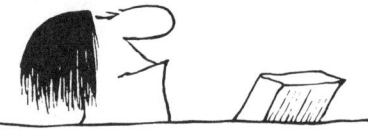

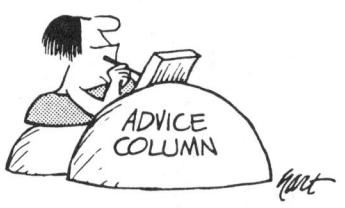

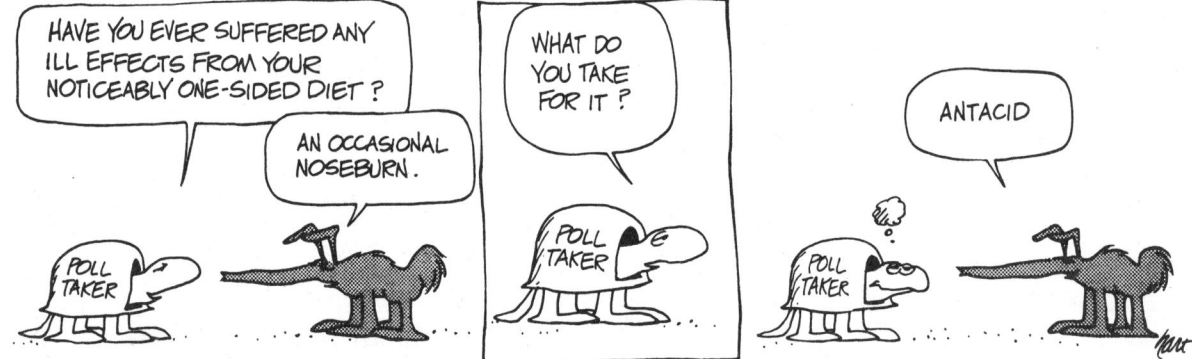

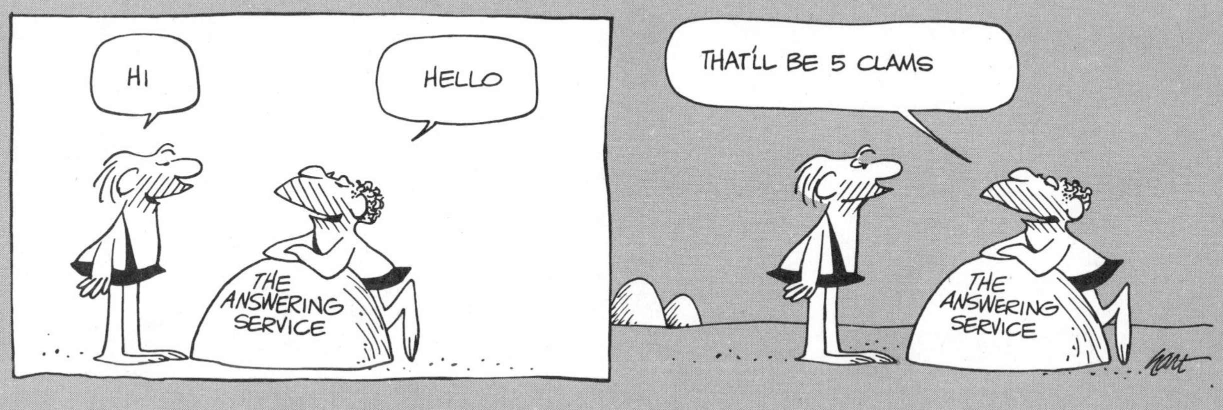
HI
HELLO
THE ANSWERING SERVICE
THAT'LL BE 5 CLAMS
THE ANSWERING SERVICE

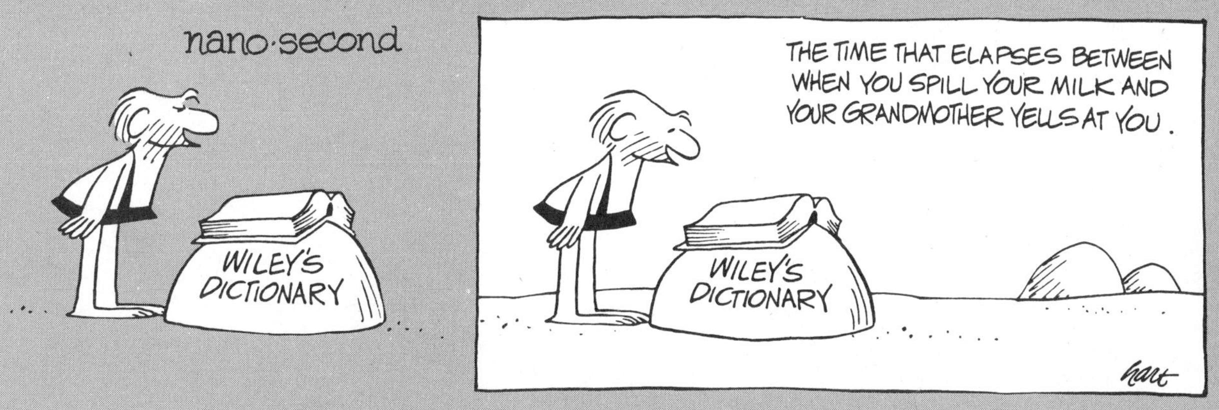
nano·second
WILEY'S DICTIONARY
THE TIME THAT ELAPSES BETWEEN WHEN YOU SPILL YOUR MILK AND YOUR GRANDMOTHER YELLS AT YOU.
WILEY'S DICTIONARY

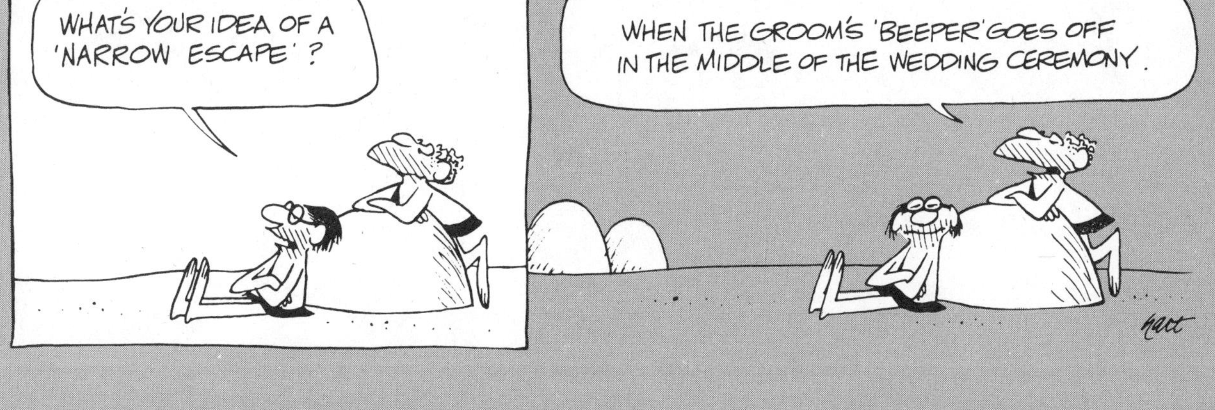
WHAT'S YOUR IDEA OF A 'NARROW ESCAPE'?
WHEN THE GROOM'S 'BEEPER' GOES OFF IN THE MIDDLE OF THE WEDDING CEREMONY.

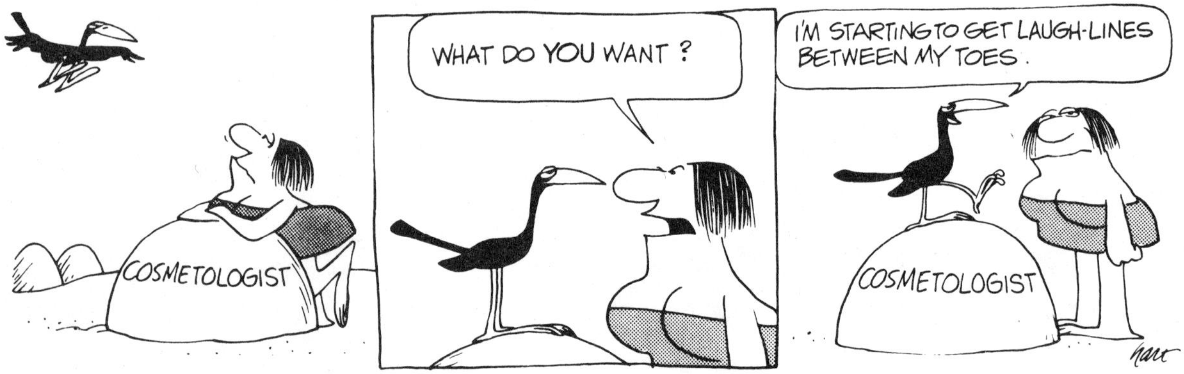
COSMETOLOGIST
WHAT DO YOU WANT ?
I'M STARTING TO GET LAUGH-LINES BETWEEN MY TOES.
COSMETOLOGIST
hart

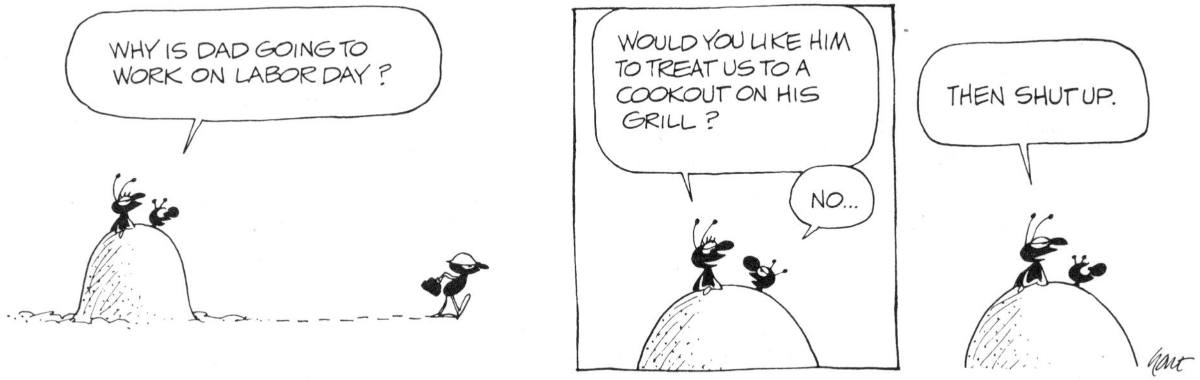
WHY IS DAD GOING TO WORK ON LABOR DAY ?
WOULD YOU LIKE HIM TO TREAT US TO A COOKOUT ON HIS GRILL ?
NO...
THEN SHUT UP.
hart

WHAT DO I NEED TO HUNT DINOSAUR WITH A SLING?
HUNTING LICENSES
YOUR HEAD EXAMINED.
HUNTING LICENSES

CAN I GET A DUCK LICENSE?
'SURE CAN.
HUNTING LICENSES
CAN I KILL ANY KIND OF DUCK I WANT TO?
LICENSE
ANYTHING THAT AIN'T WEARING A SAILOR SUIT.
HUNTING LICENSES

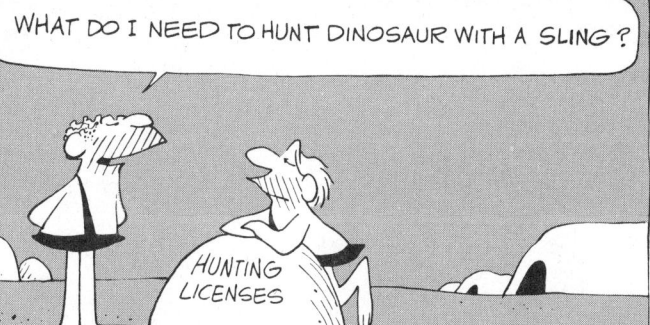

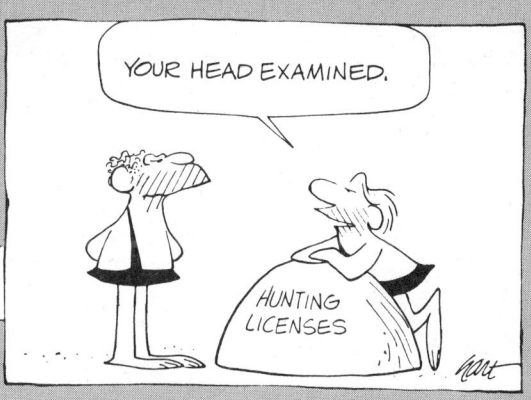

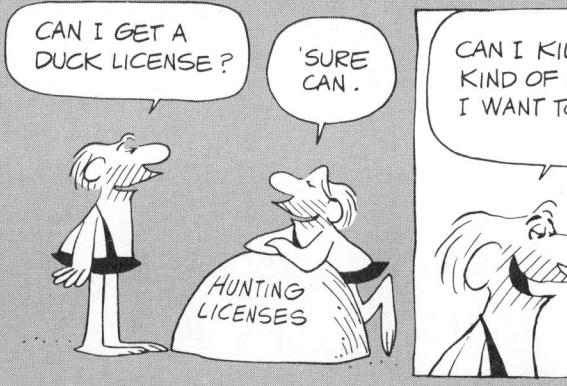

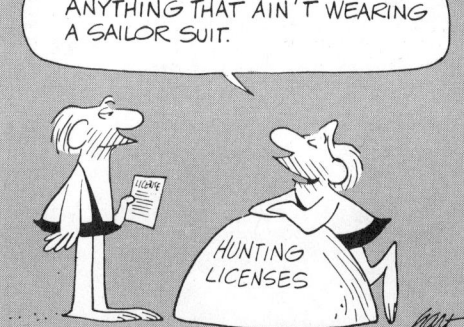

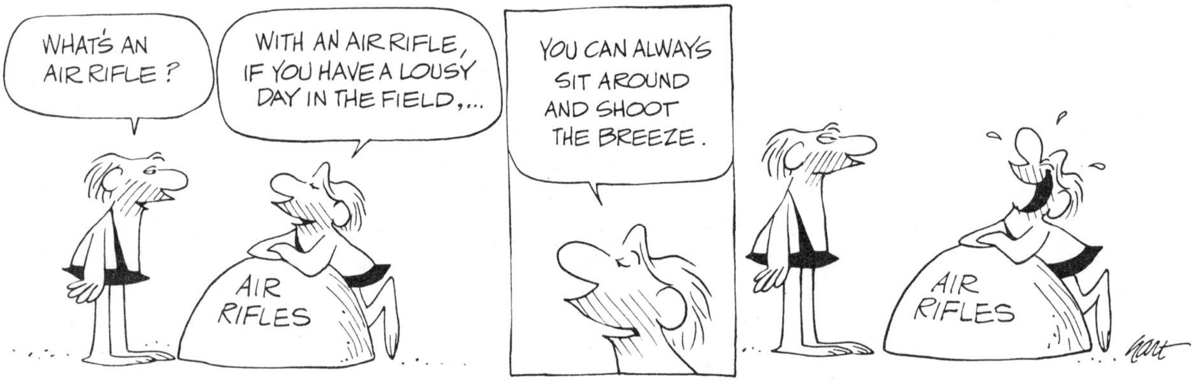
WHAT'S AN AIR RIFLE?
WITH AN AIR RIFLE, IF YOU HAVE A LOUSY DAY IN THE FIELD,...
AIR RIFLES
YOU CAN ALWAYS SIT AROUND AND SHOOT THE BREEZE.
AIR RIFLES

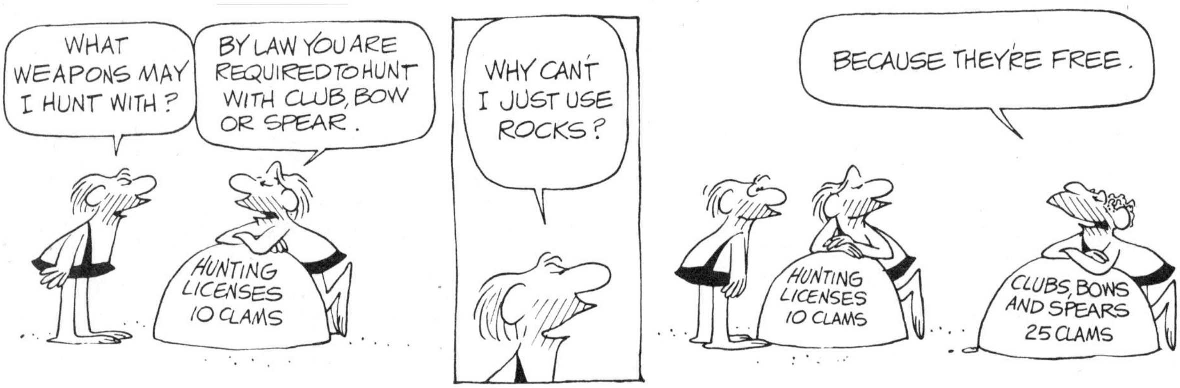
WHAT WEAPONS MAY I HUNT WITH?
BY LAW YOU ARE REQUIRED TO HUNT WITH CLUB, BOW OR SPEAR.
HUNTING LICENSES 10 CLAMS
WHY CAN'T I JUST USE ROCKS?
BECAUSE THEY'RE FREE.
HUNTING LICENSES 10 CLAMS
CLUBS, BOWS AND SPEARS 25 CLAMS

I'M CONVINCED THAT I AM BECOMING A KLEPTOMANIAC.
DR. PETER ⟷ HEAD SHRINKER
WHAT MAKES YOU SO SURE?
...I SAID, WHAT MAKES YOU.. SO....
DR. ED INKER
hart

" STICKER PRICE "

THE BOOK OF PHRASES
WHAT THE STICKEE HAS TO UNSTICK AFTER THE STICKER STICKS IT TO THE STICKEE.
THE BOOK OF PHRASES
hart

WANNA GO TO A PARTY TONIGHT AT THE FAT BROAD'S CAVE?
SURE.
WHAT DO I HAVE TO BRING?
NOTHING. I TOLD HER I'D BRING SOME DIP.
hart

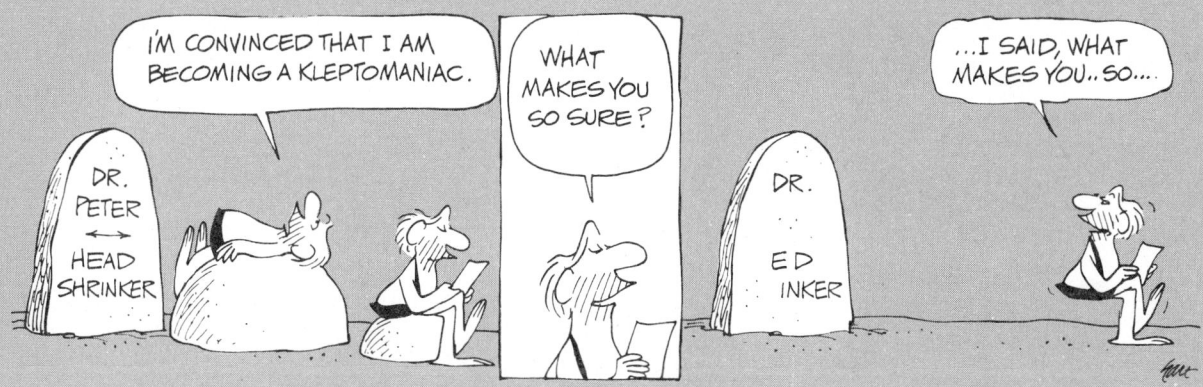

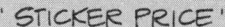

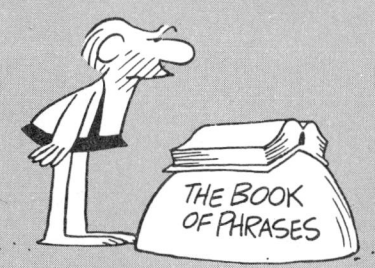

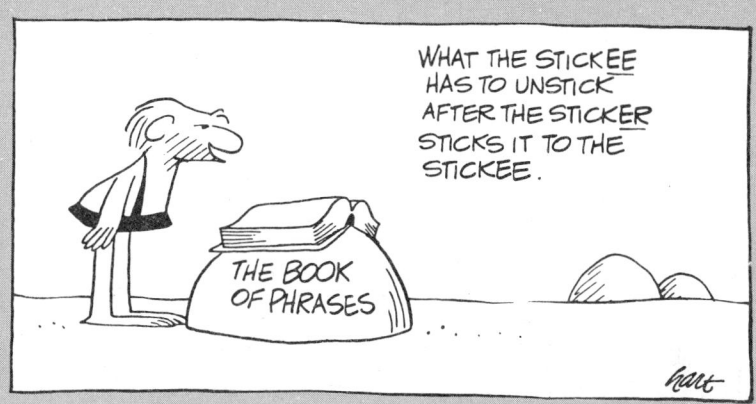

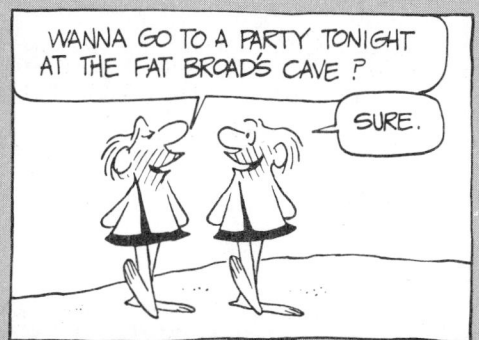

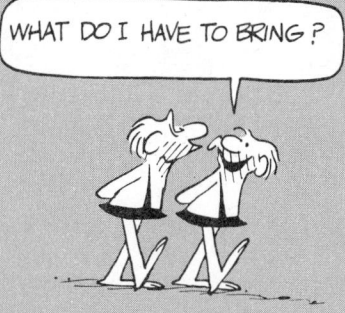

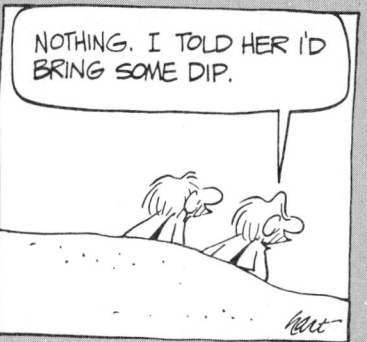

WHY THE LONG FACE ?
ZOT
I HATE THAT CLICHÉ !

WHAT ARE THE CHANCES OF RAIN ?
LESS THAN 1 %
WEATHER FORECAST

PREHISTORIC PESSIMISTIC SOCIETY
TODAY'S PICNIC CANCELLED

I THINK THE DAISY SHOULD BE THE TRADITIONAL FLOWER FOR FUNERALS.
WHY?
WHO EVER HEARD OF PUSHING-UP LILIES?

proof·reader
WILEY'S DICTIONARY
THE PERSON THAT GIVES YOU THE BREATHALYZER TEST
WILEY'S DICTIONARY

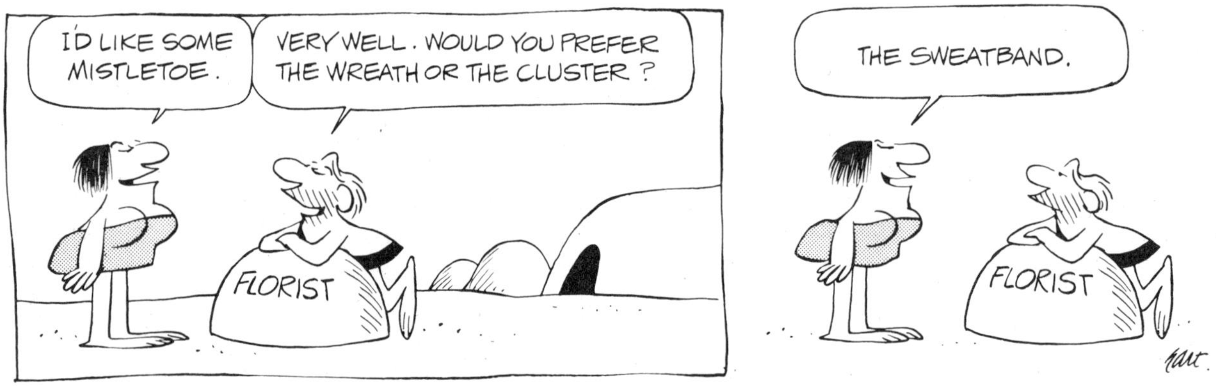
I'D LIKE SOME MISTLETOE.
VERY WELL. WOULD YOU PREFER THE WREATH OR THE CLUSTER ?
FLORIST
THE SWEATBAND.
FLORIST

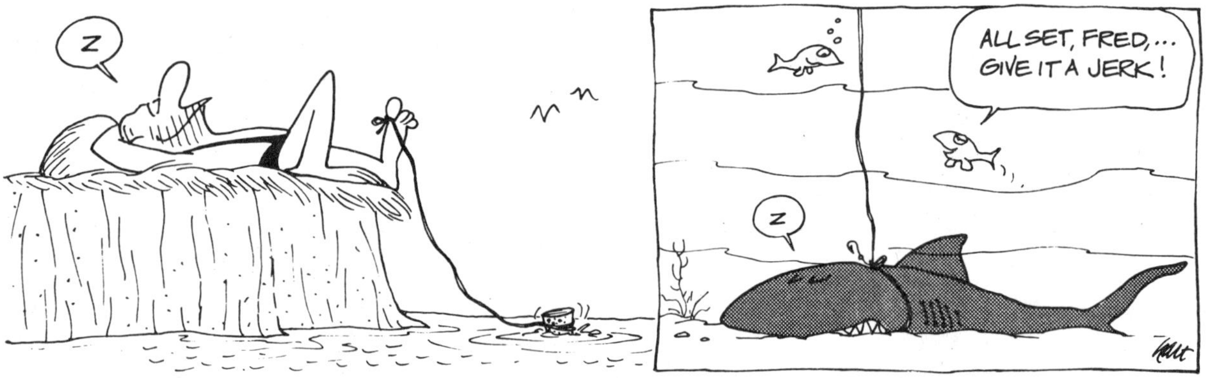
Z
Z
ALL SET, FRED,... GIVE IT A JERK!

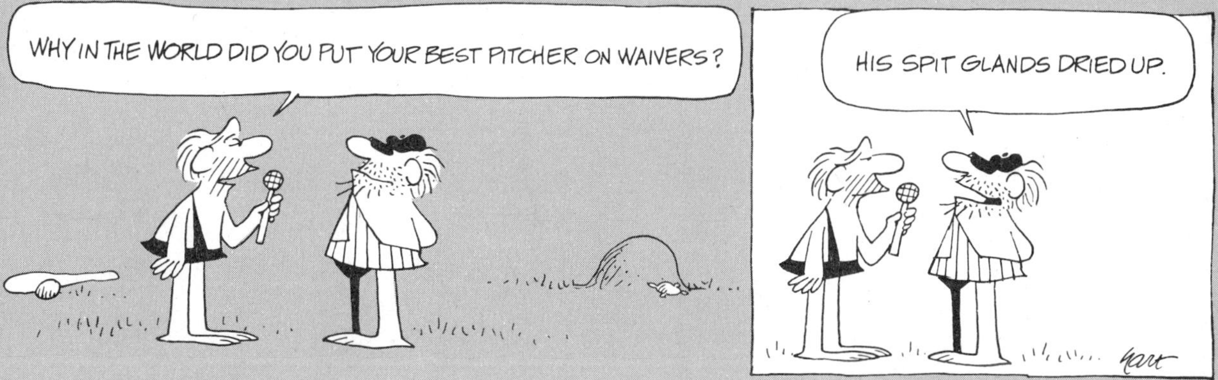
WHY IN THE WORLD DID YOU PUT YOUR BEST PITCHER ON WAIVERS?
HIS SPIT GLANDS DRIED UP.

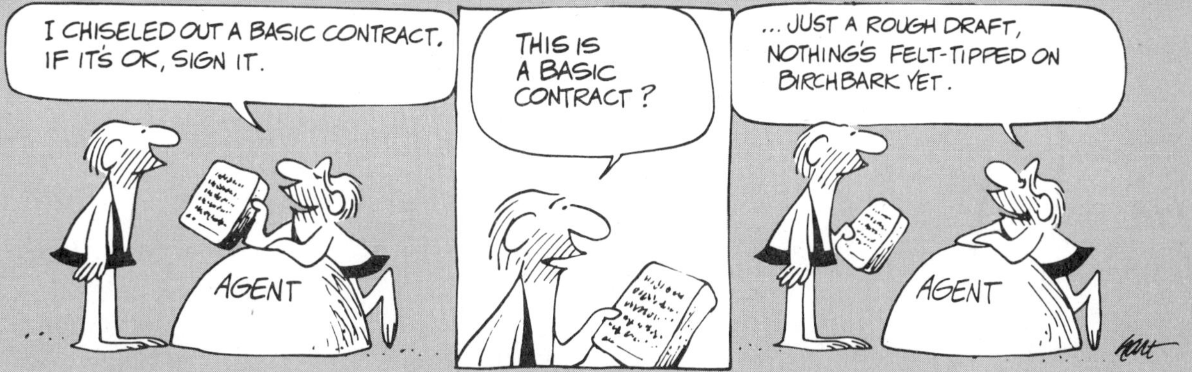
I CHISELED OUT A BASIC CONTRACT. IF IT'S OK, SIGN IT.
AGENT
THIS IS A BASIC CONTRACT?
... JUST A ROUGH DRAFT, NOTHING'S FELT-TIPPED ON BIRCHBARK YET.
AGENT

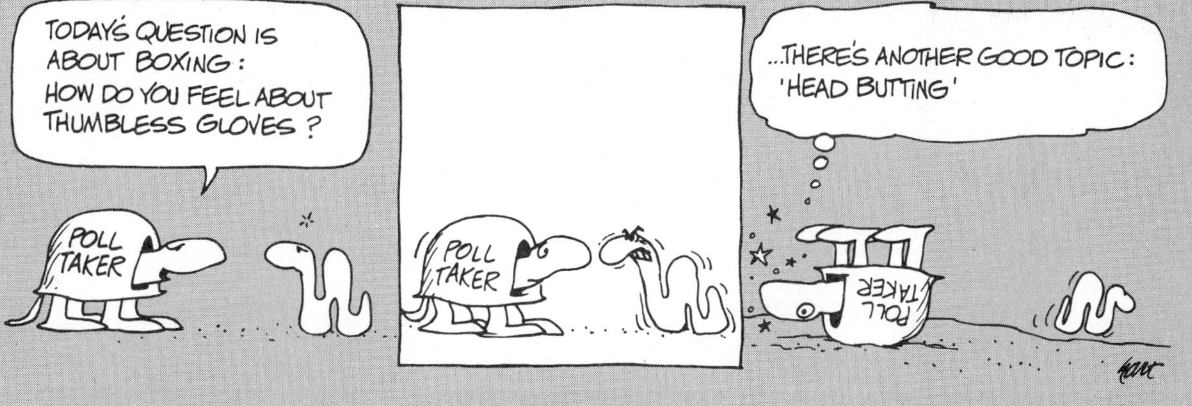
TODAY'S QUESTION IS ABOUT BOXING: HOW DO YOU FEEL ABOUT THUMBLESS GLOVES?
POLL TAKER
POLL TAKER
...THERE'S ANOTHER GOOD TOPIC: 'HEAD BUTTING'
POLL TAKER

MEN, I AM GRATEFUL THAT THE SEASON IS OVER AND I AM GRATEFUL THAT NOBODY WAS INJURED,... I HAVEN'T SEEN THE FILMS YET, SO I...
COACH
FILM HASN'T EVEN BEEN INVENTED YET!
..... AM MOST GRATEFUL FOR THAT!
COACH

Dear Fat Broad,
ADVICE COLUMN
what's the best way to tell a friend he's 'worn out his welcome' when he comes to visit?
LEAVE A NOTE ON THE DOOR THAT SAYS, 'I'M HIDING'
ADVICE COLUMN

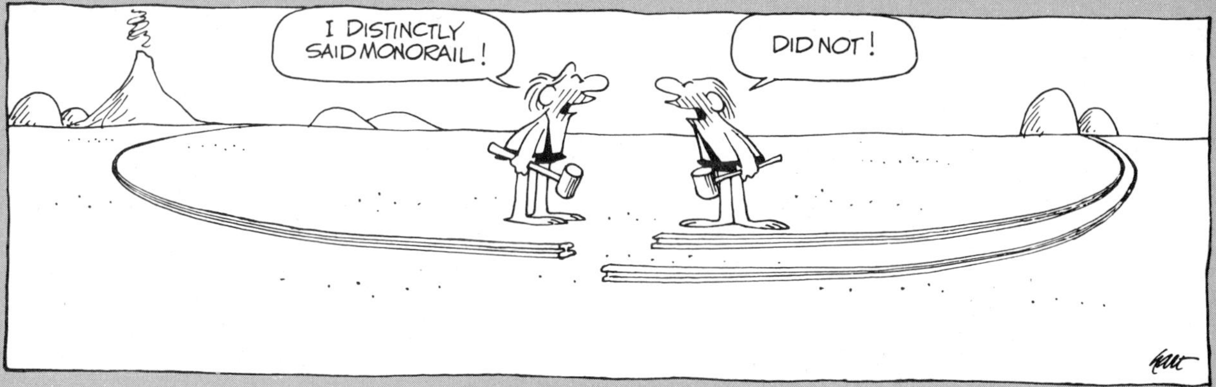
I DISTINCTLY SAID MONORAIL!
DID NOT!

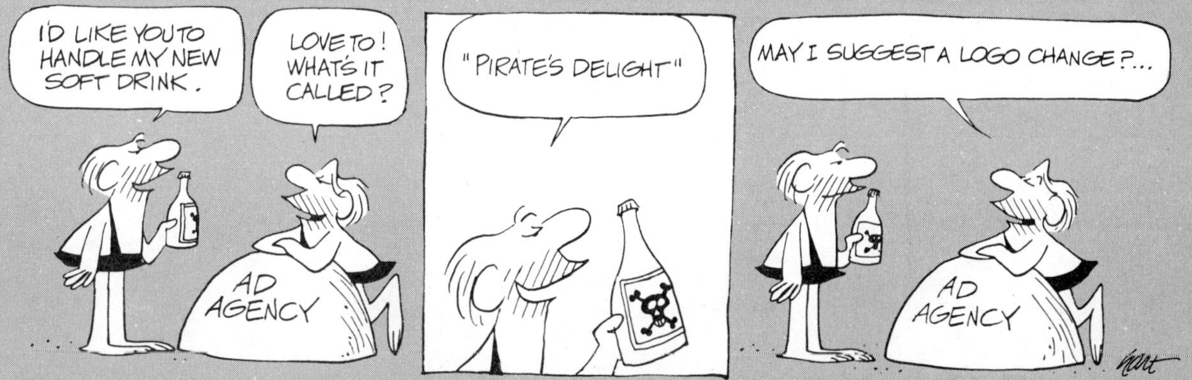
I'D LIKE YOU TO HANDLE MY NEW SOFT DRINK.
LOVE TO! WHAT'S IT CALLED?
AD AGENCY
"PIRATE'S DELIGHT"
MAY I SUGGEST A LOGO CHANGE?...
AD AGENCY

HOW RELIABLE IS YOUR NEWS ?
WE USE THE MOST UNIMPEACHABLE SOURCE KNOWN TO MAN .
NEWS DESK
HERE COMES A STORY NOW...
NEWS DESK
CLICKITY CLICK CLICKITY CLICK CLICK
the Daily Mud

DOWN WITH DRUGS
...GOT ANYTHING FOR HEAT STROKE ?
PETER'S DRUG STORE

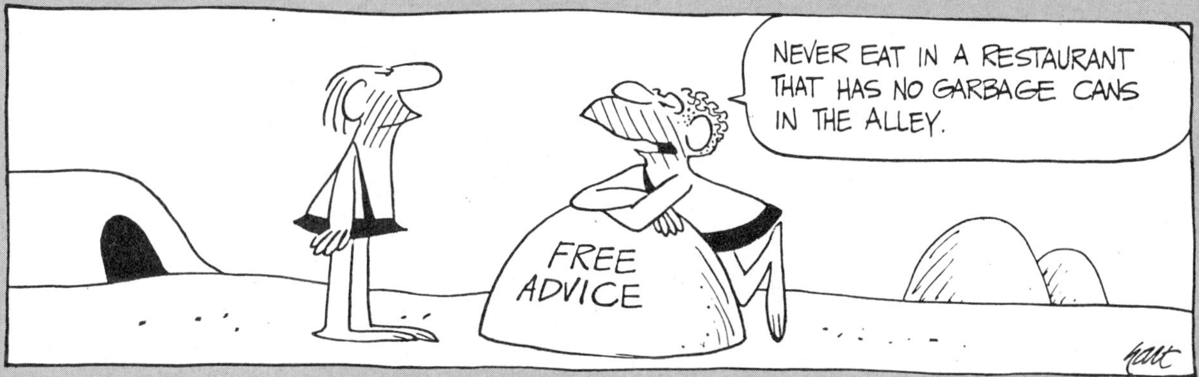
NEVER EAT IN A RESTAURANT THAT HAS NO GARBAGE CANS IN THE ALLEY.
FREE ADVICE

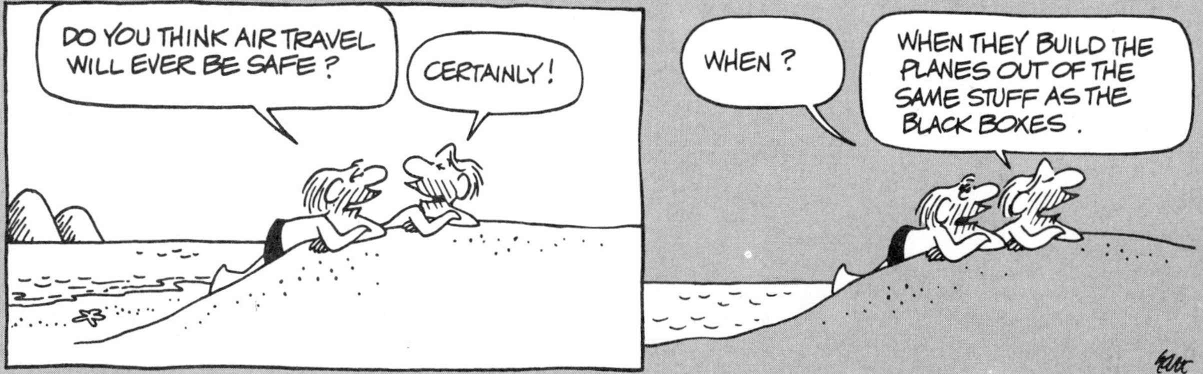
DO YOU THINK AIR TRAVEL WILL EVER BE SAFE ?
CERTAINLY !
WHEN ?
WHEN THEY BUILD THE PLANES OUT OF THE SAME STUFF AS THE BLACK BOXES .

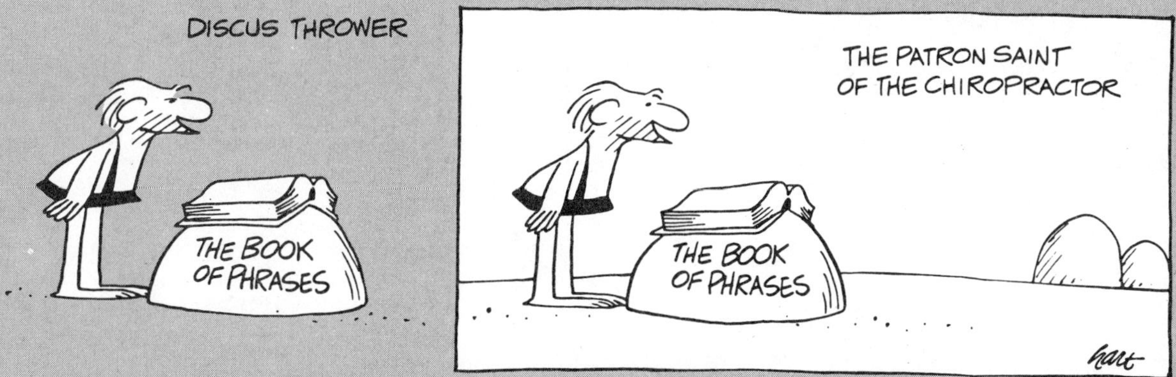
DISCUS THROWER
THE BOOK OF PHRASES
THE PATRON SAINT OF THE CHIROPRACTOR
THE BOOK OF PHRASES

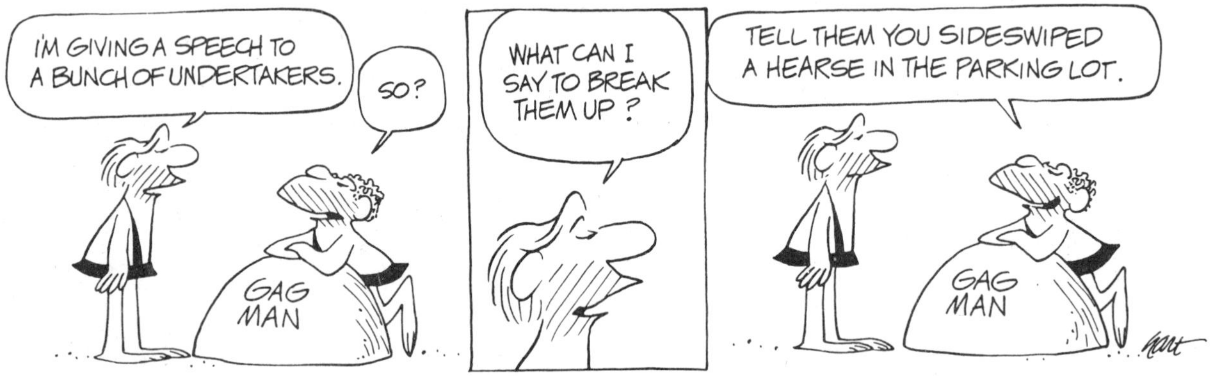
I'M GIVING A SPEECH TO A BUNCH OF UNDERTAKERS.
SO?
GAG MAN
WHAT CAN I SAY TO BREAK THEM UP ?
TELL THEM YOU SIDESWIPED A HEARSE IN THE PARKING LOT.
GAG MAN

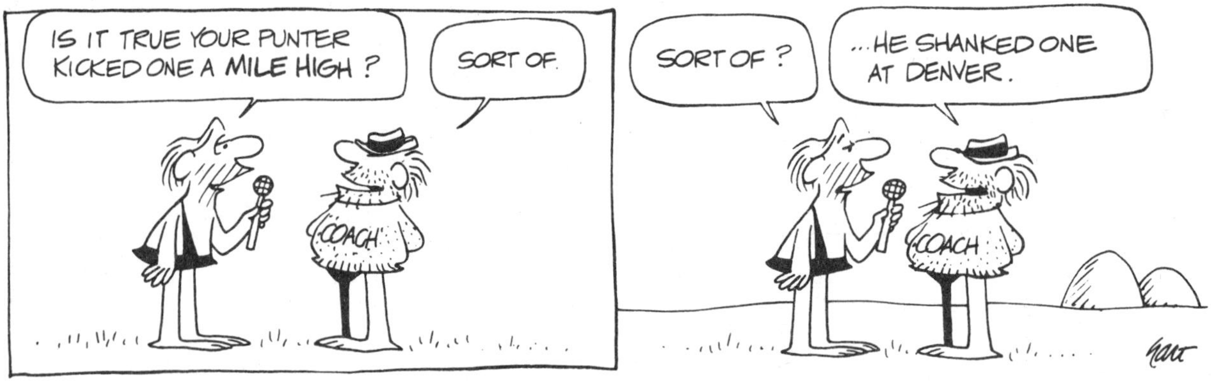
IS IT TRUE YOUR PUNTER KICKED ONE A MILE HIGH ?
SORT OF.
COACH
SORT OF ?
...HE SHANKED ONE AT DENVER.
COACH

WHAT'S IT TAKE TO BE A SUCCESSFUL P.R. MAN ?
IMAGINATION, DARING, RESOURCEFULNESS, CREATIVITY, KNOW-HOW,...
P.R. MAN
HOW MUCH LUCK ?
ABOUT 99 %
P.R. MAN
hart

'HOPE AGAINST HOPE'
THE BOOK OF PHRASES
ONE OF THE MORE HOPELESS WAYS FOR THE HOPEFUL TO HOPE
THE BOOK OF PHRASES
hart

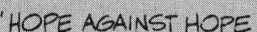

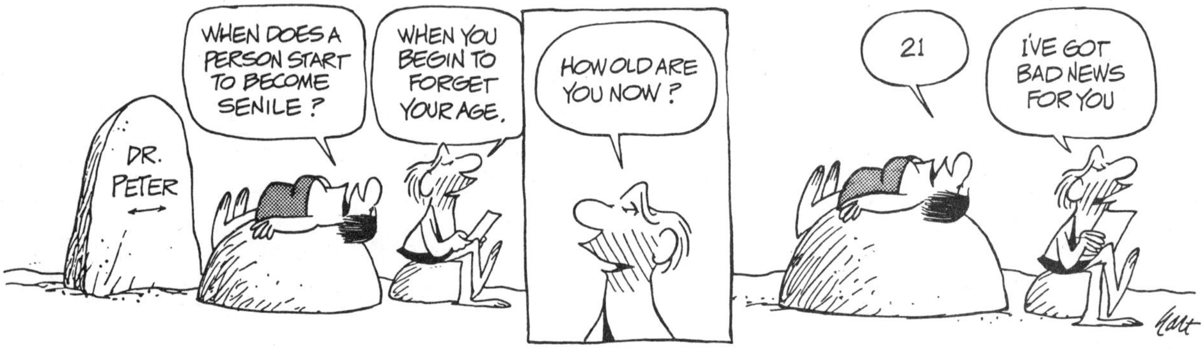
DR. PETER
WHEN DOES A PERSON START TO BECOME SENILE?
WHEN YOU BEGIN TO FORGET YOUR AGE.
HOW OLD ARE YOU NOW?
21
I'VE GOT BAD NEWS FOR YOU

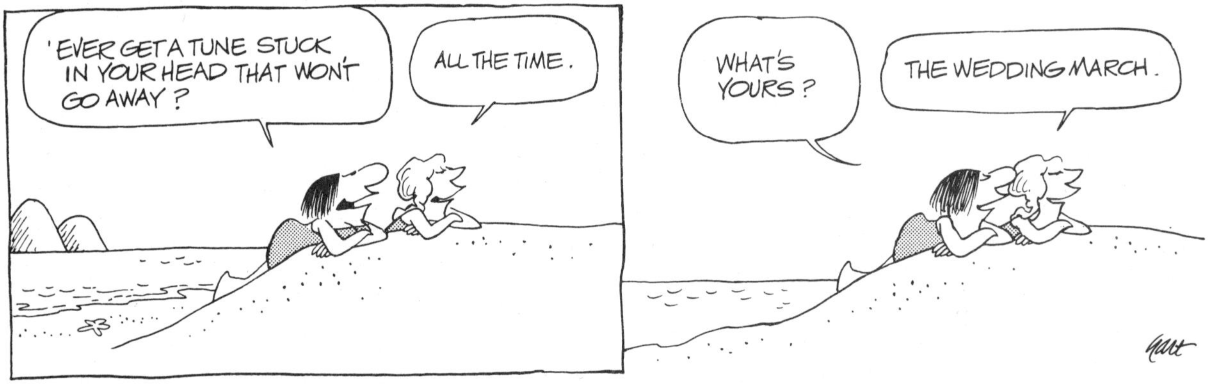
'EVER GET A TUNE STUCK IN YOUR HEAD THAT WON'T GO AWAY?
ALL THE TIME.
WHAT'S YOURS?
THE WEDDING MARCH.

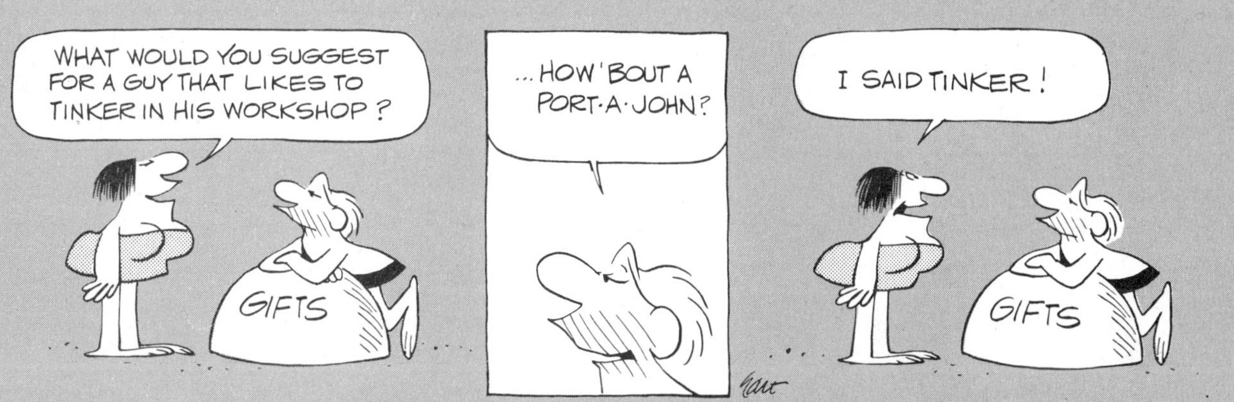
WHAT WOULD YOU SUGGEST FOR A GUY THAT LIKES TO TINKER IN HIS WORKSHOP ?
... HOW 'BOUT A PORT-A-JOHN ?
I SAID TINKER !

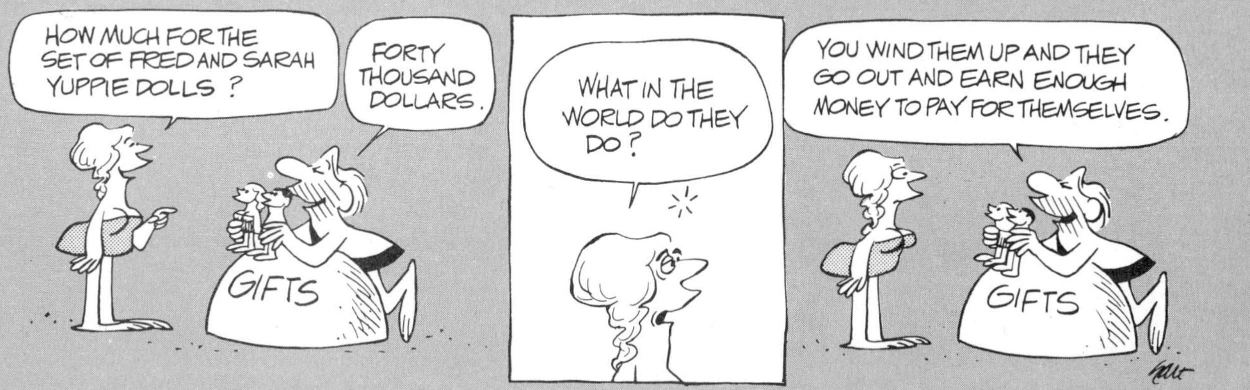
HOW MUCH FOR THE SET OF FRED AND SARAH YUPPIE DOLLS ?
FORTY THOUSAND DOLLARS.
WHAT IN THE WORLD DO THEY DO ?
YOU WIND THEM UP AND THEY GO OUT AND EARN ENOUGH MONEY TO PAY FOR THEMSELVES.
GIFTS

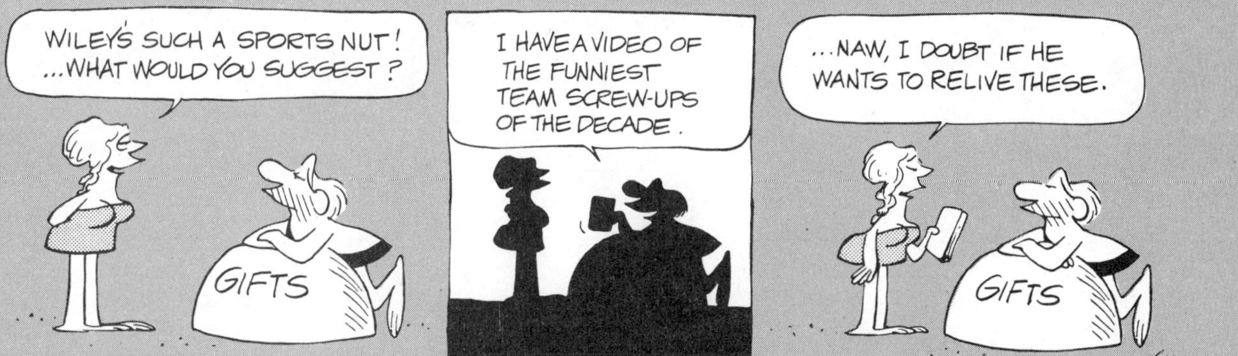
WILEY'S SUCH A SPORTS NUT ! ... WHAT WOULD YOU SUGGEST ?
I HAVE A VIDEO OF THE FUNNIEST TEAM SCREW-UPS OF THE DECADE .
... NAW, I DOUBT IF HE WANTS TO RELIVE THESE.

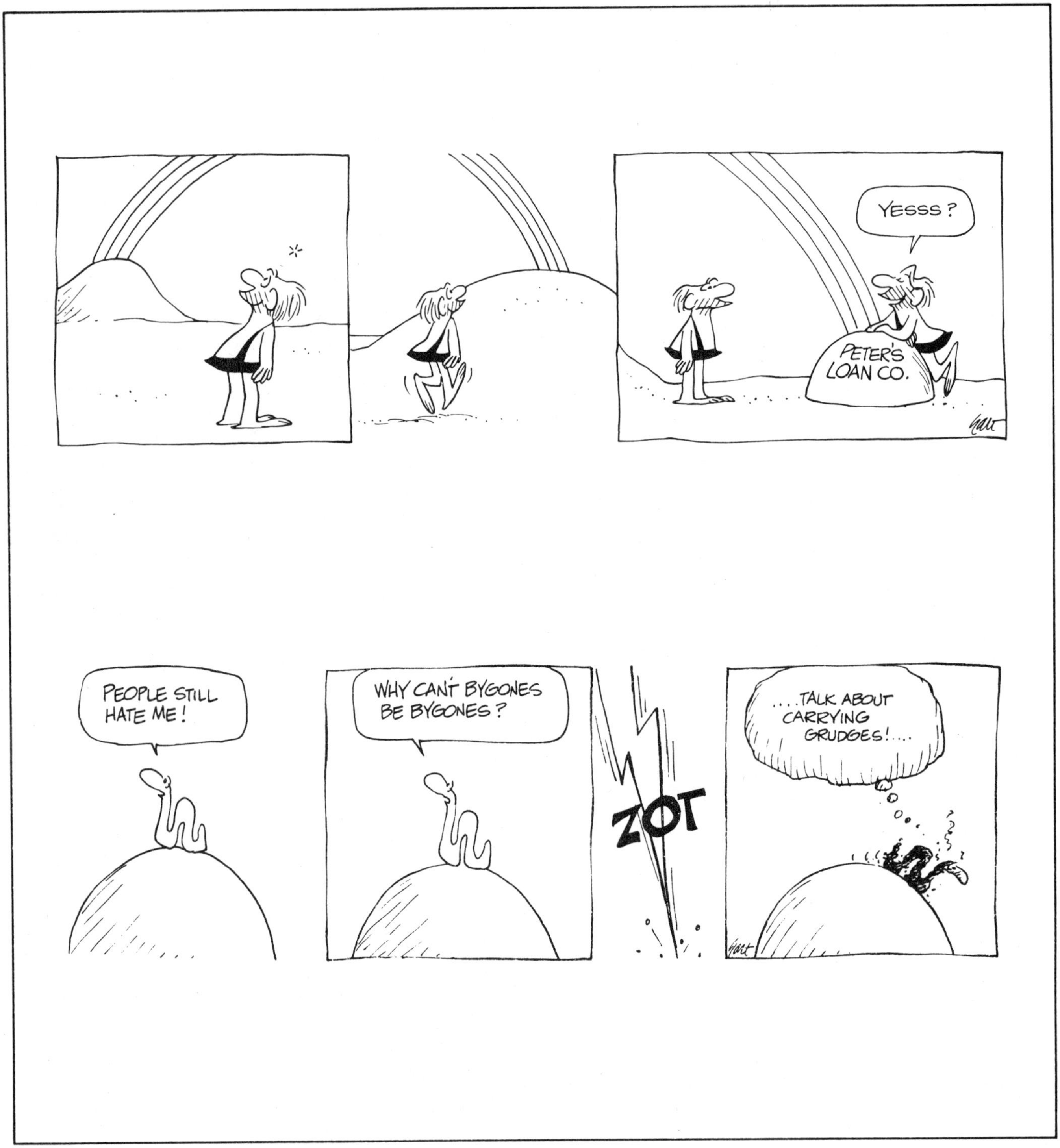
YESSS ?
PETER'S LOAN CO.
PEOPLE STILL HATE ME !
WHY CAN'T BYGONES BE BYGONES ?
ZOT
....TALK ABOUT CARRYING GRUDGES!....

I CAME FROM A REAL TOUGH SCHOOL.
HOW TOUGH WAS IT ?
THE CLASS BULLY WAS VOTED "WIMP OF THE YEAR."
hart

WILL THAT BE REGULAR DELIVERY OR EXPRESS ?
POST OFFICE
MAIL
hart

I'VE INVENTED SPRAY PAINT!
GREAT! HOW'S IT WORK?
PATENT OFFICE
PFFFFFFFFFFFF
SPLUT
STILL HAS A FEW BUGS IN IT...

ZOT
I'VE GOT TO CORRECT THAT SLICE.

IS A TOMATO A FRUIT OR A VEGETABLE ?
WHAT ARE YOU USING IT FOR ?
FRUITS AND VEGETABLES
I WAS THINKING OF PUTTING IT IN A FRUIT CAKE .
IT'S A VEGETABLE.
FRUITS AND VEGETABLES
hart

HOW DID THE INSTANT REPLAY RULE AFFECT YOU THIS YEAR ?
IT WAS EXTREMELY UNFAIR ! ....
COACH
I HAD TO PAY-OFF THE GUYS IN THE BOOTH TOO !
COACH
hart

also
WILEY'S DICTIONARY
THE STARTING CRY AT THE ANNUAL "QUILTOFF"
WILEY'S DICTIONARY
hart

THE NORDSMEN
YOU...AH...SPELLED 'NERDS' WRONG.

Dear Fat Broad,
ADVICE COLUMN
What's your secret for staying so trim and fit?
DEAR PIG BUTT, ...
ADVICE COLUMN

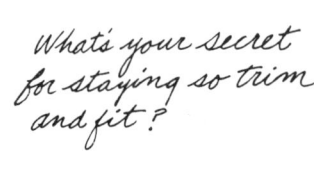

WELL, DO I GET A PATENT ON MY SPRAY PAINT OR DON'T I ?
WE DON'T JUST HAND OUT PATENTS, YOU KNOW, ...
PATENT OFFICE
THERE ARE TESTS TO BE MADE AND FORMS TO BE FILLED OUT AND...
WHICH LINE ?
...THE ONE WITH THE X .
PATENT OFFICE

MY LATEST INVENTION, 'THE BUMPER.'
FOR BUMPING THINGS !!
FOR BUMPER STICKERS .

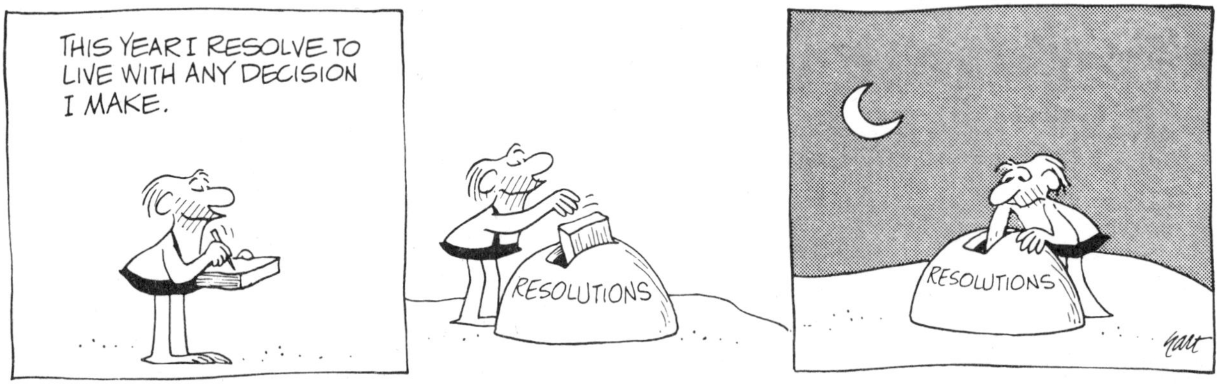
THIS YEAR I RESOLVE TO LIVE WITH ANY DECISION I MAKE.
RESOLUTIONS
RESOLUTIONS

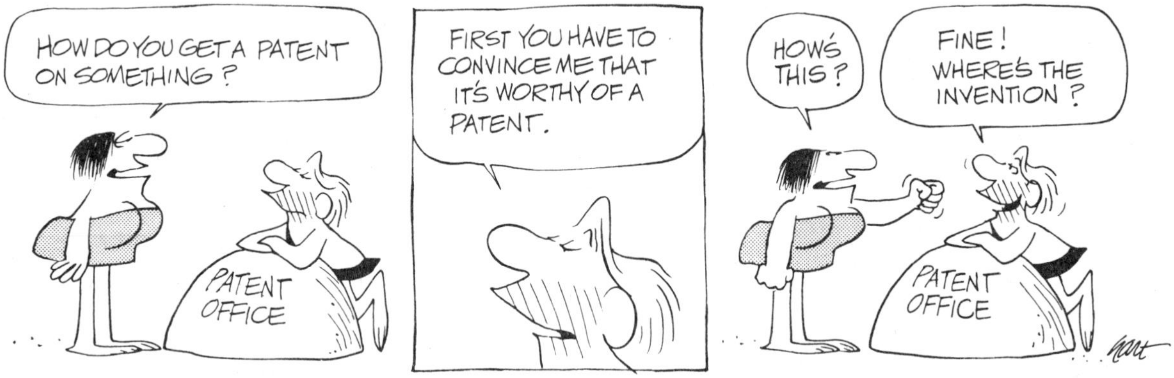
HOW DO YOU GET A PATENT ON SOMETHING?
PATENT OFFICE
FIRST YOU HAVE TO CONVINCE ME THAT IT'S WORTHY OF A PATENT.
HOW'S THIS?
FINE! WHERE'S THE INVENTION?
PATENT OFFICE

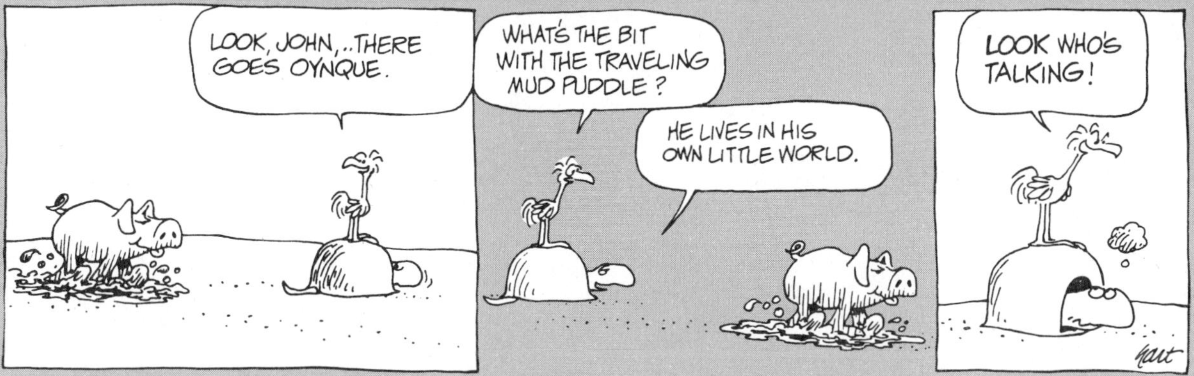
LOOK, JOHN, ..THERE GOES OYNQUE.
WHAT'S THE BIT WITH THE TRAVELING MUD PUDDLE?
HE LIVES IN HIS OWN LITTLE WORLD.
LOOK WHO'S TALKING!

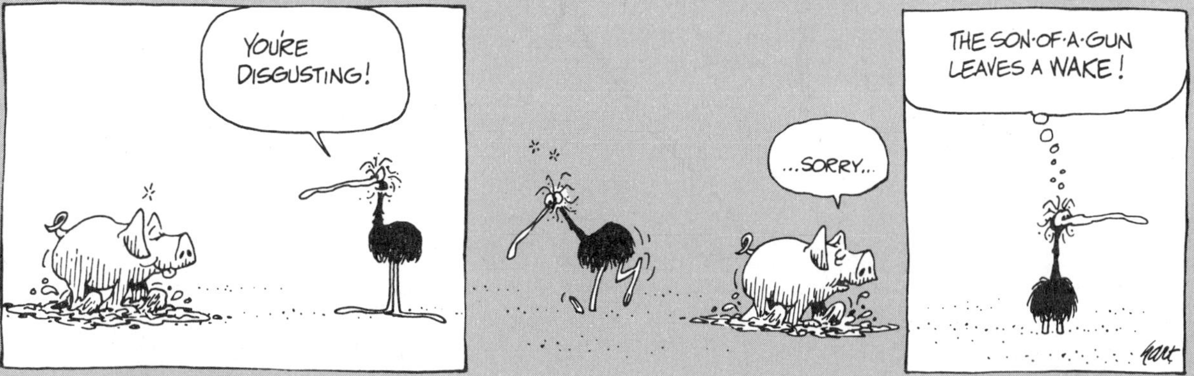
YOU'RE DISGUSTING!
...SORRY...
THE SON·OF·A·GUN LEAVES A WAKE!

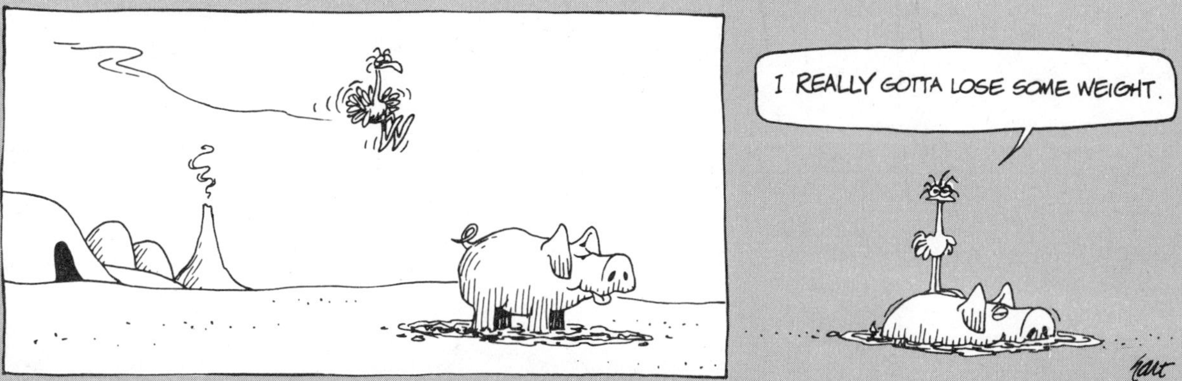
I REALLY GOTTA LOSE SOME WEIGHT.

MY FRIEND WOULD LIKE A PAIR OF GLASSES.
WE CAN'T MAKE GLASSES FOR FROGS!
OPTICIAN
WHY NOT?
'CAUSE THEY DON'T HAVE ANY EARS!
OPTICIAN

I SEE OL' CLUMSY'S AT IT AGAIN.
* JUST A MINUTE! ...HOW THE HECK DID YOU KNOW THAT WAS CLUMSY?

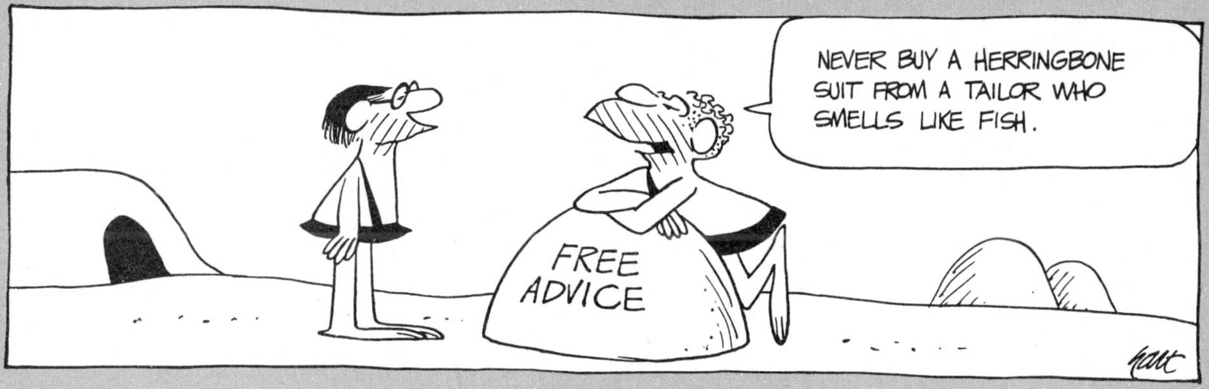
NEVER BUY A HERRINGBONE SUIT FROM A TAILOR WHO SMELLS LIKE FISH.
FREE ADVICE

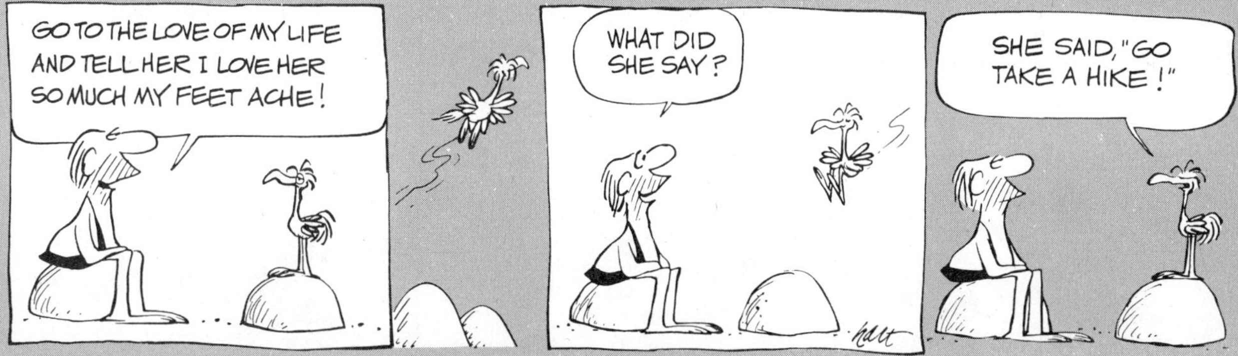
GO TO THE LOVE OF MY LIFE AND TELL HER I LOVE HER SO MUCH MY FEET ACHE!
WHAT DID SHE SAY?
SHE SAID, "GO TAKE A HIKE!"

JAKE! STOP TOSSING JUNIOR SO HIGH. YOU'LL SCARE HIM!
NONSENSE! ...HE LOVES IT.
ZOT
MANNA FROM HEAVEN!

Dear Fat Broad,
what do I do with an irresponsible lout that has nothing more to offer than Good looks and love?
ADVICE COLUMN
GIVE HIM TO ME.
ADVICE COLUMN

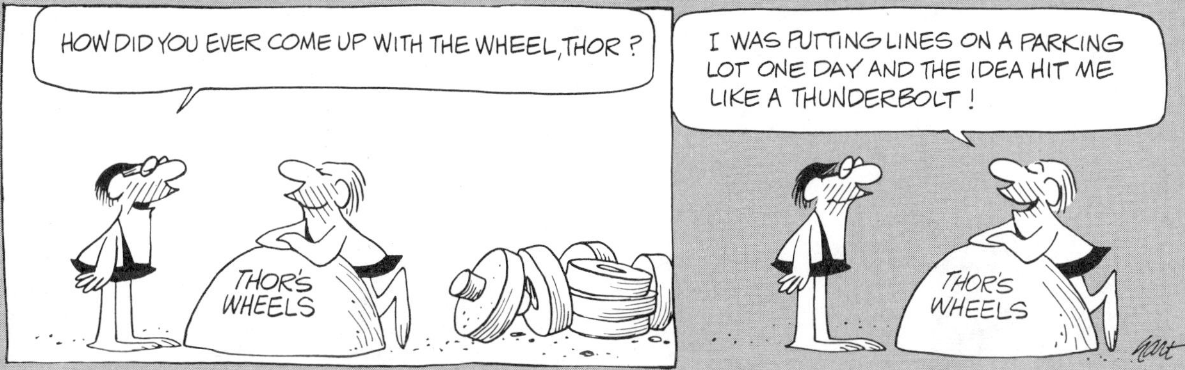
HOW DID YOU EVER COME UP WITH THE WHEEL, THOR ?
THOR'S WHEELS
I WAS PUTTING LINES ON A PARKING LOT ONE DAY AND THE IDEA HIT ME LIKE A THUNDERBOLT !
THOR'S WHEELS

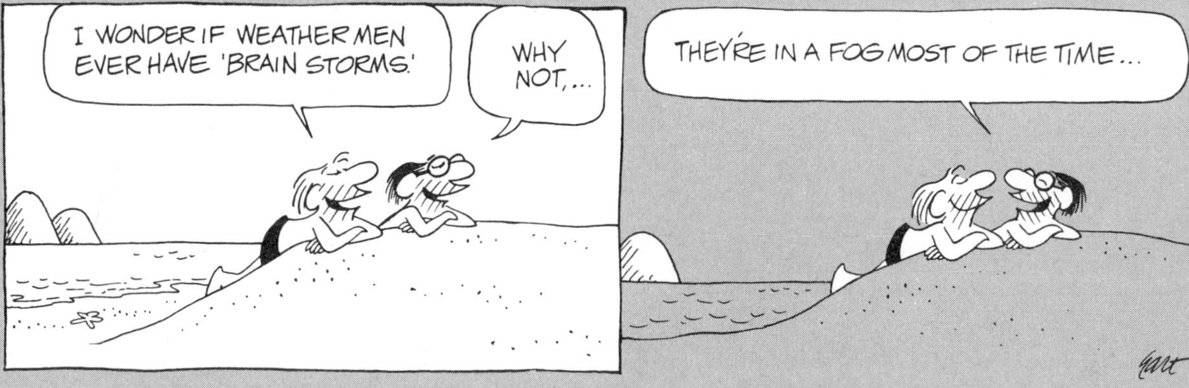
I WONDER IF WEATHER MEN EVER HAVE 'BRAIN STORMS.'
WHY NOT, ...
THEY'RE IN A FOG MOST OF THE TIME ...

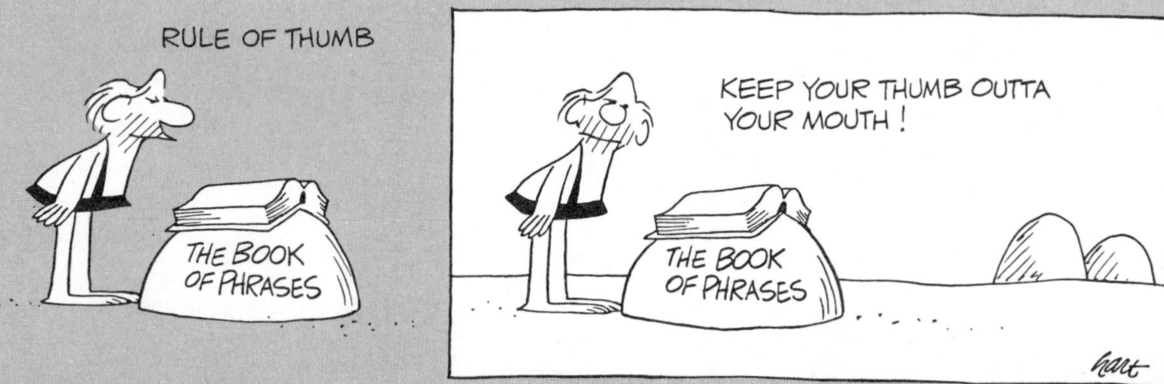
RULE OF THUMB
THE BOOK OF PHRASES
KEEP YOUR THUMB OUTTA YOUR MOUTH !
THE BOOK OF PHRASES

QUACK
QUACK
QUACK
QUACK
QUACK
QUACK
QUACK
WHAT'S THAT ?
EITHER THE GEESE ARE RETURNING OR THERE'S A MEDICAL CONVENTION IN TOWN.
hart

LET'S GO TO A MOVIE, GRAMPS.
YOU KIDDING ?... ALL THE MOVIES ARE MADE FOR KIDS!
HERE'S ONE WE CAN BOTH SEE!
WHAT IS IT ?
"I WAS A TEENAGE OCTOGENARIAN."
hart

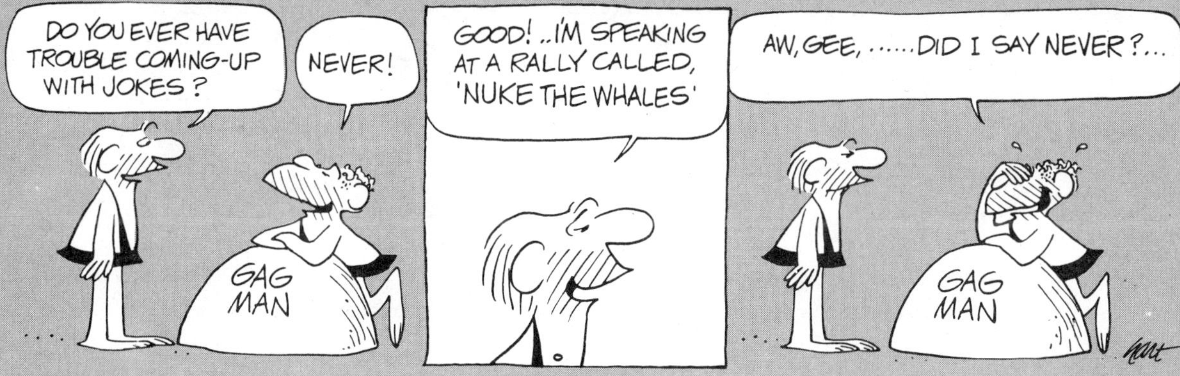
DO YOU EVER HAVE TROUBLE COMING-UP WITH JOKES ?
NEVER!
GAG MAN
GOOD! ..I'M SPEAKING AT A RALLY CALLED, 'NUKE THE WHALES'
AW, GEE, ...DID I SAY NEVER ?...
GAG MAN

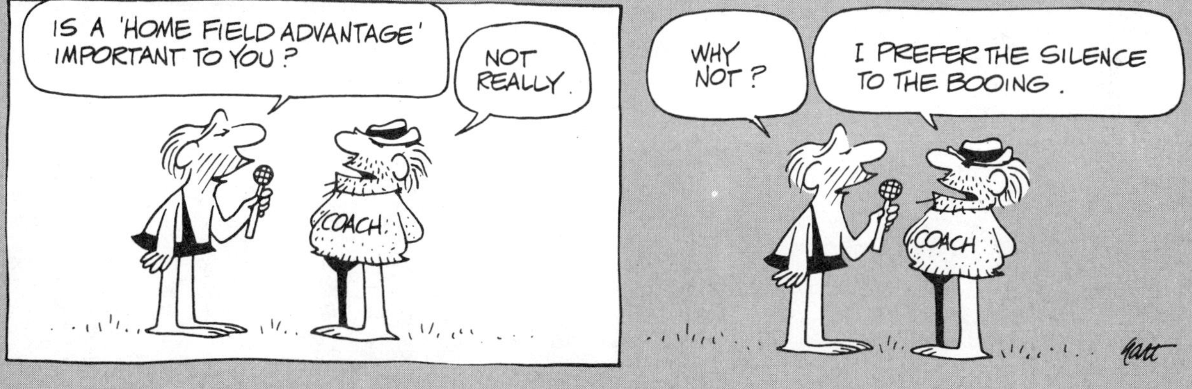
IS A 'HOME FIELD ADVANTAGE' IMPORTANT TO YOU ?
NOT REALLY.
COACH
WHY NOT ?
I PREFER THE SILENCE TO THE BOOING.
COACH

SPIDER....LADYBUG...
..ANT.....GNAT....
VERY GOOD,...NOW THE OTHER EYE.

WHAT'S IT MEAN, JOHN?
EITHER, 'DON'T EAT THE MUSHROOMS' ...OR 'BAN THE BOMB'

NEVER CHARTER AN AIRPLANE THAT HAS PONTOONS ON THE TOP OF THE WINGS.
FREE ADVICE
hart

ad infinitum

WILEY'S DICTIONARY

WHAT YOU DON'T GET ON PAY TV
WILEY'S DICTIONARY
hart

DO YOU HAVE ANY 'STEWING' CHICKENS?
MEAT
ACTUALLY THEY'VE **ALL** BEEN A LITTLE CRANKY SINCE THE ROOSTER 'FLEW THE COOP.'
MEAT
hart

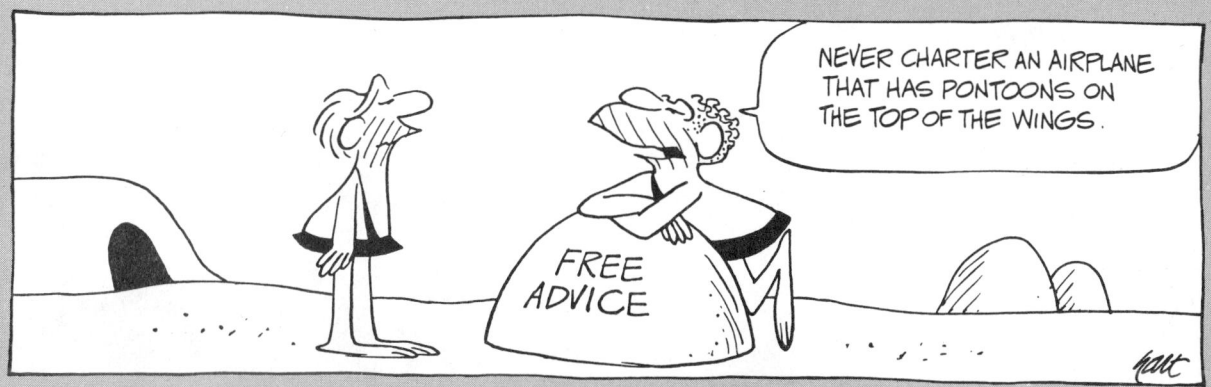

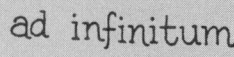

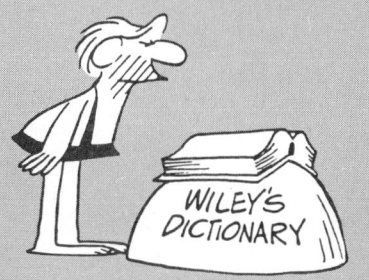

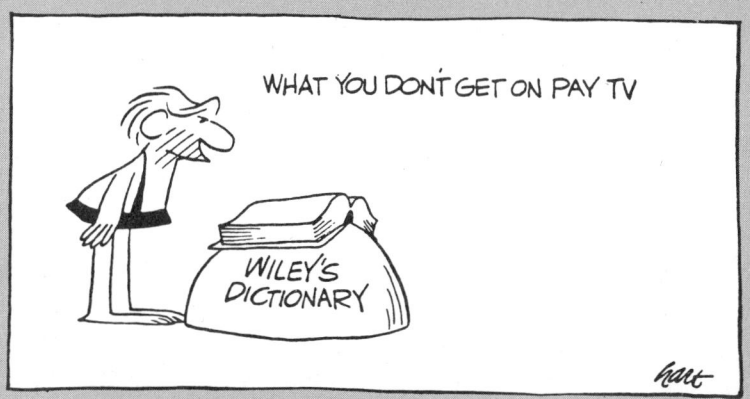

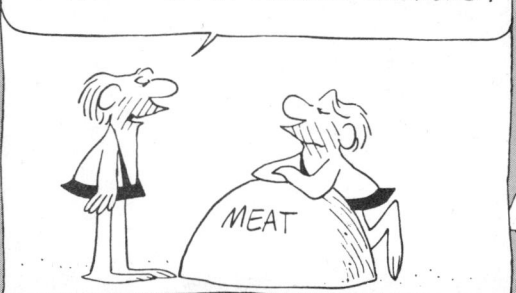

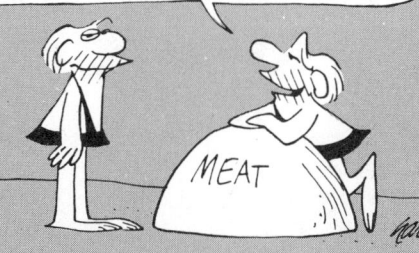

THEN THE GOOD GUY PICKED UP A BIG ROCK AND TOOK AND KILLED THE GUY THAT THOUGHT HE WAS SO SMART...
AND THEY ALL LIVED HAPPILY EVER AFTER.
SIGH.
YOU CAN'T READ, CAN YOU, DAD?

WHAT'S THAT?
A PORTABLE STOOL. ...GREAT FOR FIELD TRIPS AND SPORTING EVENTS.
CAN I TRY IT?
BE MY GUEST.
YIKES
WHAT A JERK.

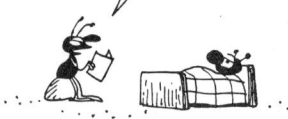

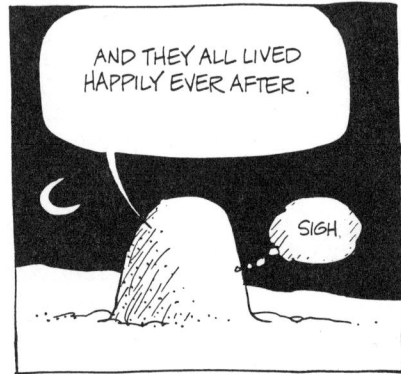

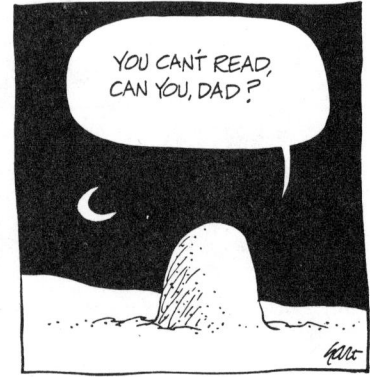

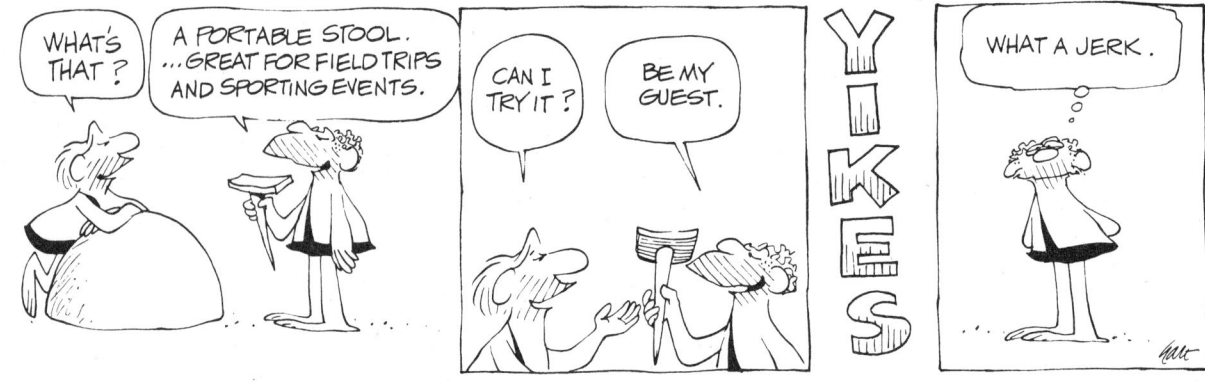

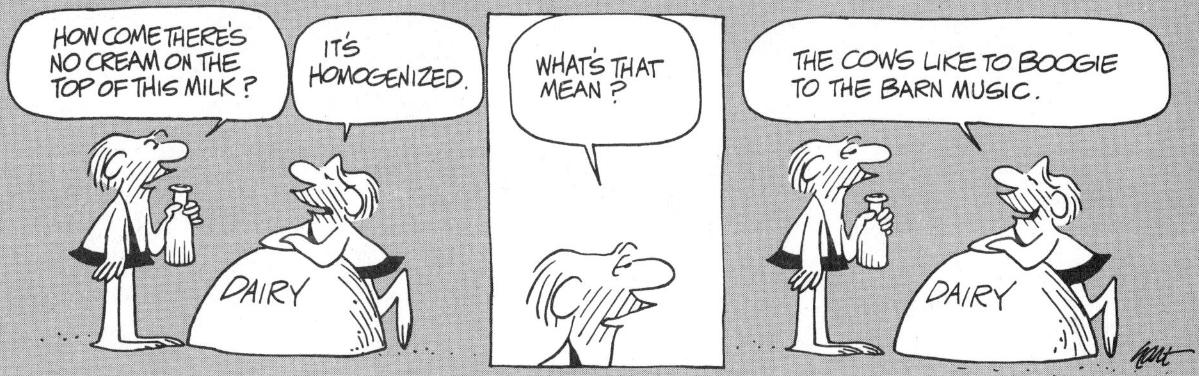
HOW COME THERE'S NO CREAM ON THE TOP OF THIS MILK ?
IT'S HOMOGENIZED.
DAIRY
WHAT'S THAT MEAN ?
THE COWS LIKE TO BOOGIE TO THE BARN MUSIC.
DAIRY

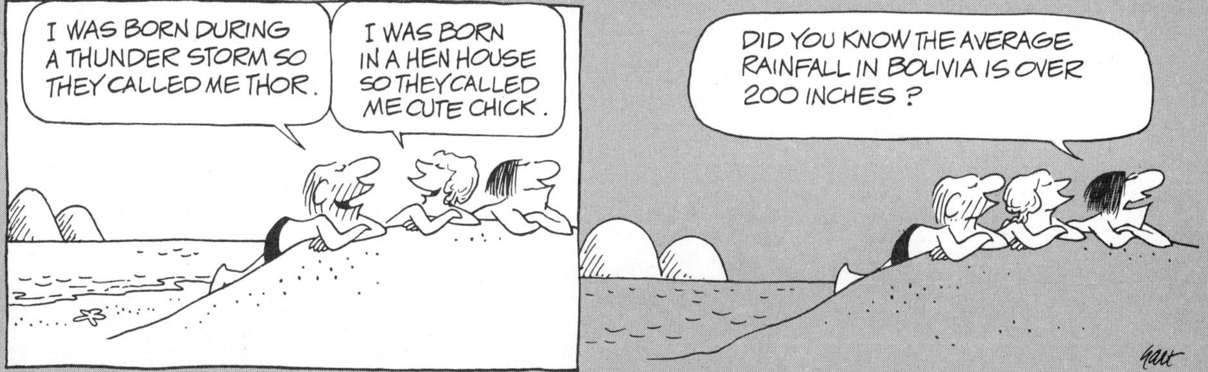
I WAS BORN DURING A THUNDER STORM SO THEY CALLED ME THOR.
I WAS BORN IN A HEN HOUSE SO THEY CALLED ME CUTE CHICK.
DID YOU KNOW THE AVERAGE RAINFALL IN BOLIVIA IS OVER 200 INCHES ?

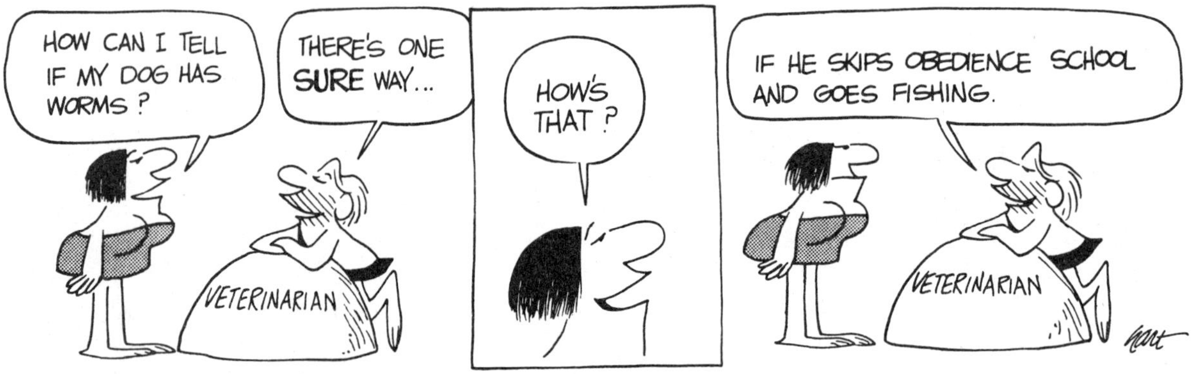
HOW CAN I TELL IF MY DOG HAS WORMS ?
THERE'S ONE SURE WAY...
VETERINARIAN
HOW'S THAT ?
IF HE SKIPS OBEDIENCE SCHOOL AND GOES FISHING.
VETERINARIAN
hart

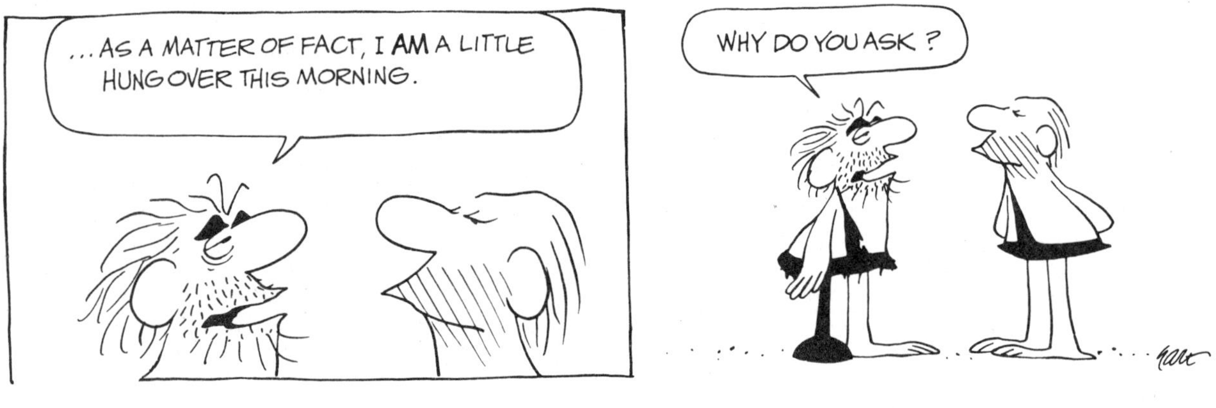
...AS A MATTER OF FACT, I AM A LITTLE HUNG OVER THIS MORNING.
WHY DO YOU ASK ?
hart

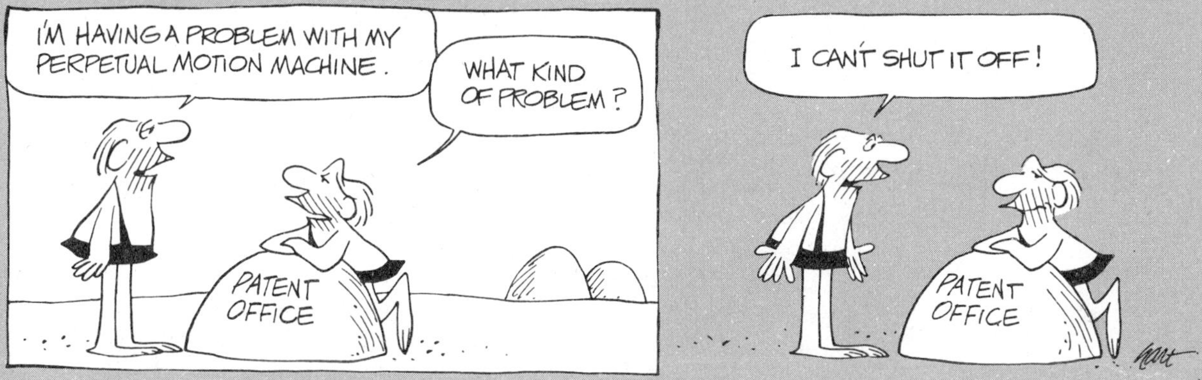
I'M HAVING A PROBLEM WITH MY PERPETUAL MOTION MACHINE.
WHAT KIND OF PROBLEM?
PATENT OFFICE
I CAN'T SHUT IT OFF!
PATENT OFFICE
hart

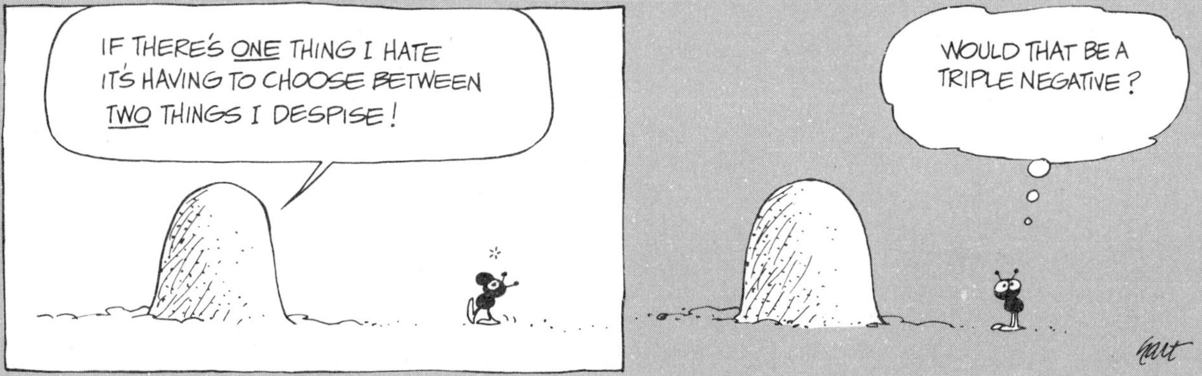
IF THERE'S ONE THING I HATE IT'S HAVING TO CHOOSE BETWEEN TWO THINGS I DESPISE!
WOULD THAT BE A TRIPLE NEGATIVE?
hart

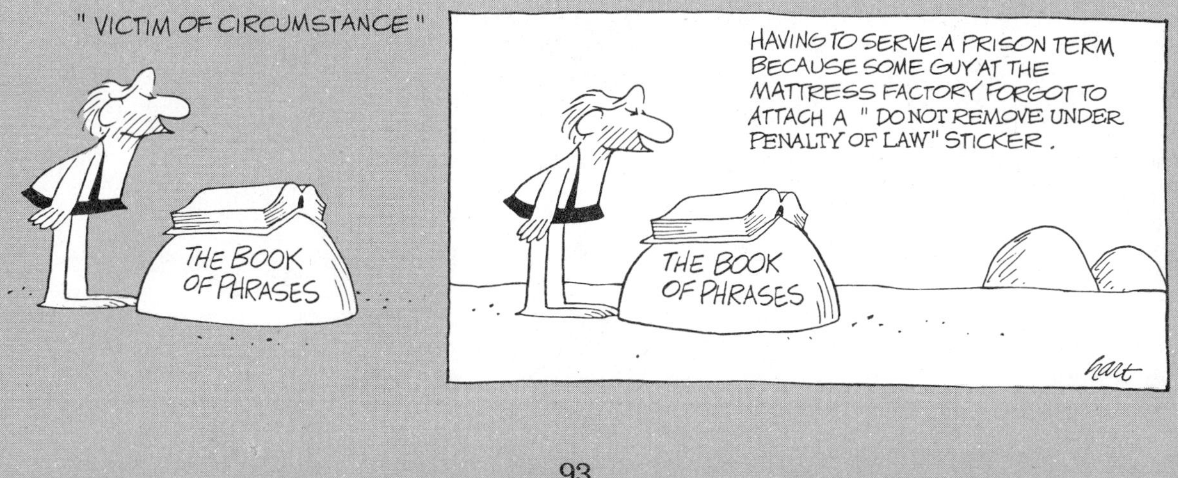
" VICTIM OF CIRCUMSTANCE "
THE BOOK OF PHRASES
HAVING TO SERVE A PRISON TERM BECAUSE SOME GUY AT THE MATTRESS FACTORY FORGOT TO ATTACH A " DO NOT REMOVE UNDER PENALTY OF LAW" STICKER.
THE BOOK OF PHRASES
hart

Dear Fat Broad,
Ever since my husband hired a new secretary, he's had to work a lot of overtime. Do you think it could just be a coincidence?
DEAR STUPID, ...
ADVICE COLUMN
ADVICE COLUMN
hart

LOVERS LEAP
?
hart

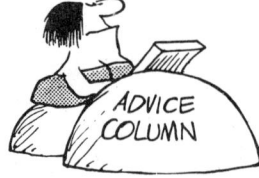

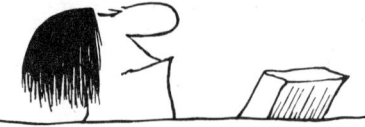

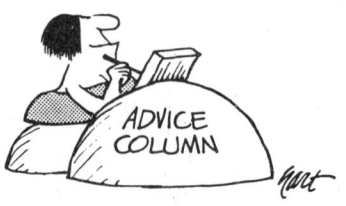

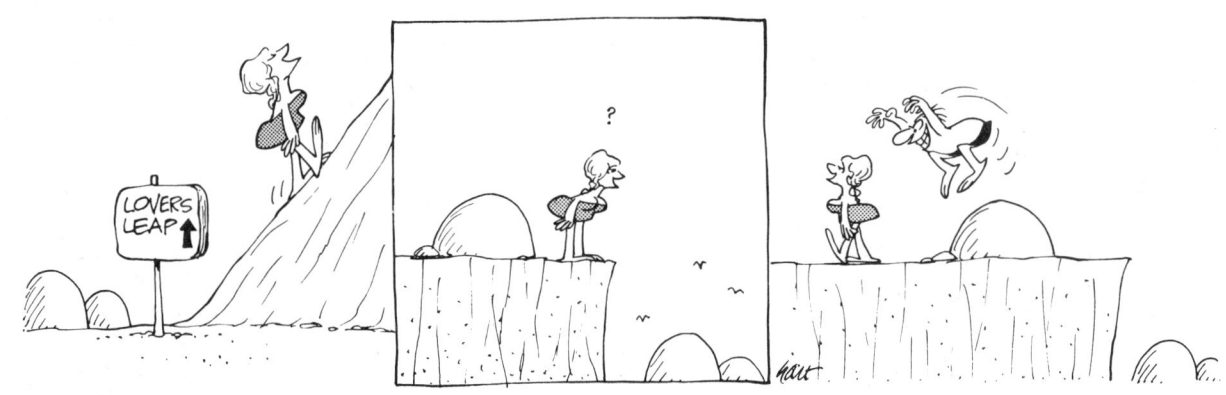

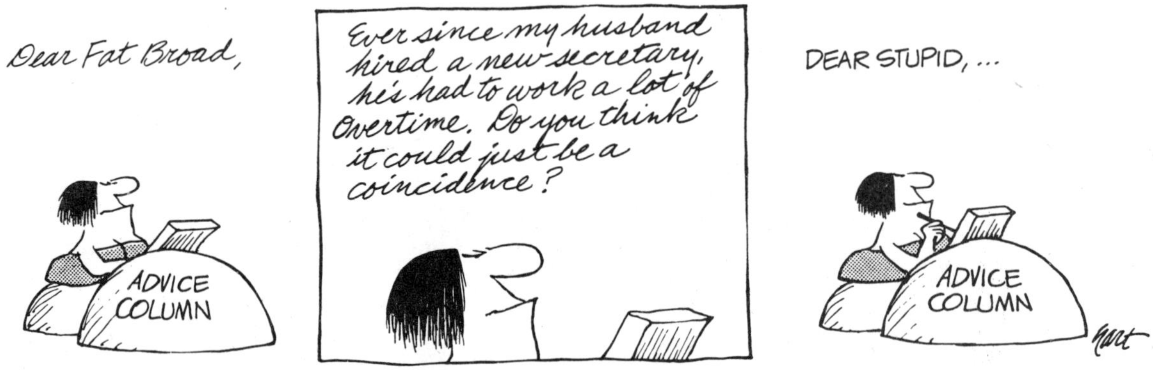

DON'T I NEED A PRESCRIPTION FOR THESE ?
NOPE.
PETER'S PHARMACY
WHY NOT ?
BECAUSE THERE'S NO LATIN WORD FOR THEM .
PETER'S PHARMACY

DO YOU HAVE OYSTERS ?
WE ONLY HAVE OYSTERS ON A MONTH WITH AN "R" IN IT.
FISH
WHAT MONTH IS THIS ?
JANUWHACKY
FISH

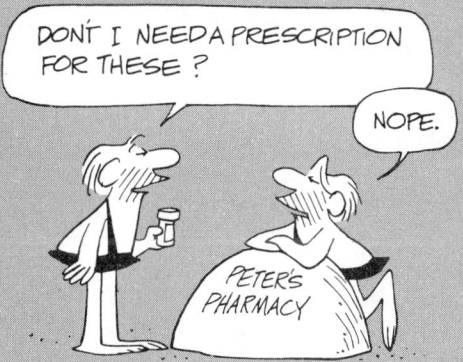

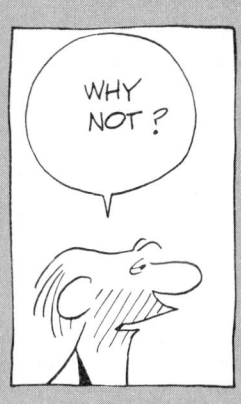

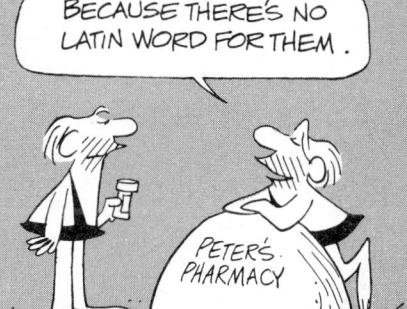

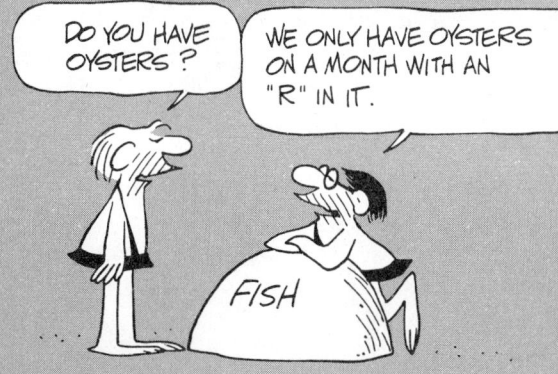

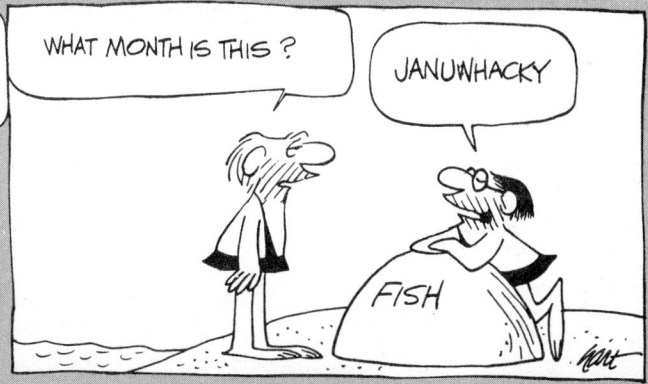

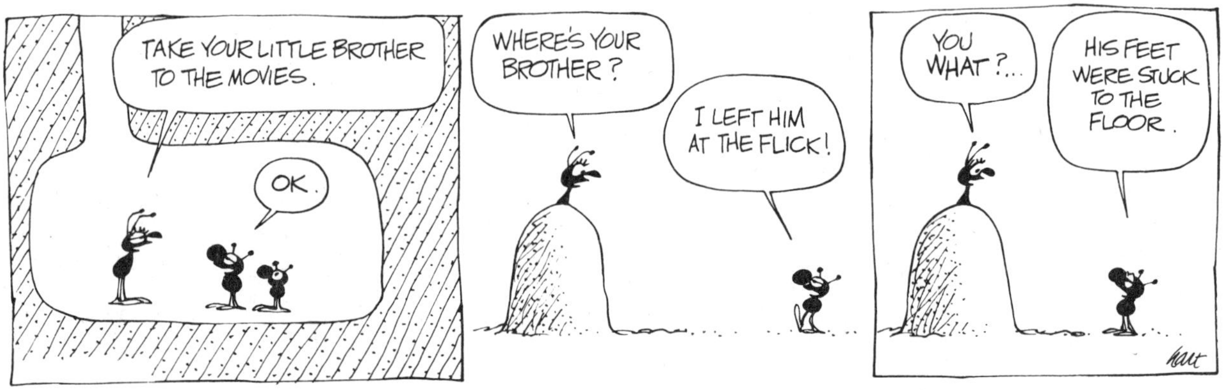
TAKE YOUR LITTLE BROTHER TO THE MOVIES.
OK.
WHERE'S YOUR BROTHER?
I LEFT HIM AT THE FLICK!
YOU WHAT?...
HIS FEET WERE STUCK TO THE FLOOR.
hart

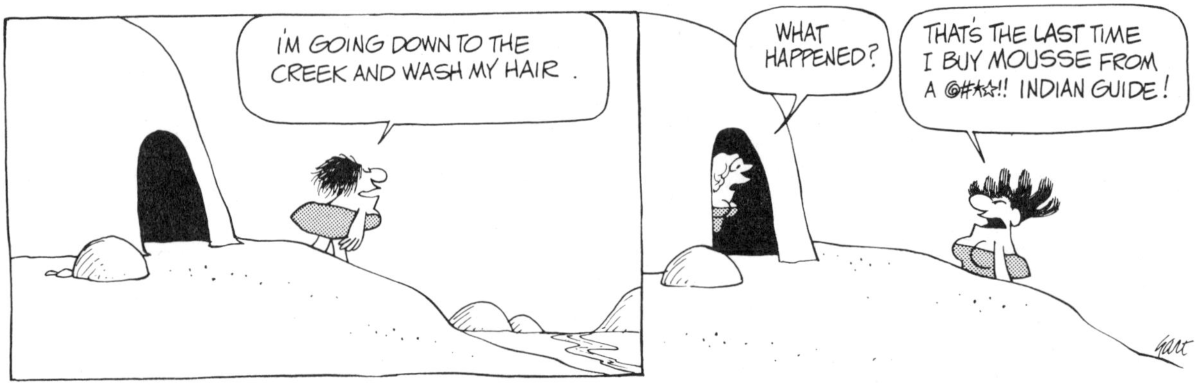
I'M GOING DOWN TO THE CREEK AND WASH MY HAIR.
WHAT HAPPENED?
THAT'S THE LAST TIME I BUY MOUSSE FROM A @#*☆!! INDIAN GUIDE!
hart

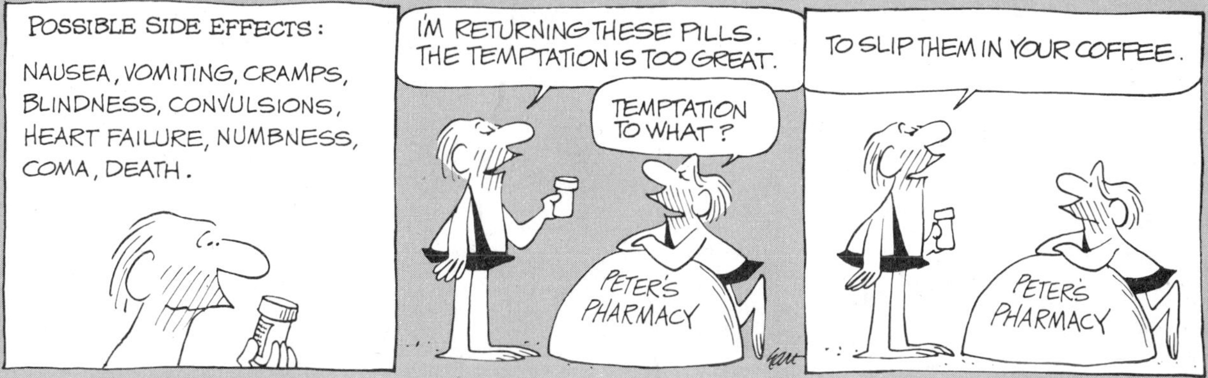
POSSIBLE SIDE EFFECTS:
NAUSEA, VOMITING, CRAMPS, BLINDNESS, CONVULSIONS, HEART FAILURE, NUMBNESS, COMA, DEATH.
I'M RETURNING THESE PILLS. THE TEMPTATION IS TOO GREAT.
TEMPTATION TO WHAT?
PETER'S PHARMACY
TO SLIP THEM IN YOUR COFFEE.
PETER'S PHARMACY

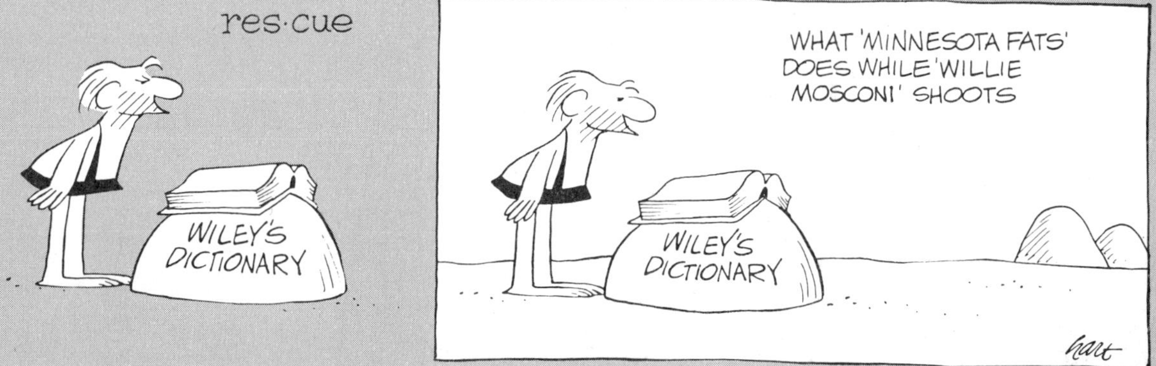
res·cue
WILEY'S DICTIONARY
WHAT 'MINNESOTA FATS' DOES WHILE 'WILLIE MOSCONI' SHOOTS
WILEY'S DICTIONARY

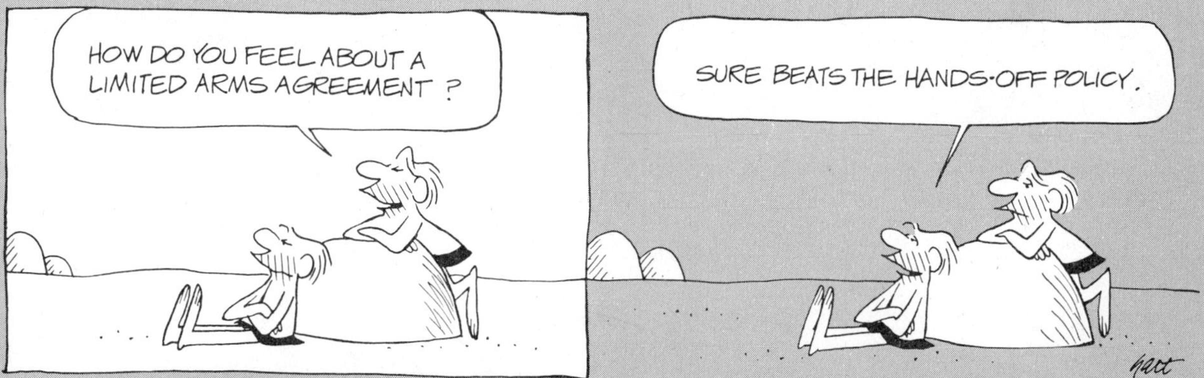
HOW DO YOU FEEL ABOUT A LIMITED ARMS AGREEMENT ?
SURE BEATS THE HANDS-OFF POLICY.

HAH! ...WHAT A NEAT LURE! THE LITTLE EYES FLASH ON AND OFF AND EVERYTHING!
LURES
CLUMSY'S BAIT SHOP
WORMS
WHO CAME UP WITH THIS ?
THE 'PUNK TUXEDO RENTAL'
CLUMSY'S

OPERA TRYOUTS TODAY
CRACK
THAT'S WHAT I CALL ENDING YOUR CAREER ON A HIGH NOTE.
TODAY

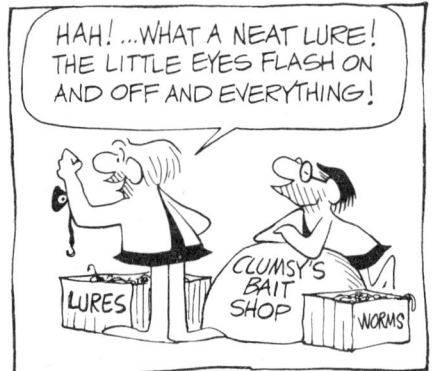

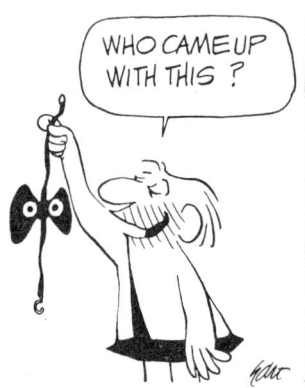

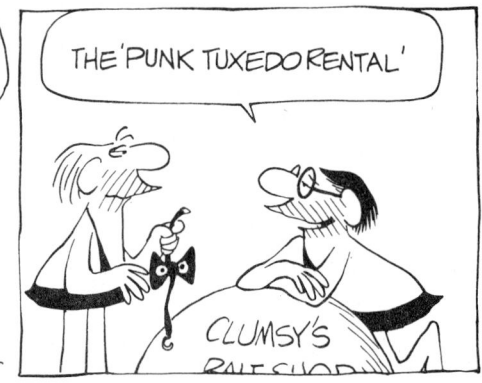

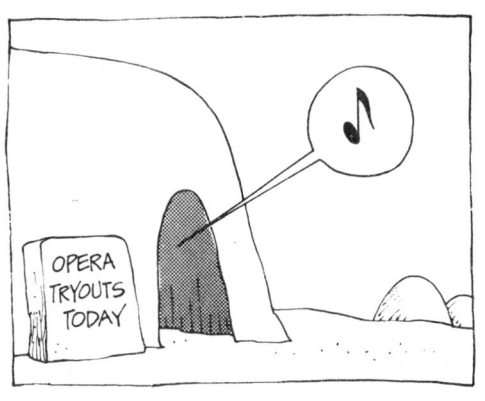

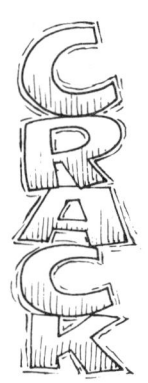

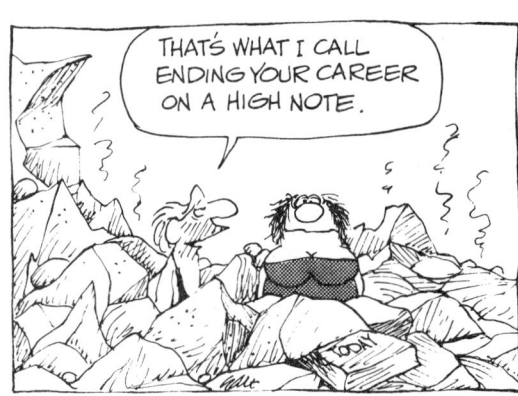

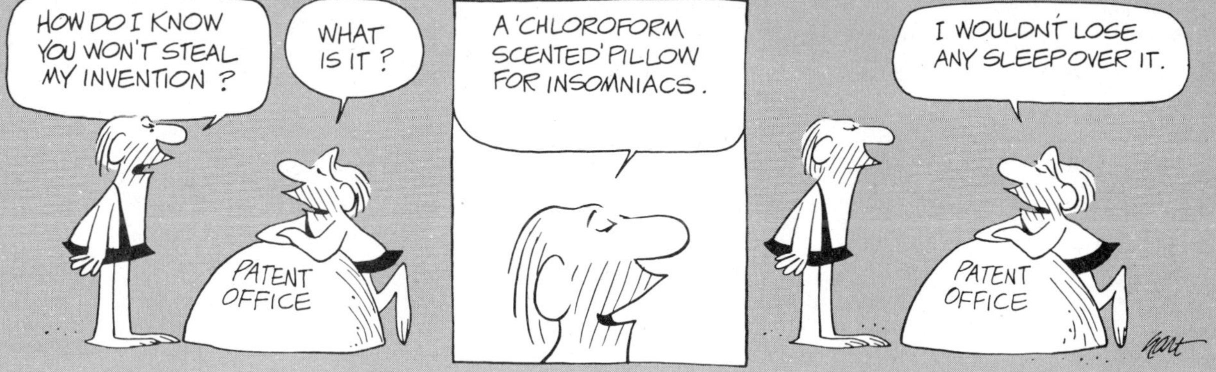
HOW DO I KNOW YOU WON'T STEAL MY INVENTION ?
WHAT IS IT ?
PATENT OFFICE
A 'CHLOROFORM SCENTED' PILLOW FOR INSOMNIACS .
I WOULDN'T LOSE ANY SLEEP OVER IT.
PATENT OFFICE

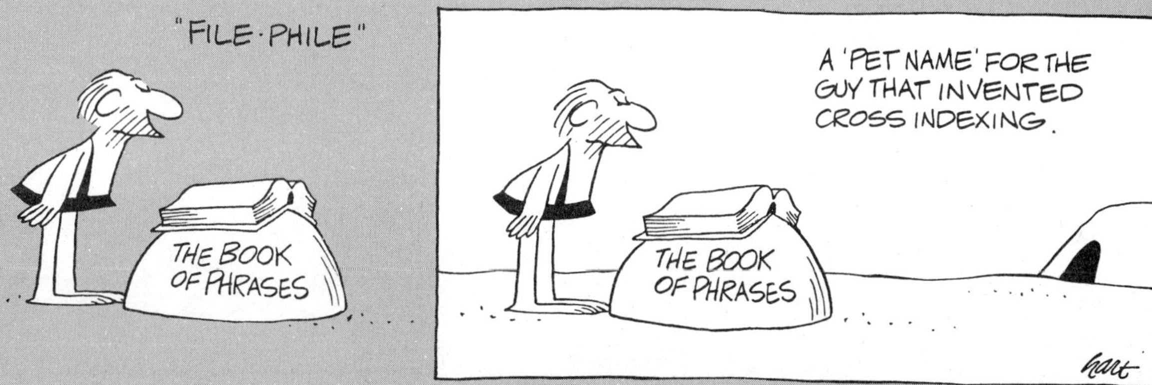
"FILE · PHILE"
THE BOOK OF PHRASES
A 'PET NAME' FOR THE GUY THAT INVENTED CROSS INDEXING .
THE BOOK OF PHRASES

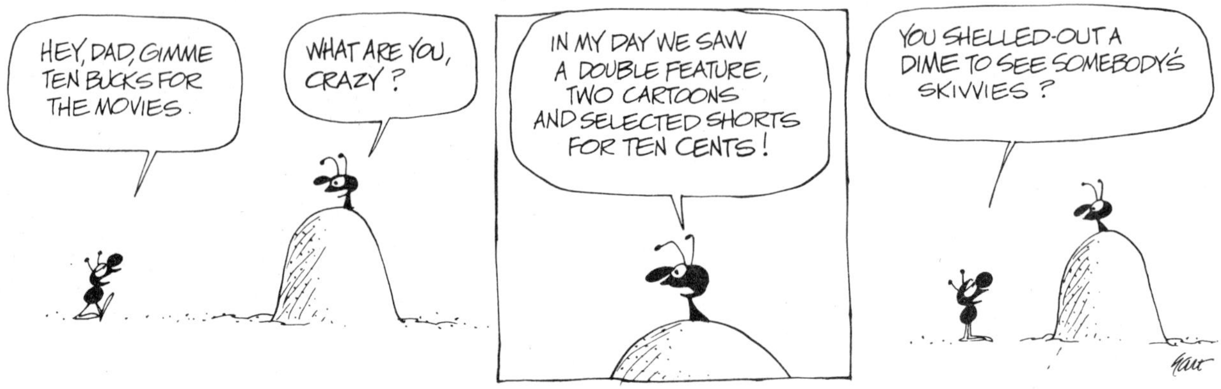
HEY, DAD, GIMME TEN BUCKS FOR THE MOVIES.
WHAT ARE YOU, CRAZY ?
IN MY DAY WE SAW A DOUBLE FEATURE, TWO CARTOONS AND SELECTED SHORTS FOR TEN CENTS !
YOU SHELLED-OUT A DIME TO SEE SOMEBODY'S SKIVVIES ?
hart

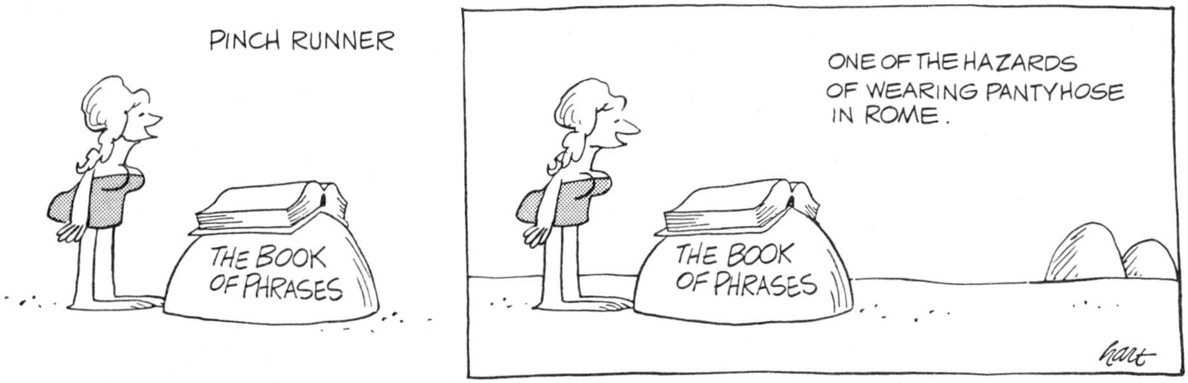
PINCH RUNNER
THE BOOK OF PHRASES
ONE OF THE HAZARDS OF WEARING PANTYHOSE IN ROME.
THE BOOK OF PHRASES
hart

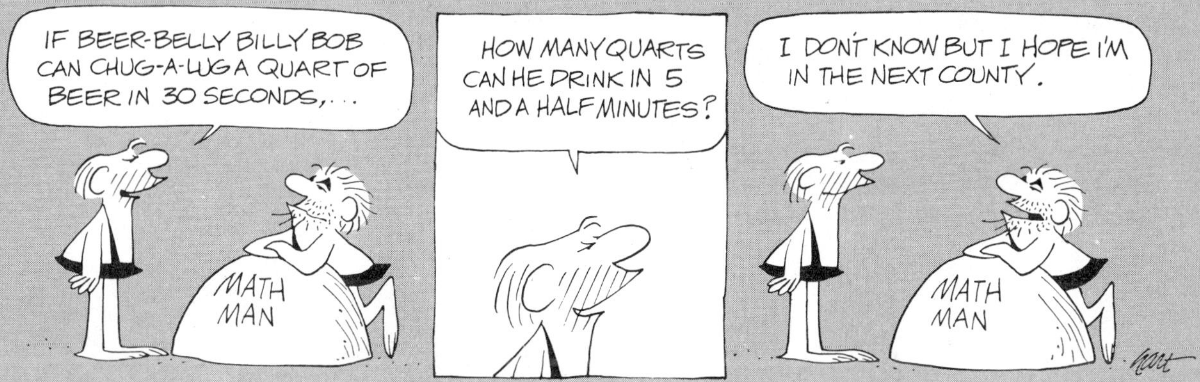
IF BEER-BELLY BILLY BOB CAN CHUG-A-LUG A QUART OF BEER IN 30 SECONDS, . . .
MATH MAN
HOW MANY QUARTS CAN HE DRINK IN 5 AND A HALF MINUTES?
I DON'T KNOW BUT I HOPE I'M IN THE NEXT COUNTY.
MATH MAN
hart

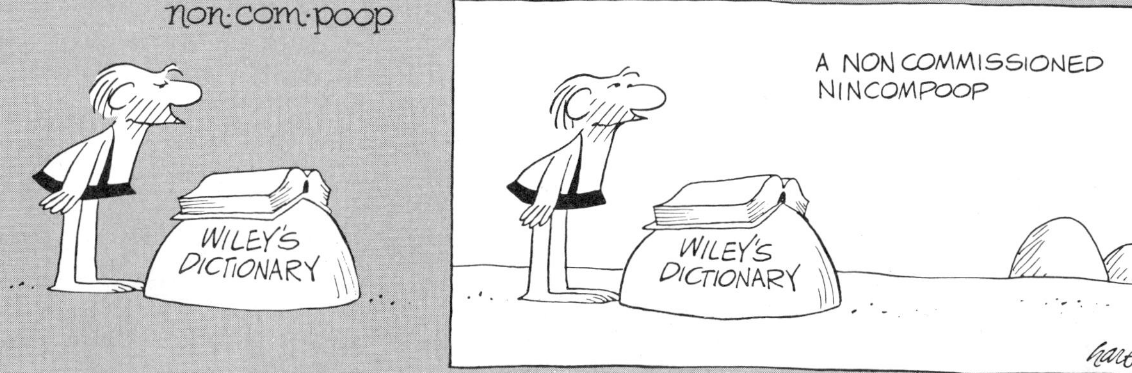
non·com·poop
WILEY'S DICTIONARY
A NON COMMISSIONED NINCOMPOOP
WILEY'S DICTIONARY
hart

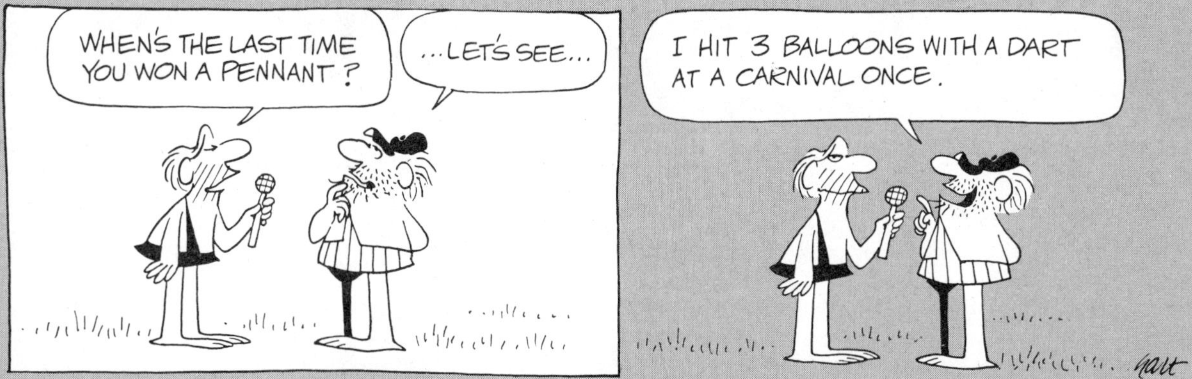
WHEN'S THE LAST TIME YOU WON A PENNANT?
. . . LET'S SEE . . .
I HIT 3 BALLOONS WITH A DART AT A CARNIVAL ONCE.
hart

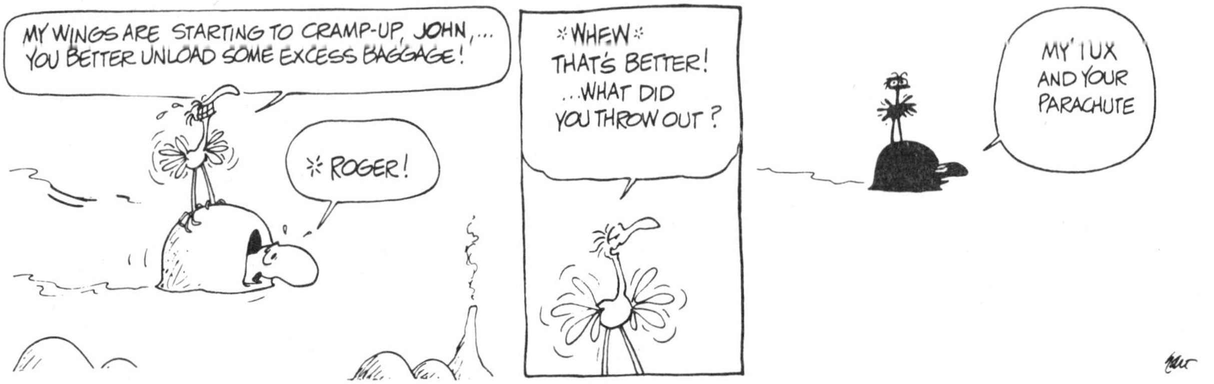
MY WINGS ARE STARTING TO CRAMP-UP, JOHN,... YOU BETTER UNLOAD SOME EXCESS BAGGAGE!
* ROGER!
* WHEW *
THAT'S BETTER! ...WHAT DID YOU THROW OUT?
MY 'LUX AND YOUR PARACHUTE

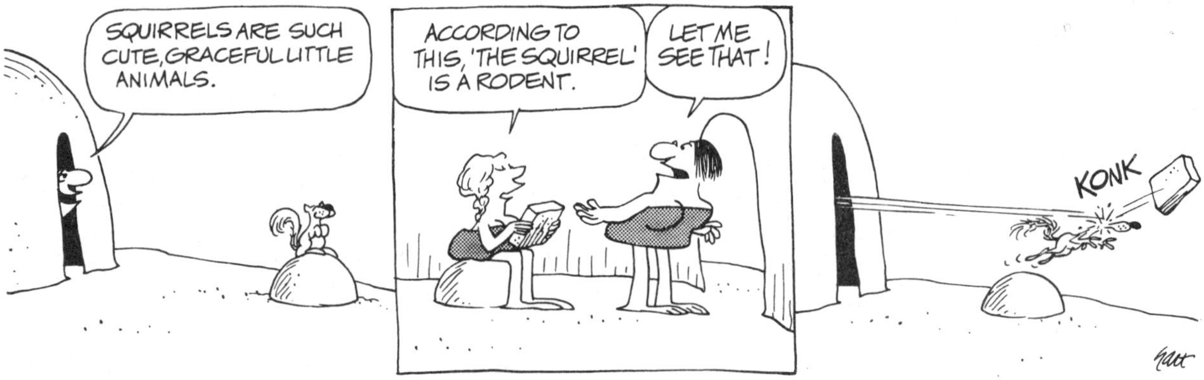
SQUIRRELS ARE SUCH CUTE, GRACEFUL LITTLE ANIMALS.
ACCORDING TO THIS, 'THE SQUIRREL' IS A RODENT.
LET ME SEE THAT!
KONK

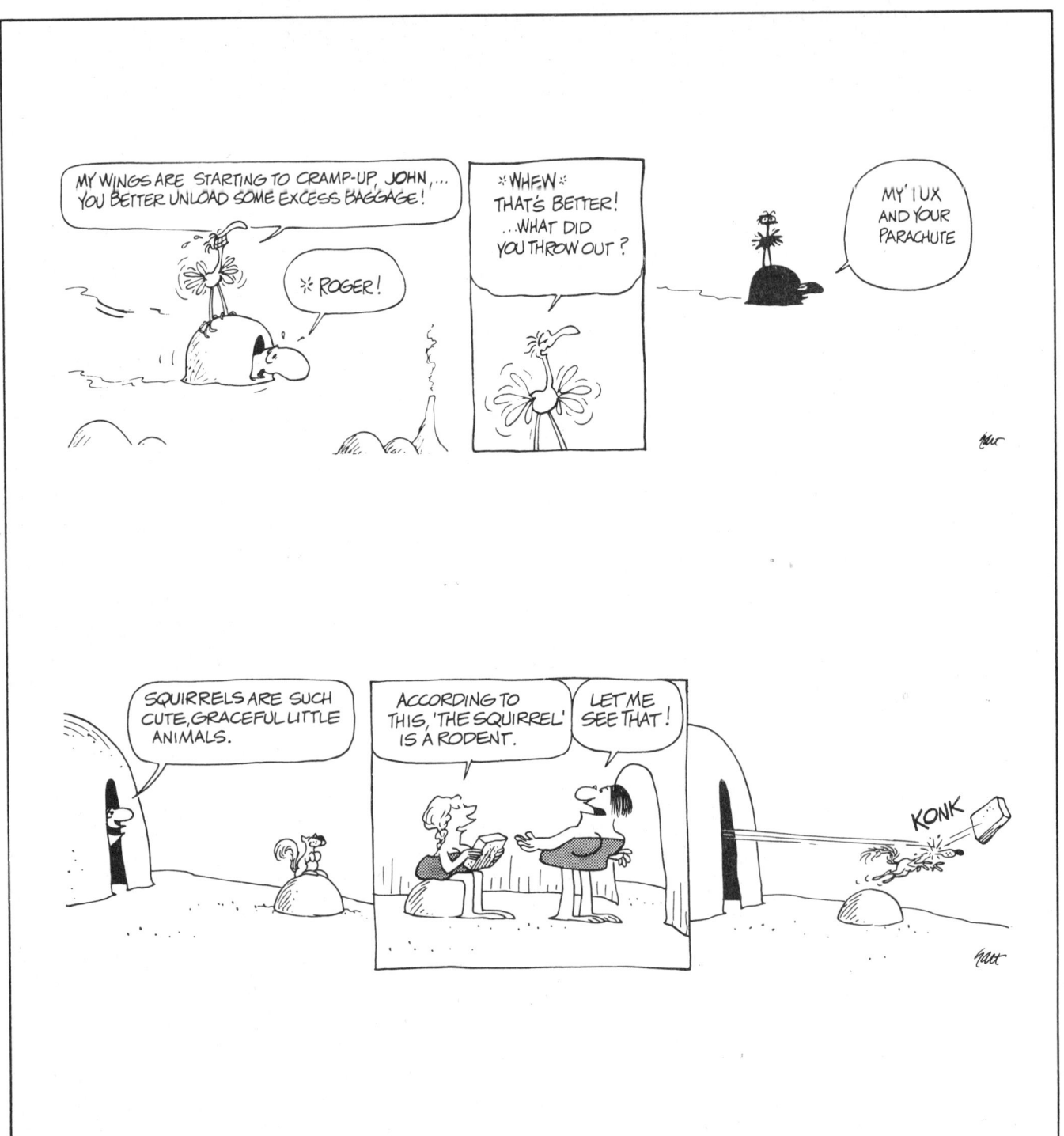

DO YOU BELIEVE IN REINCARNATION ?
I SURE DO. AND NEXT TIME I'M GONNA TAKE LIFE A LITTLE SLOWER.
WHAT DO YOU PLAN TO COME BACK AS, A GLACIER ?

WHAT'S THE BEST MEDIA TOOL FOR ADVERTISING A BRAND NEW PRODUCT ?
WHAT'S YOUR ADVERTISING BUDGET ?
AD AGENCY
TEN CLAMS
ARE YOU FAMILIAR WITH A DEVICE CALLED THE MEGAPHONE ?
AD AGENCY

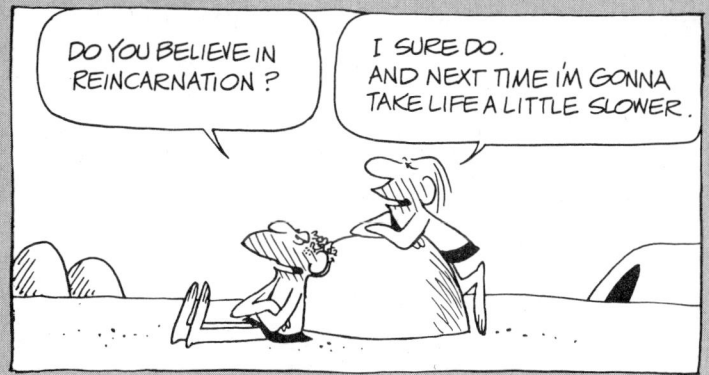

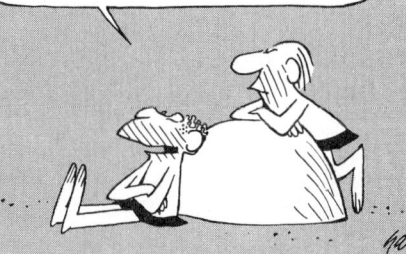

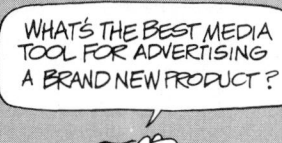

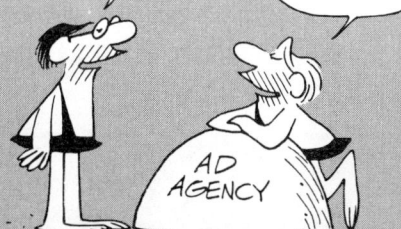

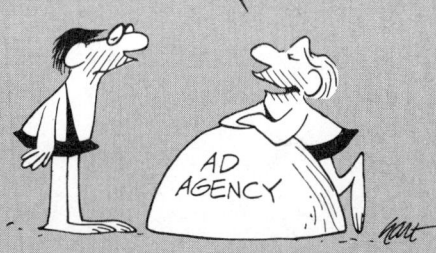

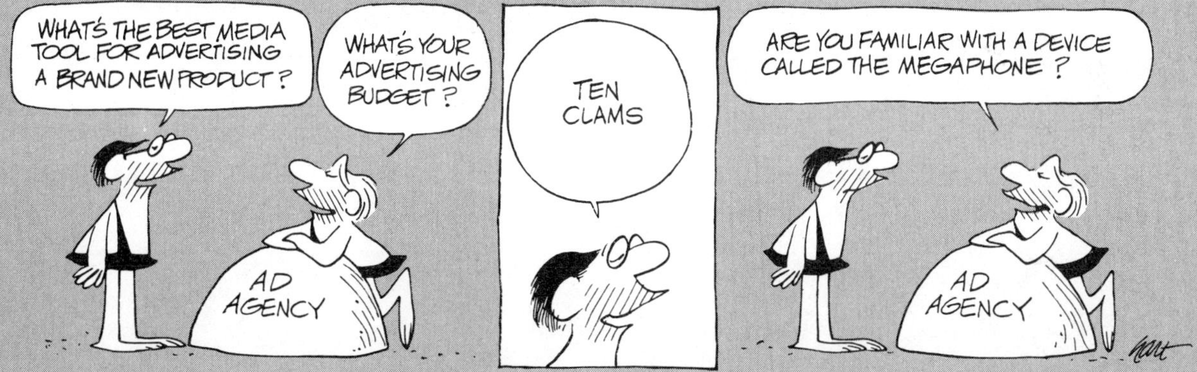

Dear Fat Broad,
ADVICE COLUMN
what do you think of a husband that works in a mine all day and brings me flowers every night?
I THINK THE RASCAL IS UNDERMINING A HOTHOUSE.
ADVICE COLUMN
hart

POPSICLES THAT GLOW IN THE DARK.
AMAZING!
PATENT OFFICE
WHAT'S THE SECRET?
YOU JUST USE THE WATER DOWNSTREAM FROM THE NUCLEAR POWER PLANT!
PATENT OFFICE
hart

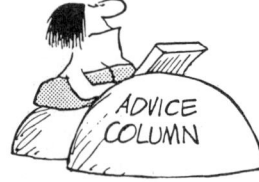

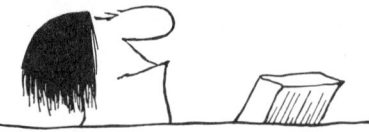

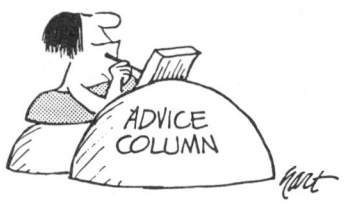

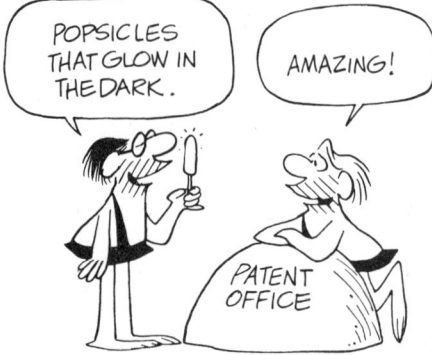

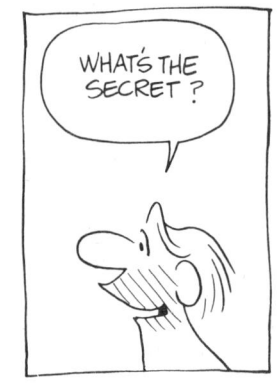

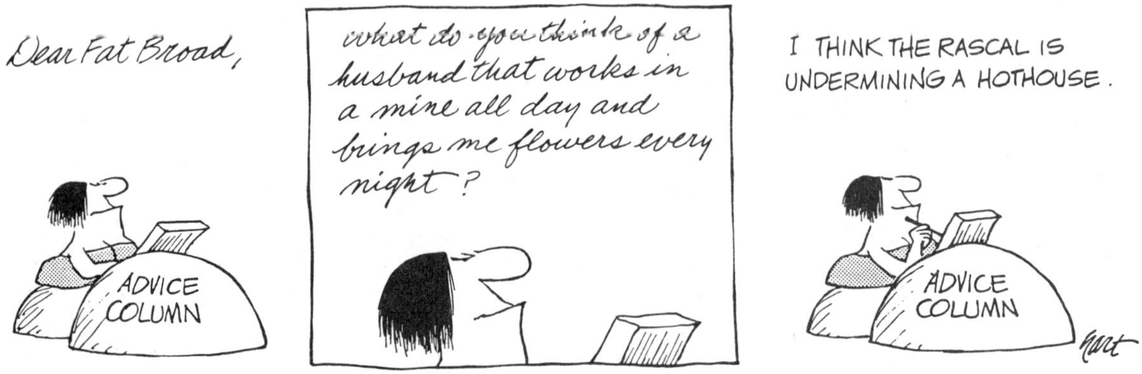

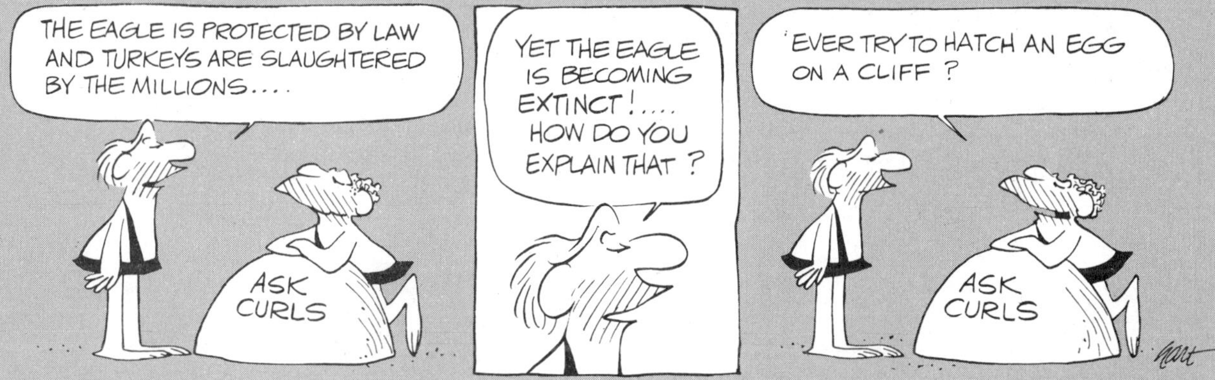
THE EAGLE IS PROTECTED BY LAW AND TURKEYS ARE SLAUGHTERED BY THE MILLIONS....
ASK CURLS
YET THE EAGLE IS BECOMING EXTINCT!.... HOW DO YOU EXPLAIN THAT?
EVER TRY TO HATCH AN EGG ON A CLIFF?
ASK CURLS
hart

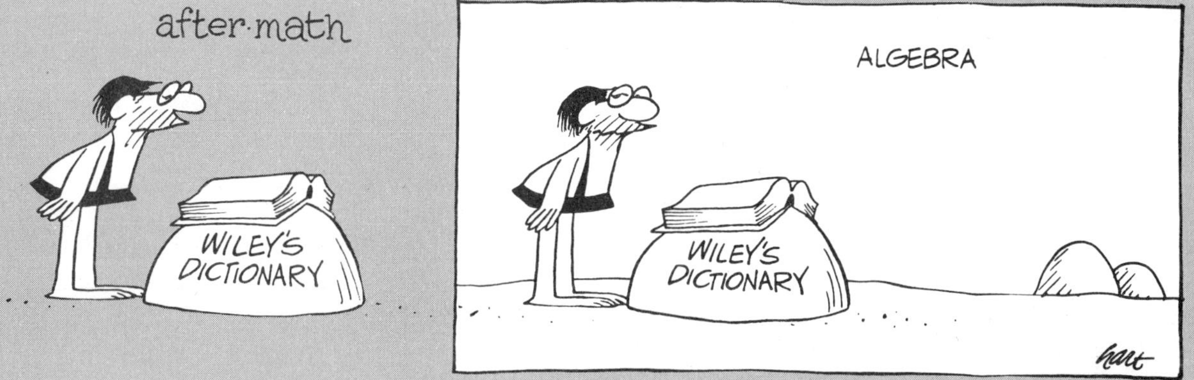
after·math
WILEY'S DICTIONARY
ALGEBRA
WILEY'S DICTIONARY
hart

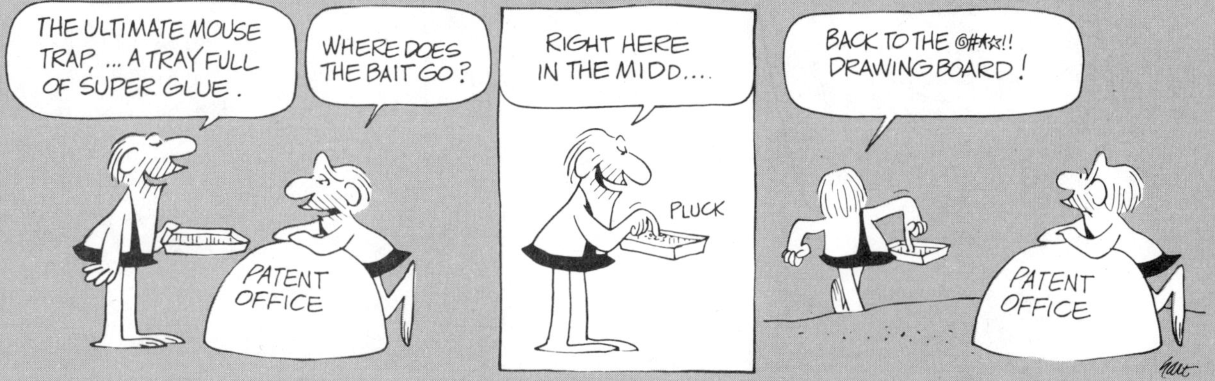
THE ULTIMATE MOUSE TRAP, ... A TRAY FULL OF SUPER GLUE.
WHERE DOES THE BAIT GO?
PATENT OFFICE
RIGHT HERE IN THE MIDD....
PLUCK
BACK TO THE @#*☆!! DRAWING BOARD!
PATENT OFFICE
hart

WHAT'S THE WEATHER ?
PARTLY CLOUDY WITH WINDS FROM THE NORTH, EAST, SOUTH AND WEST.
WEATHER FORECAST
THAT'S A EUPHEMISM FOR A CYCLONE, ISN'T IT ?
YES!
WEATHER FORECAST

OH, NO ... HERE COMES THE CUTE CHICK ....
HOW SWEET ! .. WHAT PROMPTED YOU TO DO THAT ?
.. IT'S ONE OF THE ASSIGNMENTS IN MY EGO COURSE.
C.C. LOVES C.C.

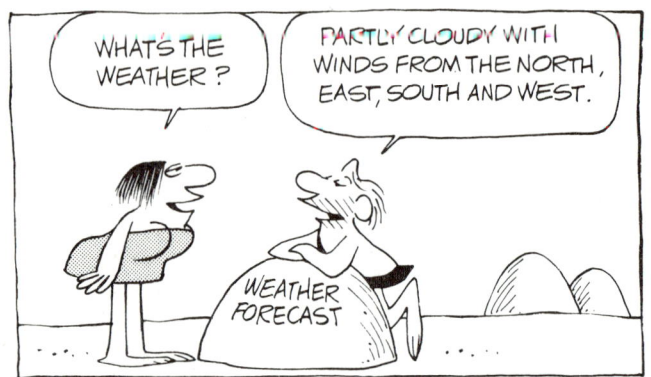

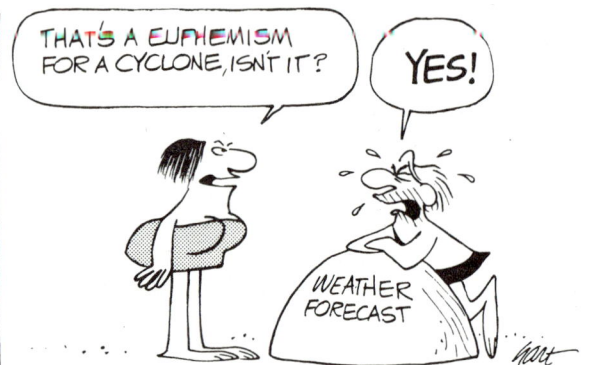

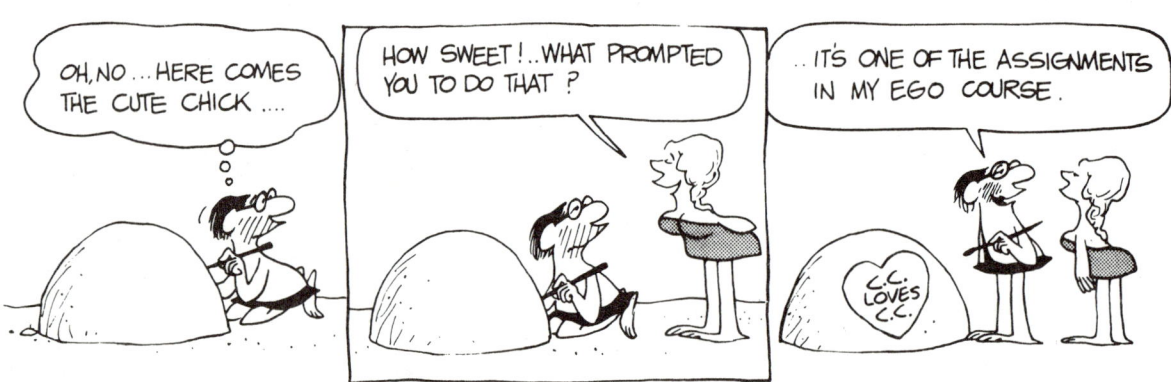

SORRY, ... I CAN'T ACCEPT THIS!
WHY NOT ?
RAT POISON
PETER'S DRUG STORE
THE TAMPER-PROOF SEAL HAS BEEN BROKEN
RAT POISON
PETER'S DRUG STORE

HOW WAS THE CROWD LAST NIGHT ?
TERRIBLE.
COACH
.. BUT LAST NIGHT WAS 'WHOOPIE CUSHION NIGHT.'
... THAT EXPLAINS THE 2 HOUR 'RAZZBERRY DELAY.'
COACH

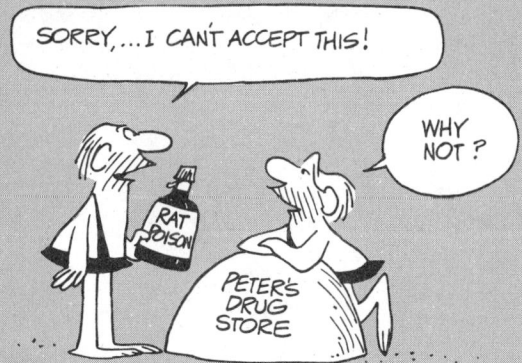

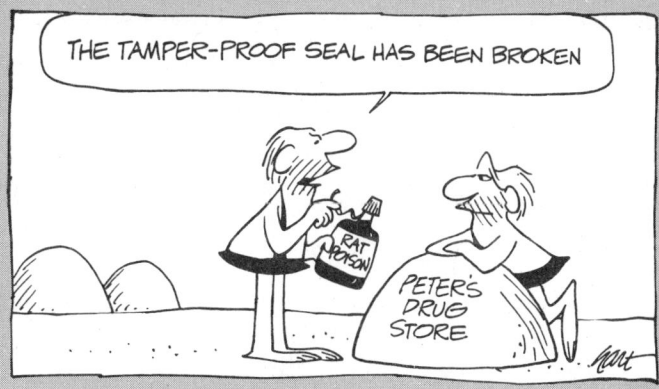

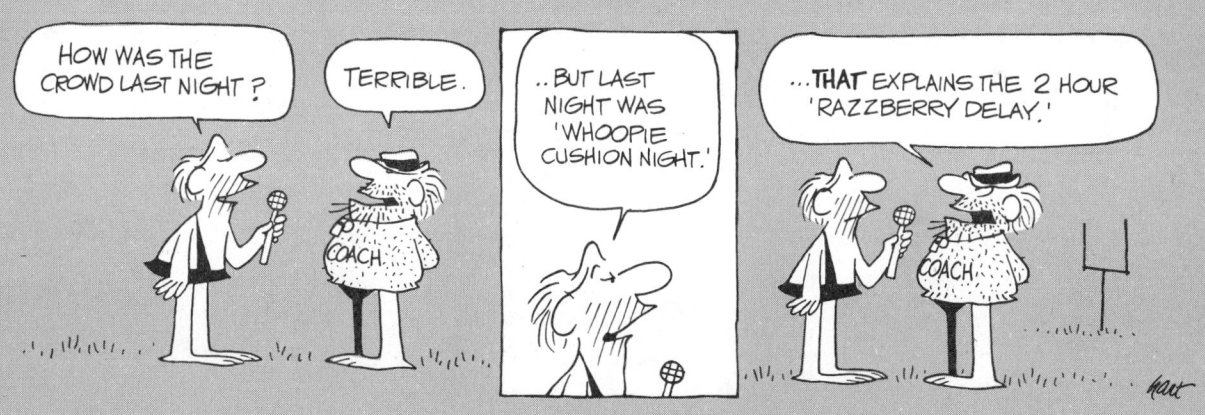

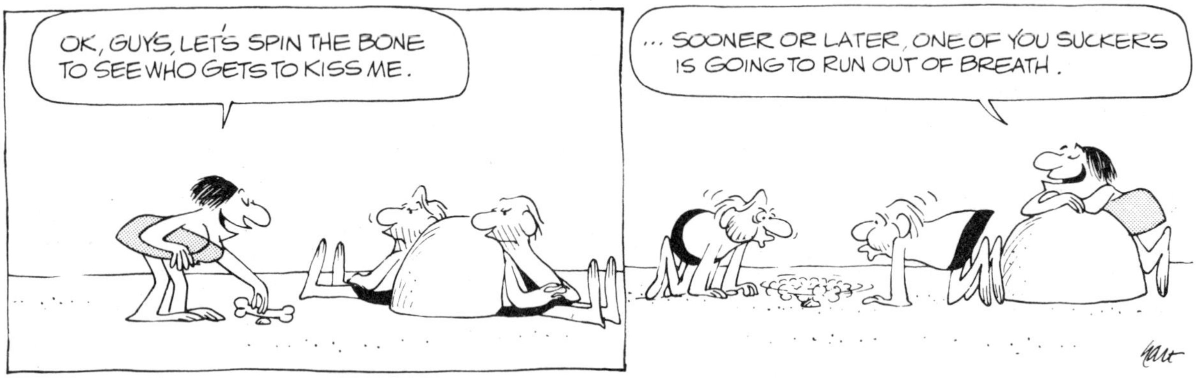
OK, GUYS, LET'S SPIN THE BONE TO SEE WHO GETS TO KISS ME.
... SOONER OR LATER, ONE OF YOU SUCKERS IS GOING TO RUN OUT OF BREATH.

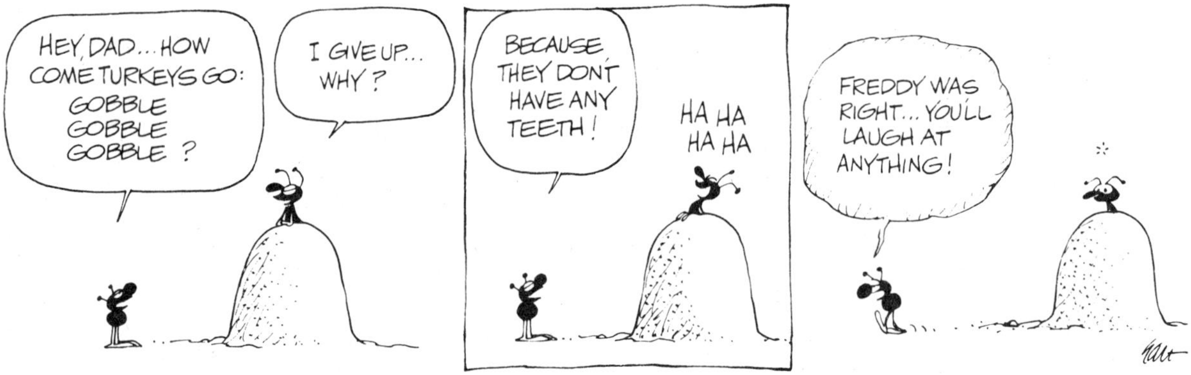
HEY, DAD... HOW COME TURKEYS GO: GOBBLE GOBBLE GOBBLE ?
I GIVE UP... WHY ?
BECAUSE THEY DON'T HAVE ANY TEETH !
HA HA HA HA
FREDDY WAS RIGHT... YOU'LL LAUGH AT ANYTHING!

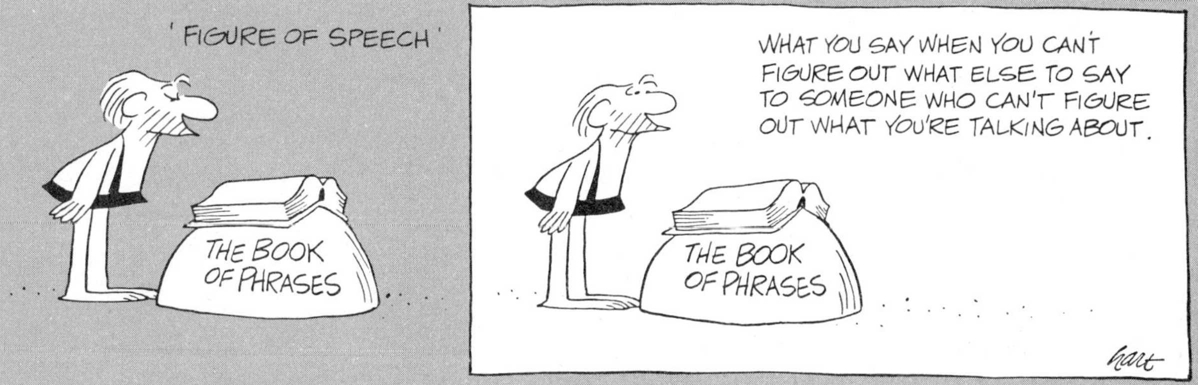
'FIGURE OF SPEECH'
THE BOOK OF PHRASES
WHAT YOU SAY WHEN YOU CAN'T FIGURE OUT WHAT ELSE TO SAY TO SOMEONE WHO CAN'T FIGURE OUT WHAT YOU'RE TALKING ABOUT.
THE BOOK OF PHRASES
hart

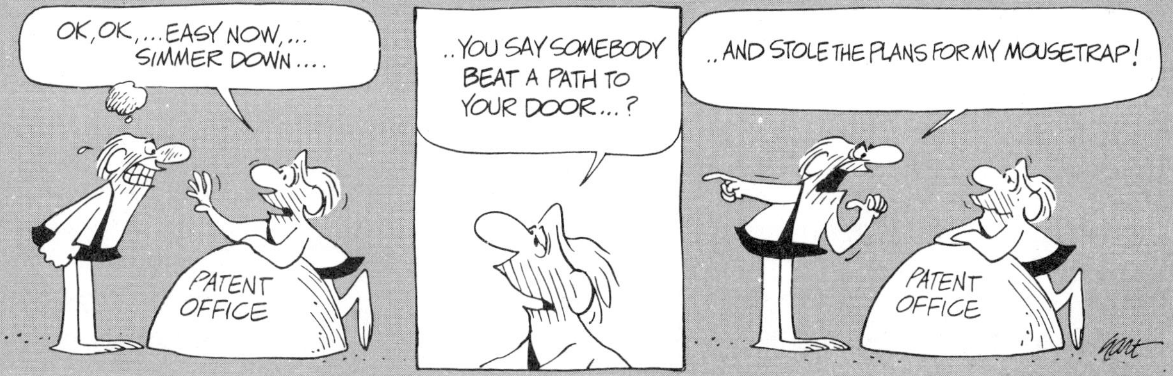
OK, OK, ... EASY NOW, ... SIMMER DOWN....
PATENT OFFICE
..YOU SAY SOMEBODY BEAT A PATH TO YOUR DOOR...?
..AND STOLE THE PLANS FOR MY MOUSETRAP!
PATENT OFFICE
hart

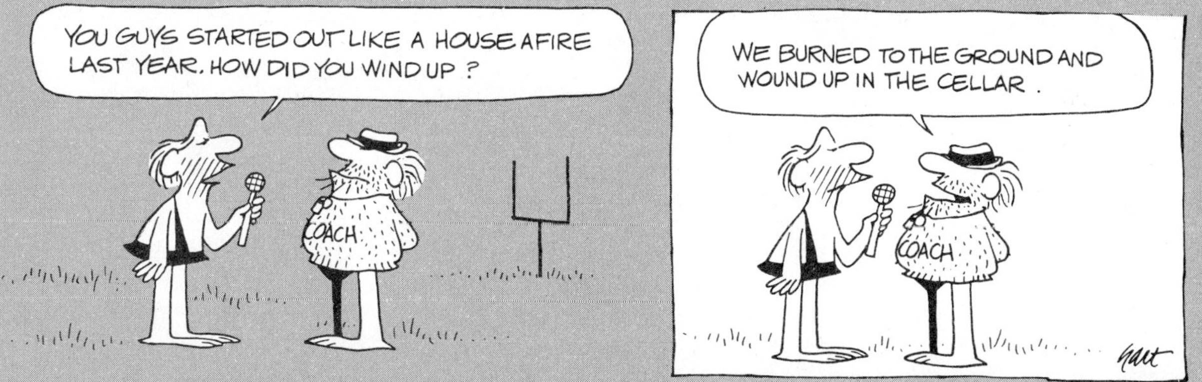
YOU GUYS STARTED OUT LIKE A HOUSE AFIRE LAST YEAR. HOW DID YOU WIND UP ?
COACH
WE BURNED TO THE GROUND AND WOUND UP IN THE CELLAR.
COACH
hart

Dear Fat Broad,
"My best friend has terrible breath. How do I tell her?
THROUGH A 15-FOOT CARDBOARD TUBE.
ADVICE COLUMN
ADVICE COLUMN

MUNCH MUNCH MUNCH MUNCH
ACCORDING TO THIS ... COWS HAVE FOUR STOMACHS.
.. PARDON?
I DIDN'T SAY NOTHING.
SORRY ... I THOUGHT YOU MOOED.

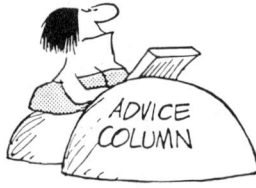

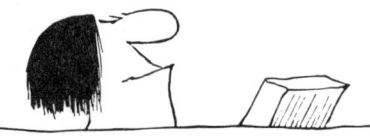

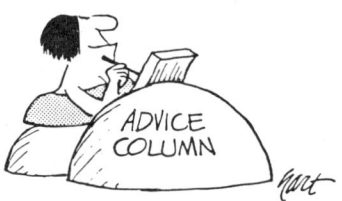

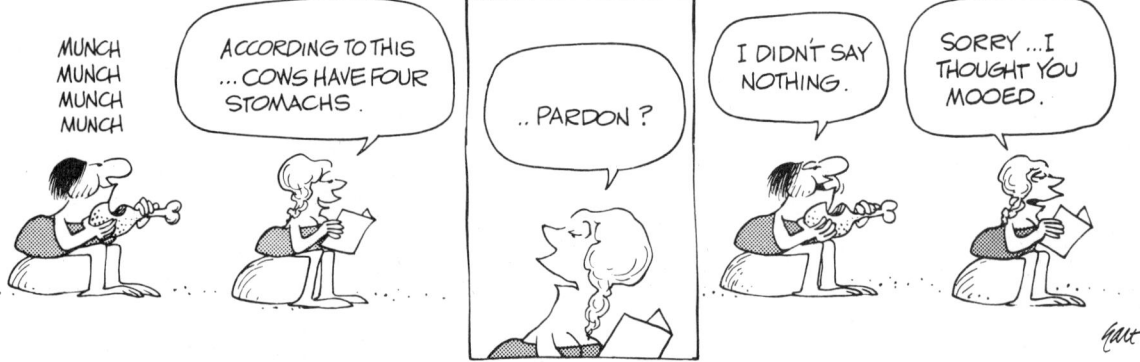

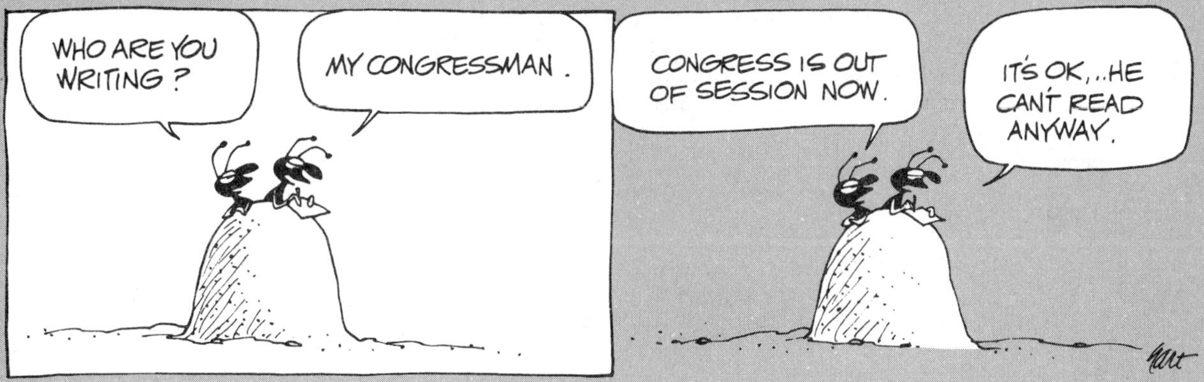
WHO ARE YOU WRITING ?
MY CONGRESSMAN .
CONGRESS IS OUT OF SESSION NOW.
IT'S OK, ..HE CAN'T READ ANYWAY.

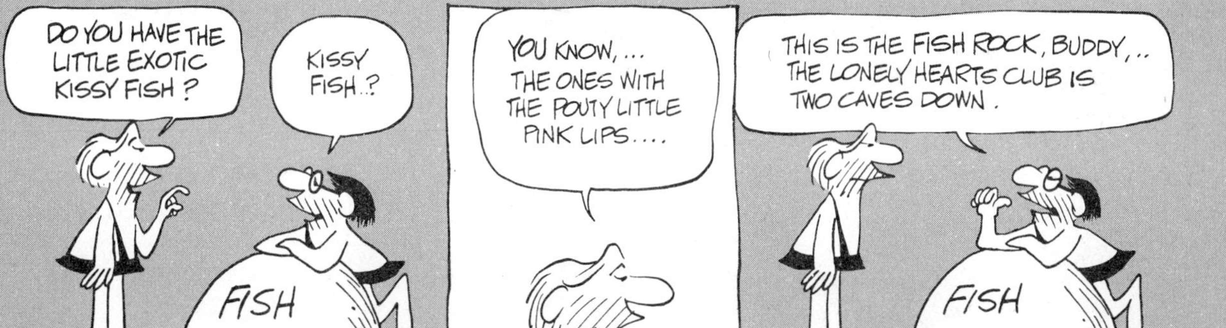
DO YOU HAVE THE LITTLE EXOTIC KISSY FISH ?
KISSY FISH..?
YOU KNOW, ... THE ONES WITH THE POUTY LITTLE PINK LIPS....
THIS IS THE FISH ROCK, BUDDY, .. THE LONELY HEARTS CLUB IS TWO CAVES DOWN .
FISH
FISH

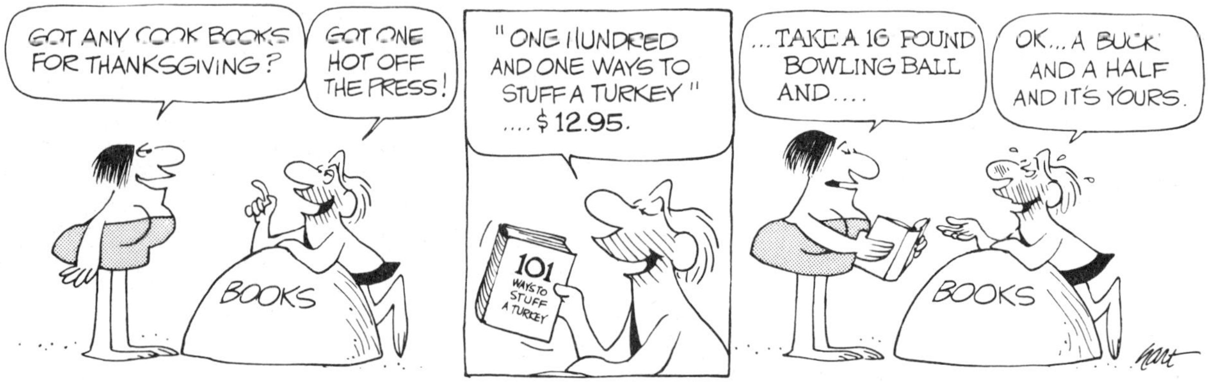
GOT ANY COOK BOOKS FOR THANKSGIVING?
GOT ONE HOT OFF THE PRESS!
BOOKS
"ONE HUNDRED AND ONE WAYS TO STUFF A TURKEY" .... $12.95.
101 WAYS TO STUFF A TURKEY
...TAKE A 16 POUND BOWLING BALL AND....
OK... A BUCK AND A HALF AND IT'S YOURS.
BOOKS

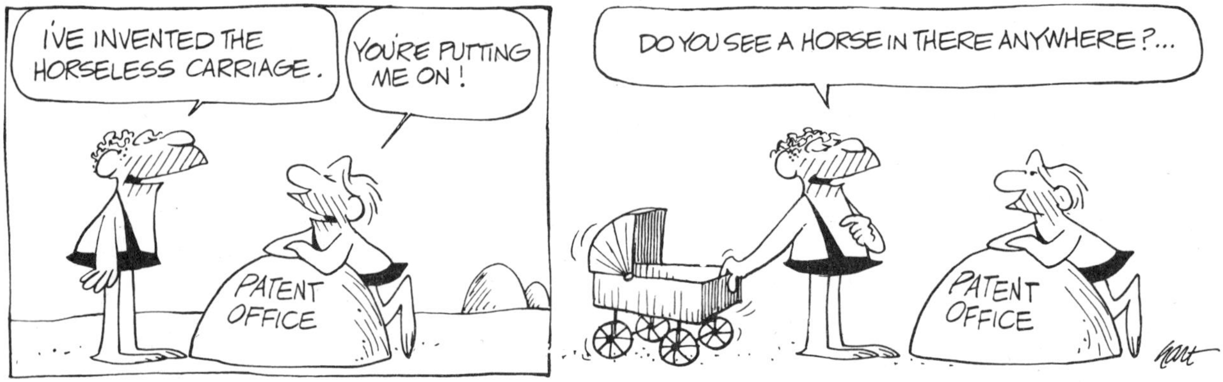
I'VE INVENTED THE HORSELESS CARRIAGE.
YOU'RE PUTTING ME ON!
PATENT OFFICE
DO YOU SEE A HORSE IN THERE ANYWHERE?...
PATENT OFFICE

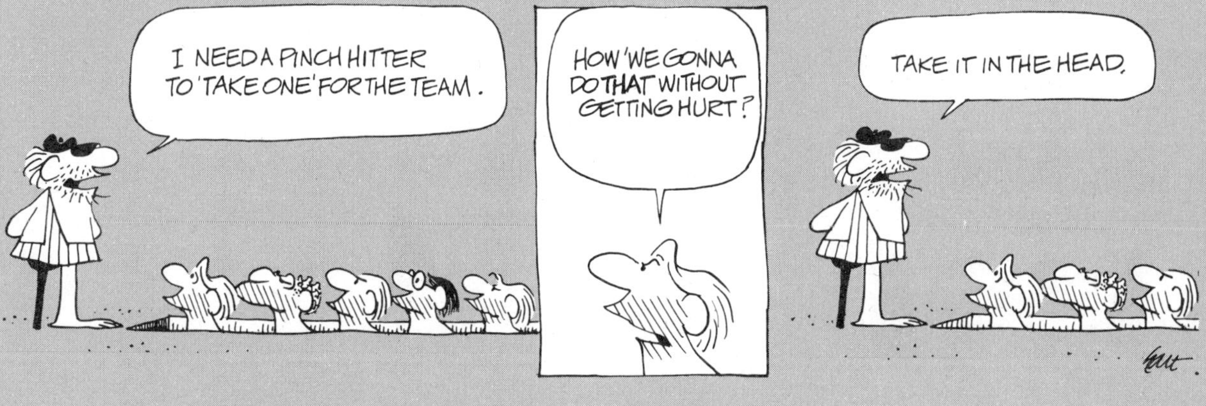
I NEED A PINCH HITTER TO 'TAKE ONE' FOR THE TEAM.
HOW 'WE GONNA DO **THAT** WITHOUT GETTING HURT?
TAKE IT IN THE HEAD.

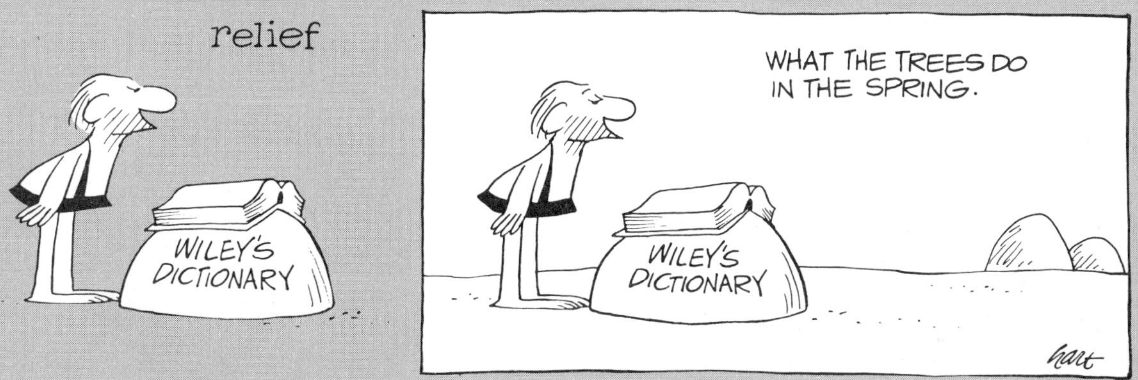
relief
WILEY'S DICTIONARY
WHAT THE TREES DO IN THE SPRING.
WILEY'S DICTIONARY

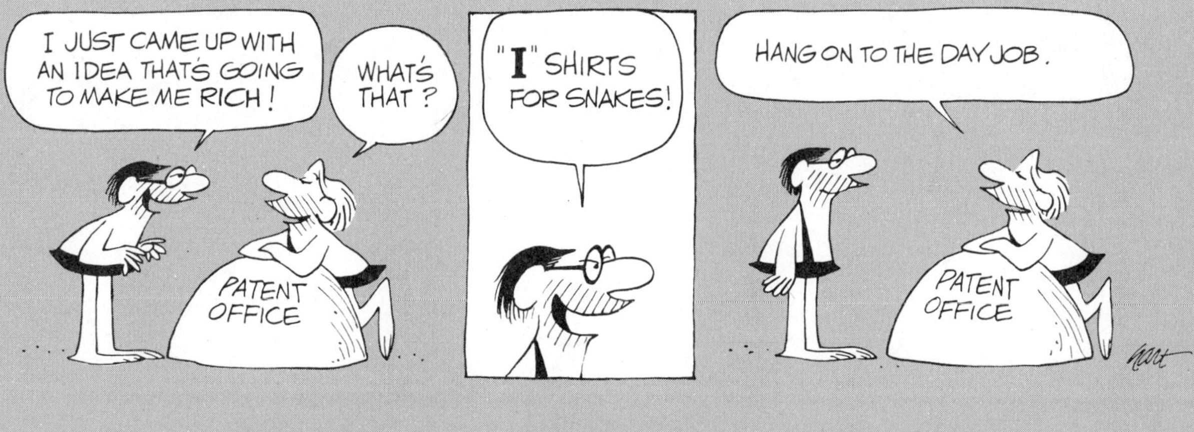
I JUST CAME UP WITH AN IDEA THAT'S GOING TO MAKE ME RICH!
WHAT'S THAT?
PATENT OFFICE
"I" SHIRTS FOR SNAKES!
HANG ON TO THE DAY JOB.
PATENT OFFICE

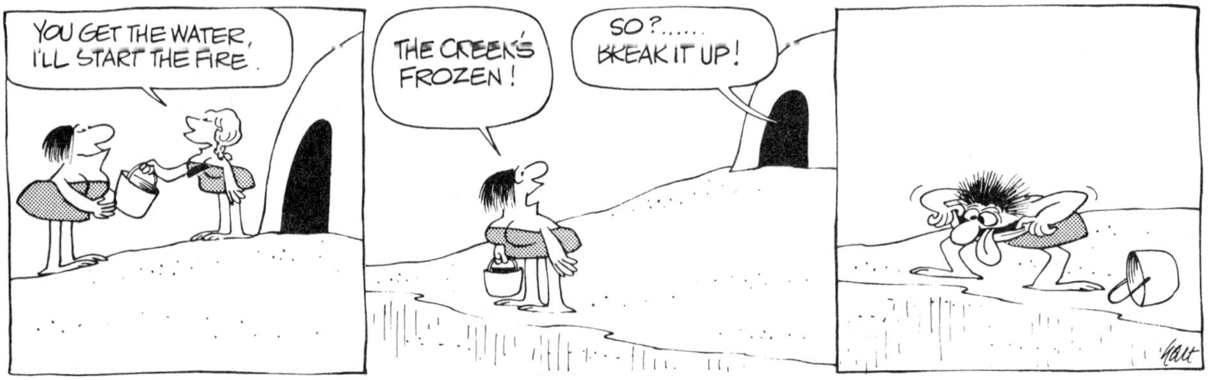
YOU GET THE WATER, I'LL START THE FIRE.
THE CREEK'S FROZEN!
SO?...... BREAK IT UP!

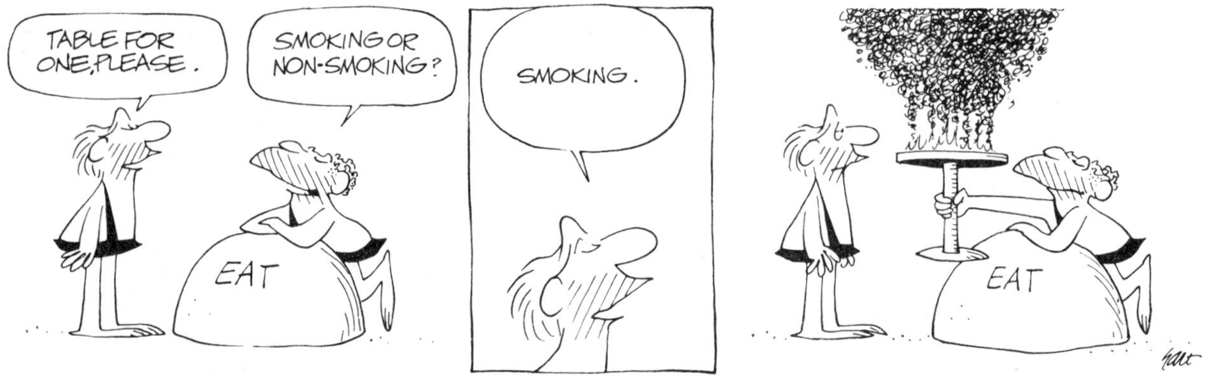
TABLE FOR ONE, PLEASE.
SMOKING OR NON-SMOKING?
EAT
SMOKING.
EAT

I HEAR SNAKESKIN IS BECOMING THE NEW FASHION RAGE.
DOES THAT MEAN WE'LL FINALLY BE IN VOGUE?
....ONE WAY OR ANOTHER.

WHY DOESN'T MOM WEAR MAKE-UP, DAD?
LEAVE HER ALONE. SHE'S UNATTRACTIVE ENOUGH AS IT IS.

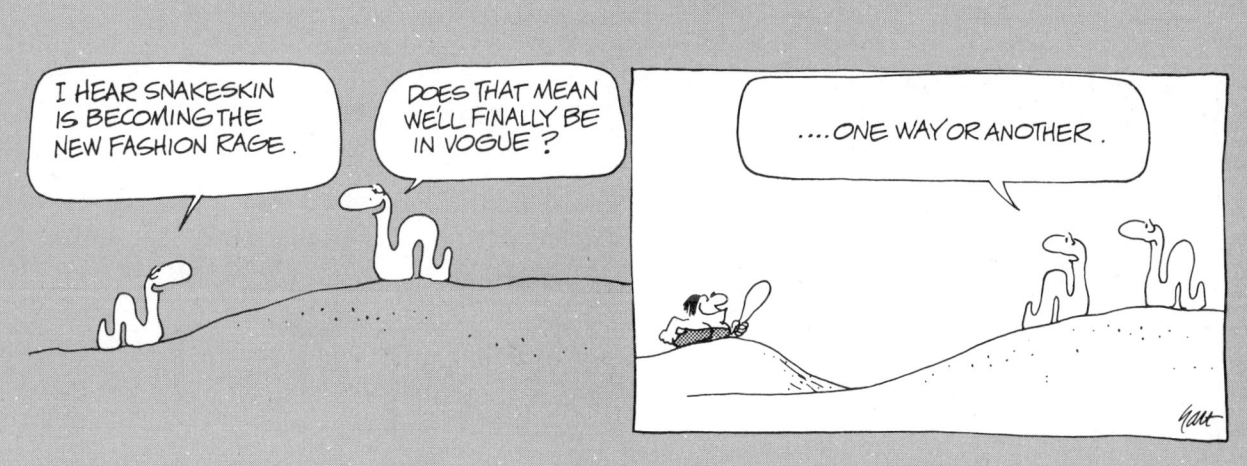

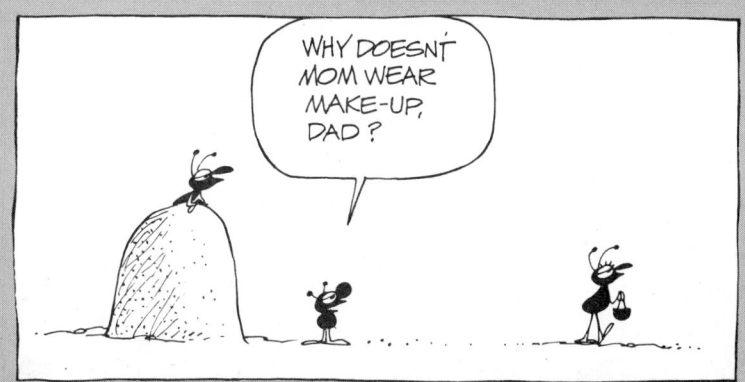

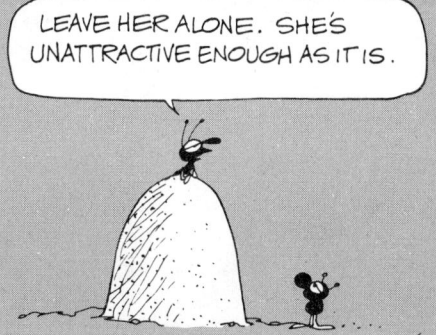

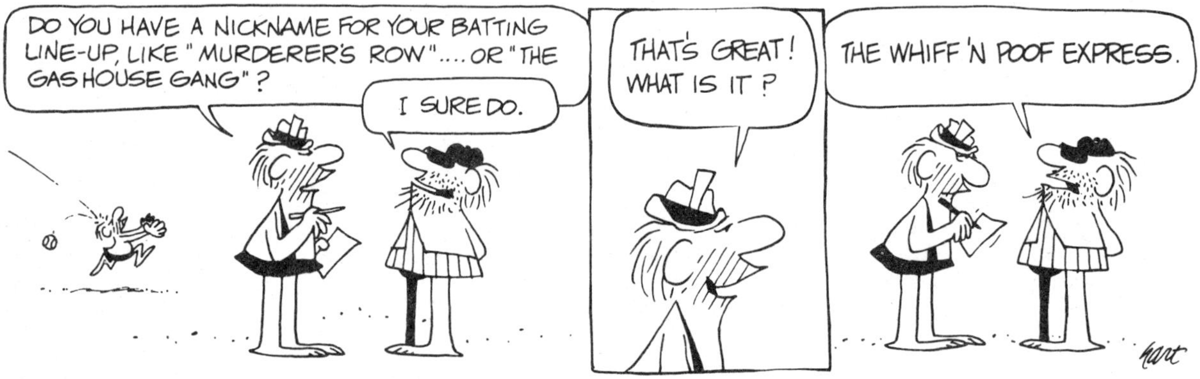
DO YOU HAVE A NICKNAME FOR YOUR BATTING LINE-UP, LIKE "MURDERER'S ROW"....OR "THE GAS HOUSE GANG"?
I SURE DO.
THAT'S GREAT! WHAT IS IT?
THE WHIFF 'N POOF EXPRESS.

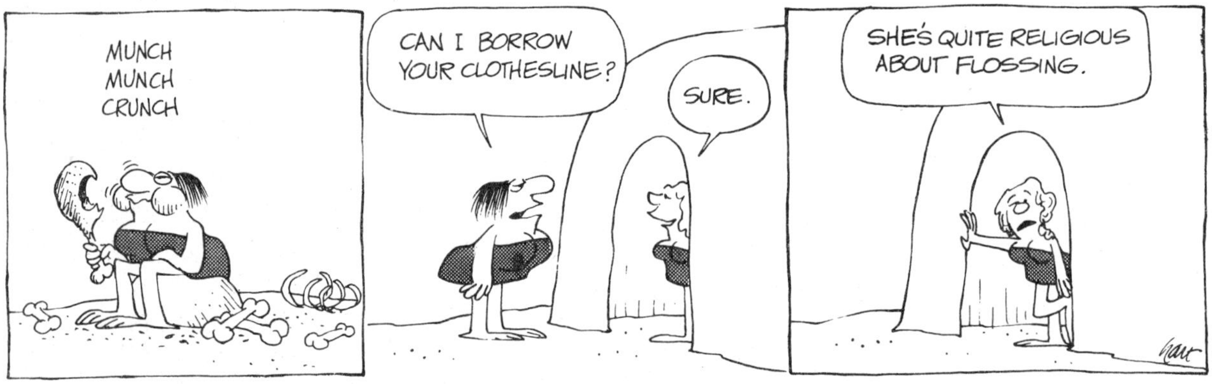
MUNCH
MUNCH
CRUNCH
CAN I BORROW YOUR CLOTHESLINE?
SURE.
SHE'S QUITE RELIGIOUS ABOUT FLOSSING.

I'VE INVENTED A CHILDPROOF COCKROACH TRAP.
PATENT OFFICE
WHAT MAKES IT CHILDPROOF ?
NO CHILD ALIVE CAN CRAWL THROUGH AN OPENING THAT SMALL.
PATENT OFFICE

BORK
WILEY'S DICTIONARY
THE SOUND OF A BUSTED GAVEL
WILEY'S DICTIONARY

DID MY SNAILS COME IN YET ?
WHEN DID YOU ORDER THEM ?
FISH
LAST AUGUST
WHAT DO YOU THINK THIS IS, A FAST-FOOD JOINT ?
FISH

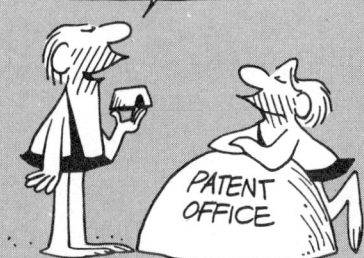

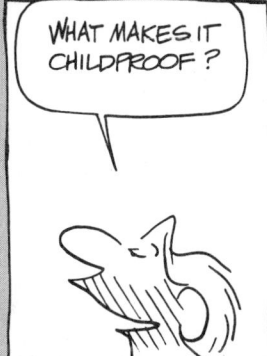

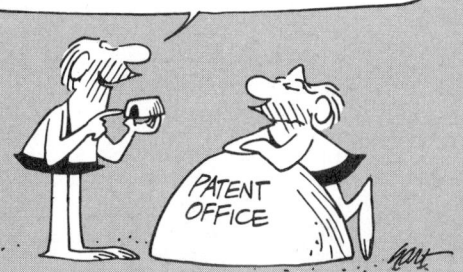

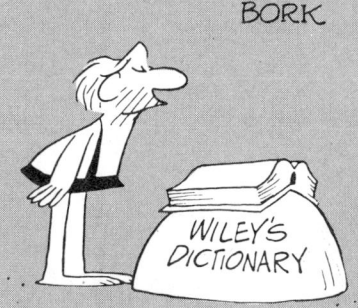

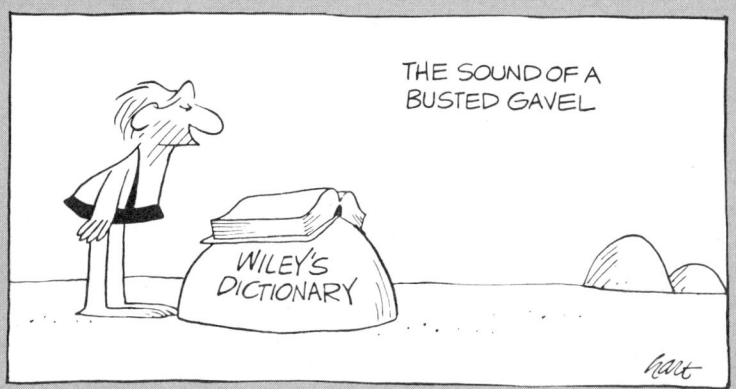

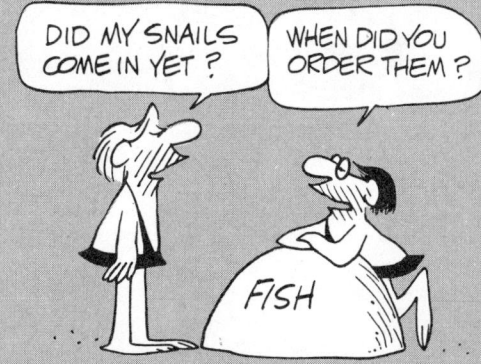

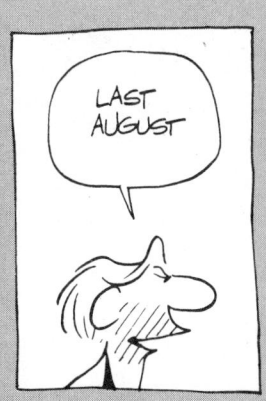

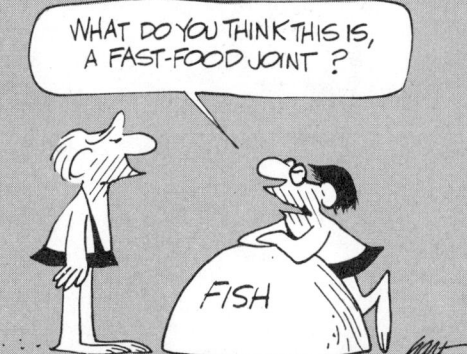

Dear Fat Broad,
my husband insists on eating his soup with a fork. what can I do ?
ADVICE COLUMN
START HIM OFF 3 HOURS AHEAD OF THE OTHERS.
ADVICE COLUMN
hart

HERE'S A SURE-FIRE LURE FOR YOU.
CLUMSY'S BAIT SHOP
...ONCE INFLATED, IT WHISTLES SEDUCTIVE LITTLE FISH TUNES.
WHAT SHOULD I USE TO BLOW IT UP ?
GOSH, I DONT KNOW....HOW 'BOUT A HAND GRENADE ?
CLUMSY'S BAIT SHOP
hart

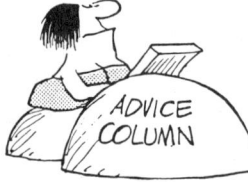

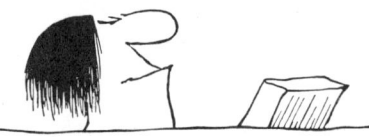

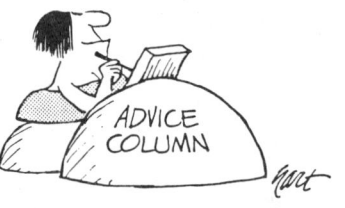

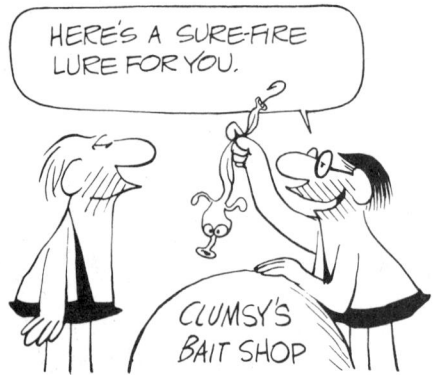

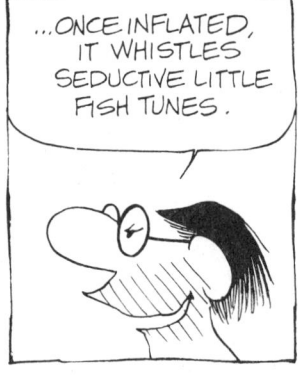

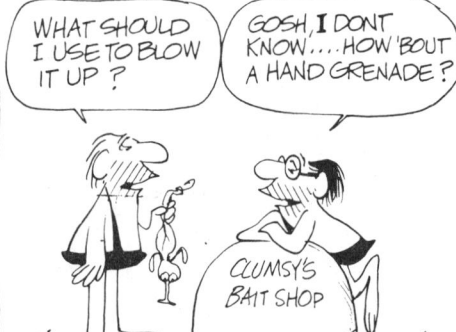

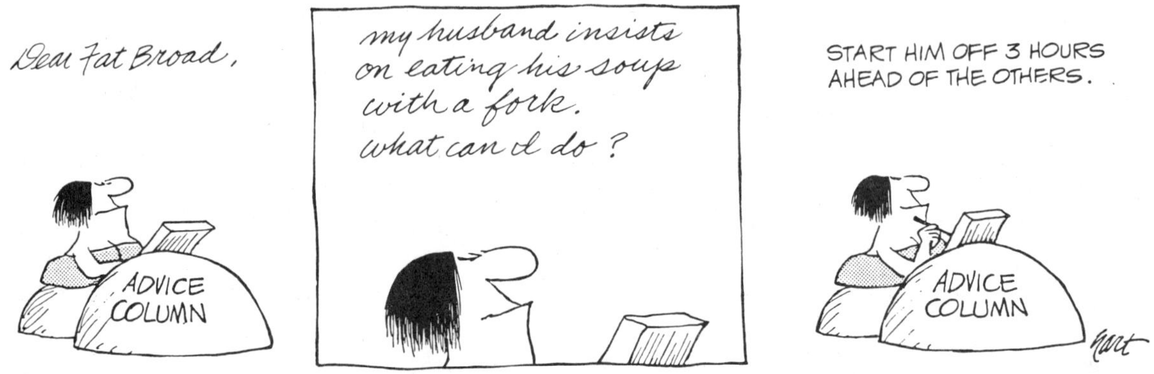

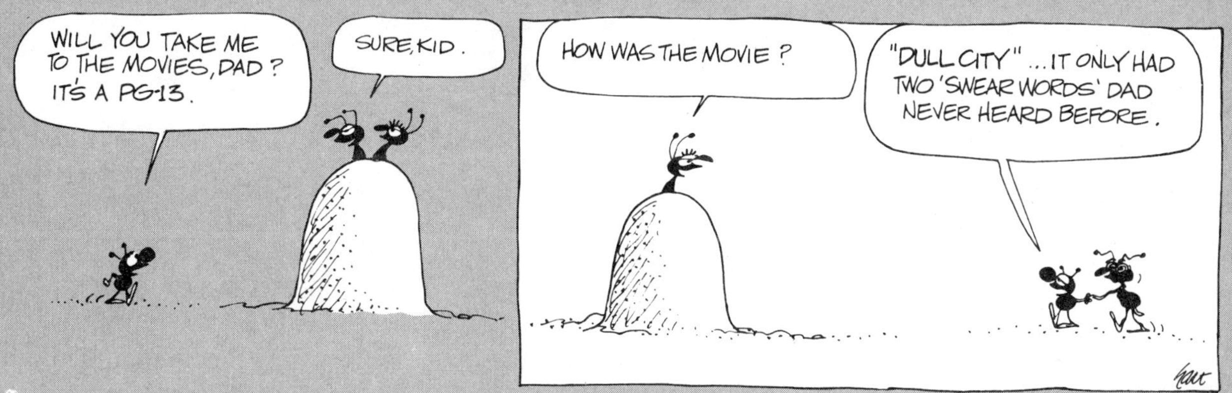
WILL YOU TAKE ME TO THE MOVIES, DAD? IT'S A PG-13.
SURE, KID.
HOW WAS THE MOVIE?
"DULL CITY"...IT ONLY HAD TWO 'SWEAR WORDS' DAD NEVER HEARD BEFORE.

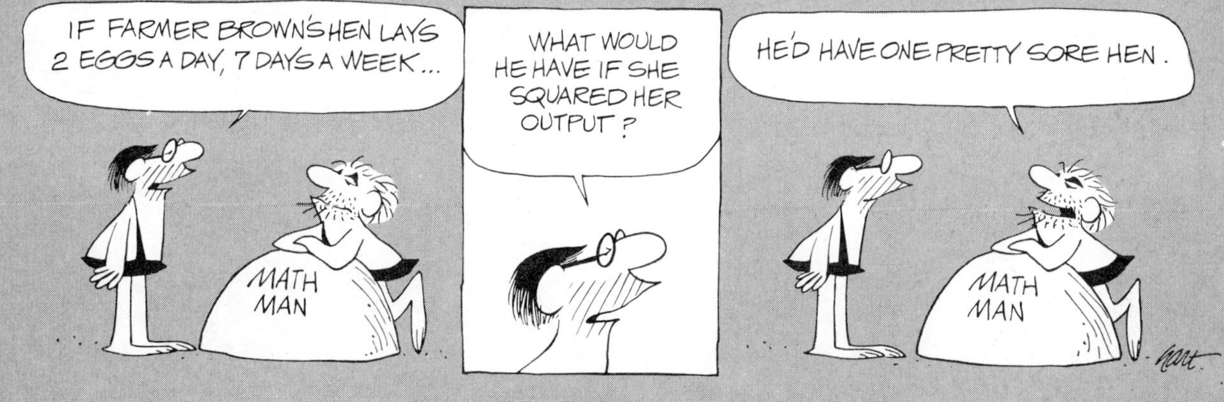
IF FARMER BROWN'S HEN LAYS 2 EGGS A DAY, 7 DAYS A WEEK...
MATH MAN
WHAT WOULD HE HAVE IF SHE SQUARED HER OUTPUT?
HE'D HAVE ONE PRETTY SORE HEN.
MATH MAN

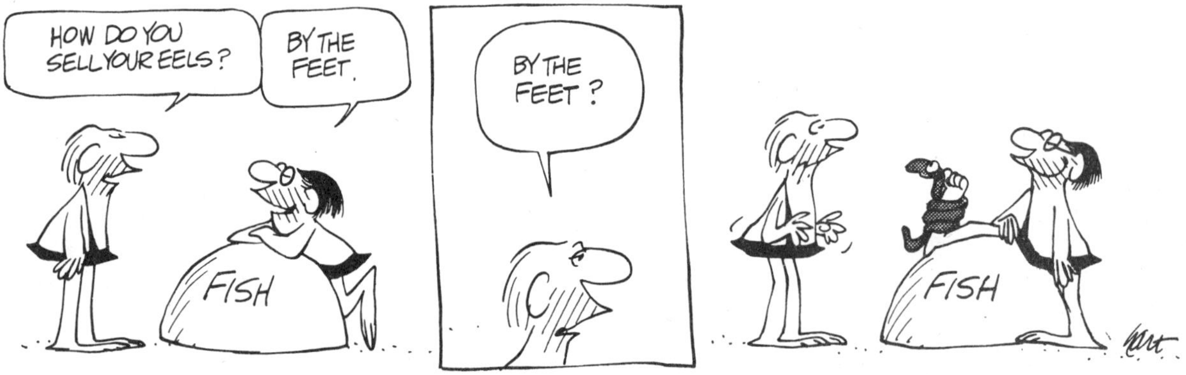
HOW DO YOU SELL YOUR EELS?
BY THE FEET.
BY THE FEET?
FISH
FISH

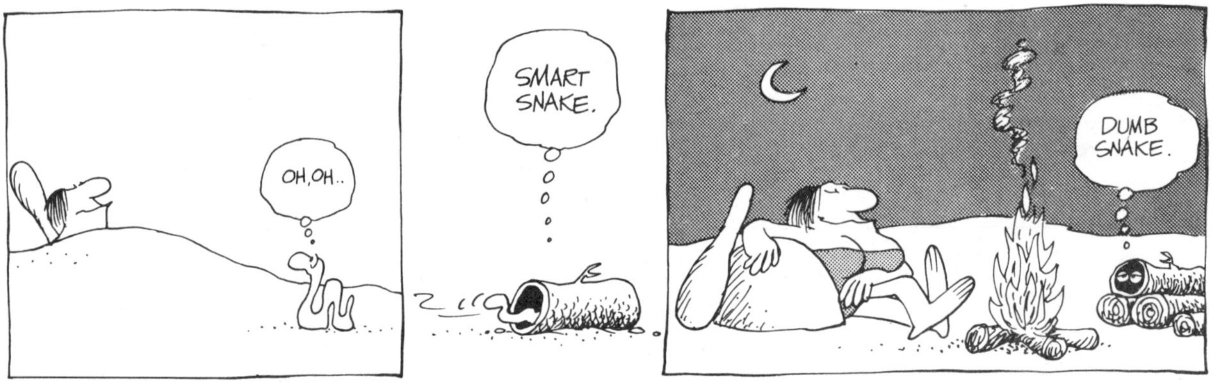
OH, OH..
SMART SNAKE.
DUMB SNAKE.

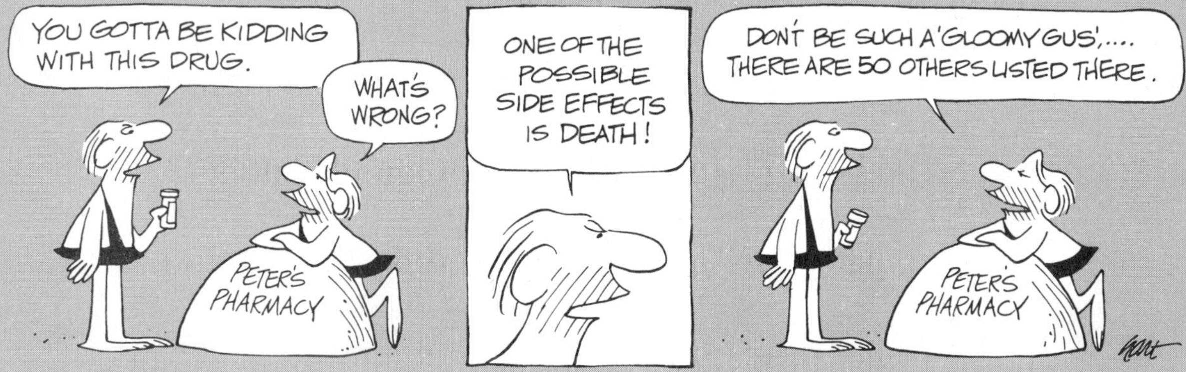
YOU GOTTA BE KIDDING WITH THIS DRUG.
WHAT'S WRONG?
PETER'S PHARMACY
ONE OF THE POSSIBLE SIDE EFFECTS IS DEATH!
DON'T BE SUCH A 'GLOOMY GUS',.... THERE ARE 50 OTHERS LISTED THERE.
PETER'S PHARMACY

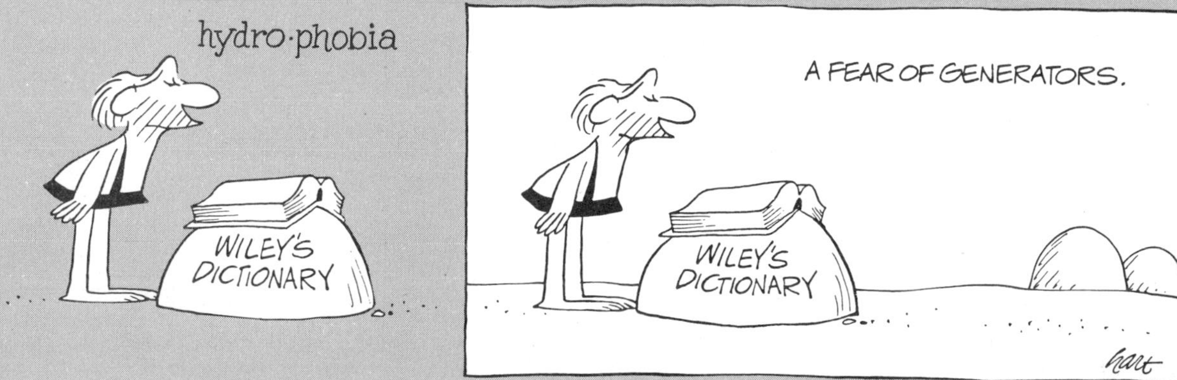
hydro·phobia
WILEY'S DICTIONARY
A FEAR OF GENERATORS.
WILEY'S DICTIONARY

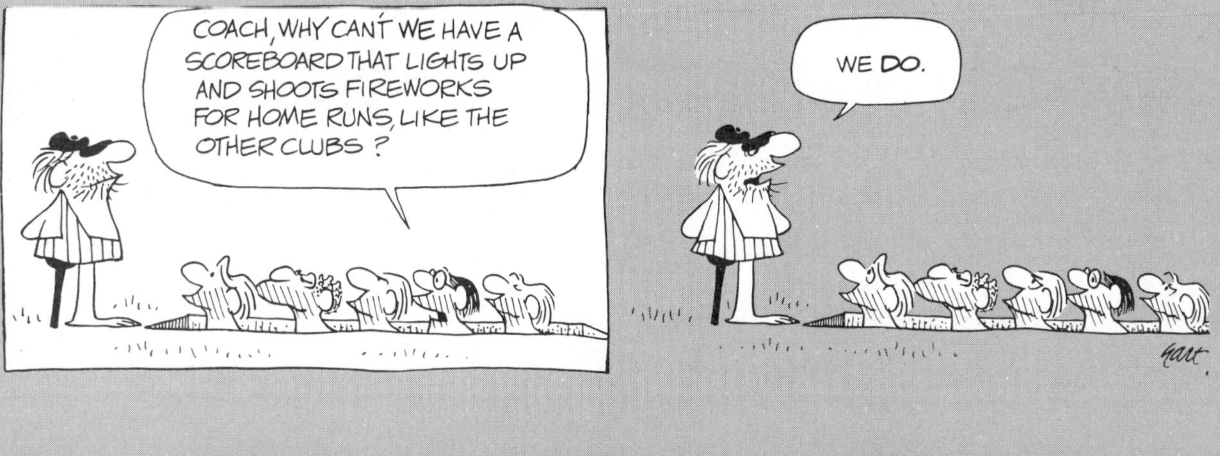
COACH, WHY CAN'T WE HAVE A SCOREBOARD THAT LIGHTS UP AND SHOOTS FIREWORKS FOR HOME RUNS, LIKE THE OTHER CLUBS?
WE DO.

AH... WHAT'S THAT ?
PICKLED DINOSAUR KNUCKLES.
I PLAN TO GIVE EVERYONE A JAR FOR CHRISTMAS !
THAT OUGHTA DO IT.

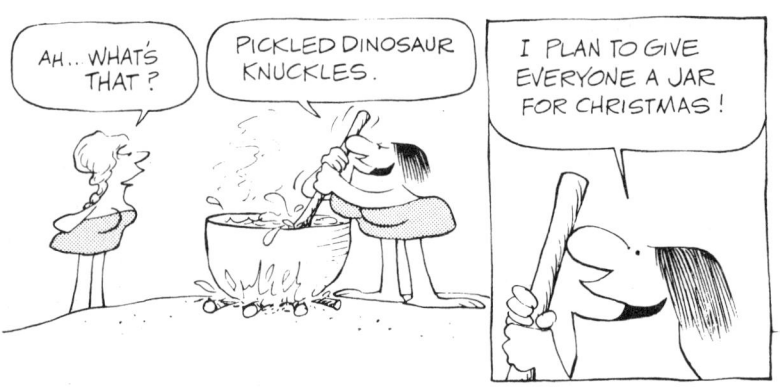

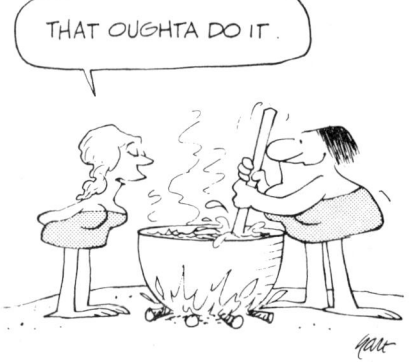

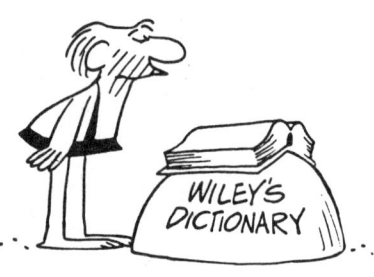

KISHU, HATCHU AND HUISHI
WILEY'S DICTIONARY
THE 3 MOST POPULAR JAPANESE SNEEZES
WILEY'S DICTIONARY

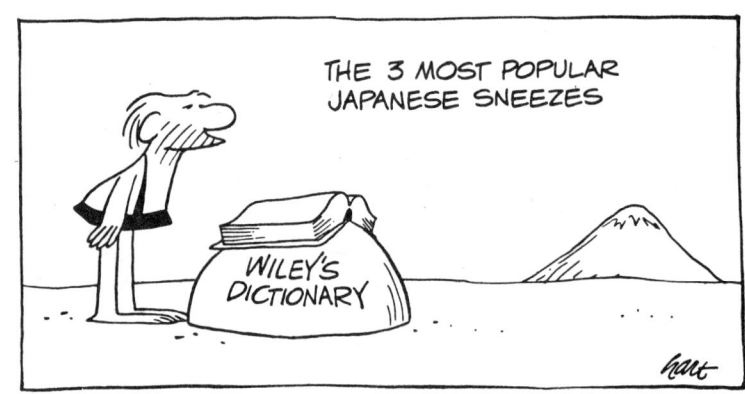

WHAT MEASURES ARE YOU TAKING TO STRENGTHEN YOUR BULLPEN THIS YEAR ?
I'VE BEEN THINKING ALONG THE LINES OF A CHAIN LINK FENCE .

GOT ANY AFRICAN LOBSTER ?
ONE CAME IN THIS MORNING
FISH
FRESH OR FROZEN ?
FRESH
HOW CAN IT BE FRESH ?
THEY KEEL-HAULED THE SUCKER, ALL THE WAY FROM MADAGASCAR .
FISH

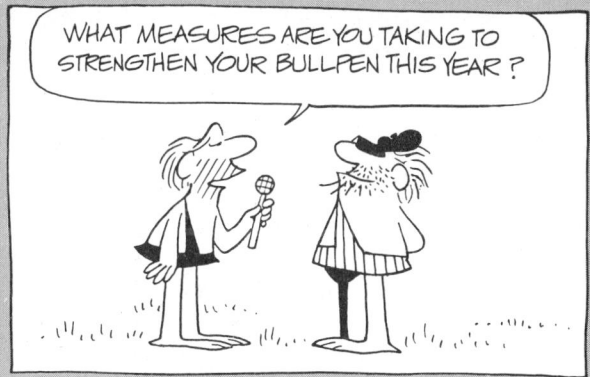

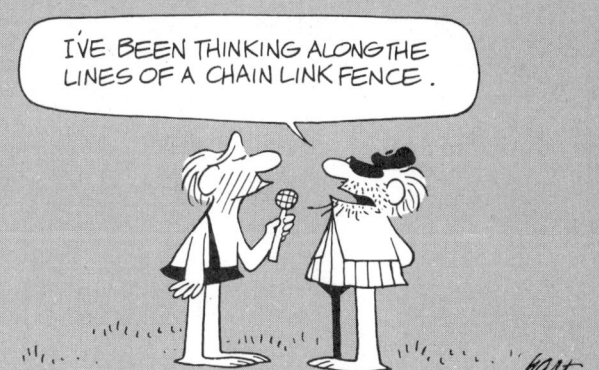

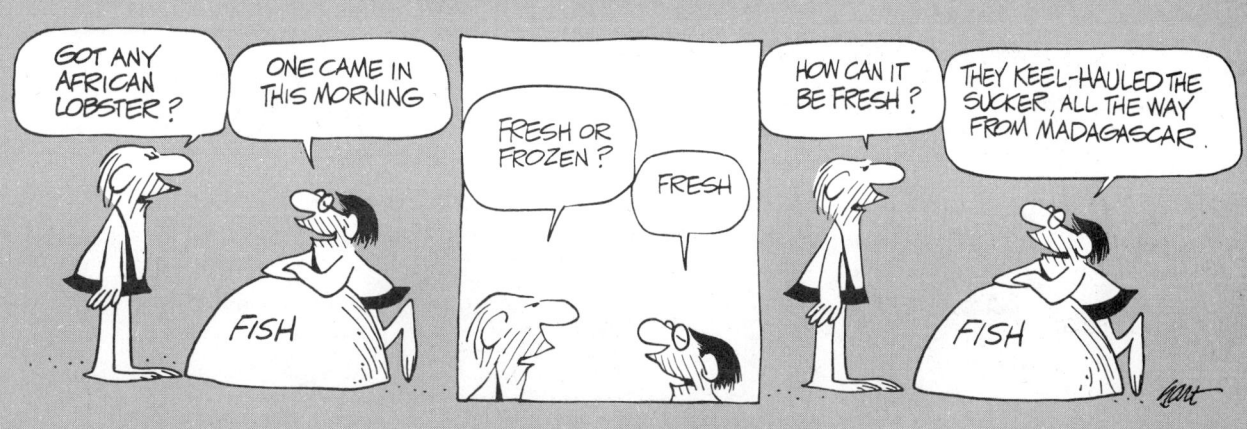

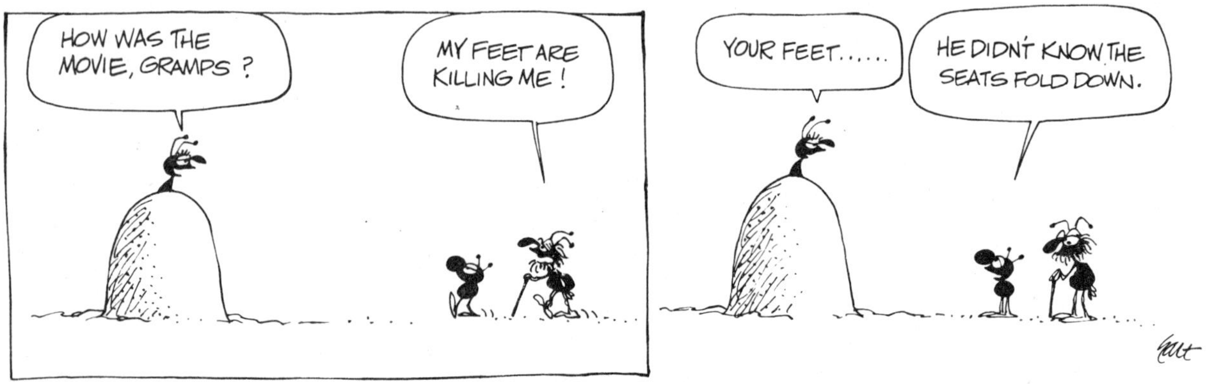
HOW WAS THE MOVIE, GRAMPS ?
MY FEET ARE KILLING ME !
YOUR FEET.....
HE DIDN'T KNOW THE SEATS FOLD DOWN.
hart

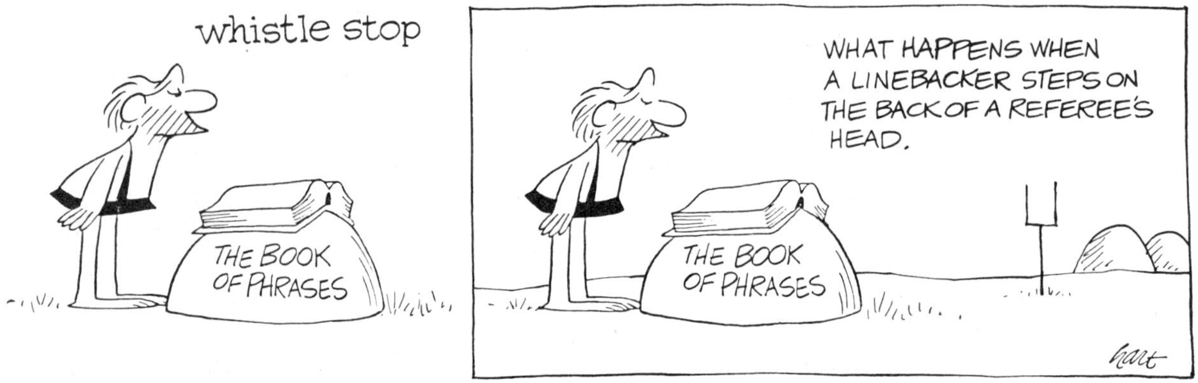
whistle stop
THE BOOK OF PHRASES
WHAT HAPPENS WHEN A LINEBACKER STEPS ON THE BACK OF A REFEREE'S HEAD.
THE BOOK OF PHRASES
hart

" SIX OF ONE AND A HALF DOZEN OF THE OTHER ."
THE BOOK OF PHRASES
AN APPPOPRIATE WAY TO ORDER A DOZEN APPLES AND ORANGES .
THE BOOK OF PHRASES
hart

THIS IS OUR HUMANE MODEL. ... NO HOOKS !
CLUMSY'S BAIT SHOP
HOW DOES IT WORK ?
IT DON'T. THAT'S WHAT MAKES IT SO HUMANE .
CLUMSY'S BAIT SHOP
hart

IF YOU COULD LEGISLATE A NEW RULE FOR BASEBALL, WHAT WOULD IT BE ?
TO STOP OUR FANS FROM PUTTING THOSE PAPER BAGS OVER THEIR HEADS .
hart

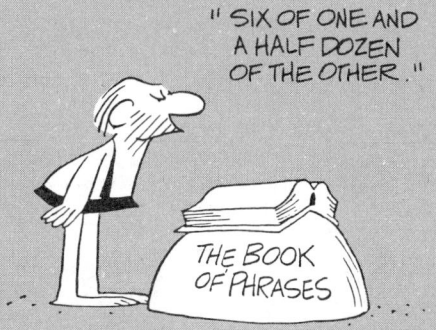

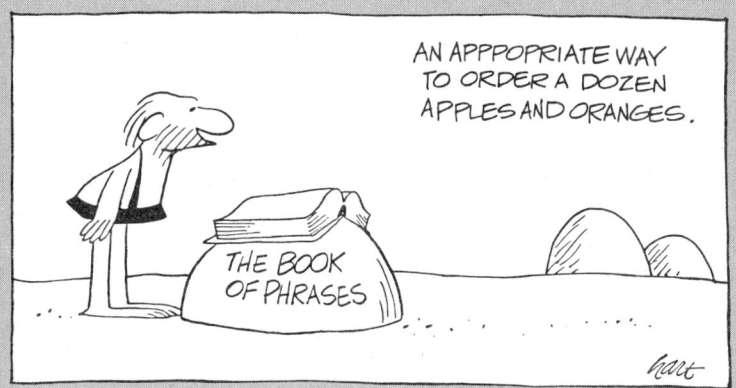

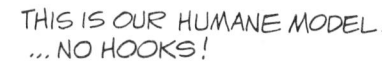

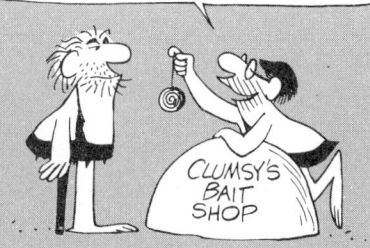

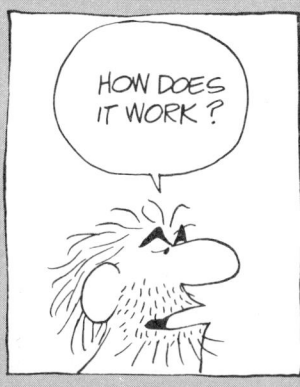

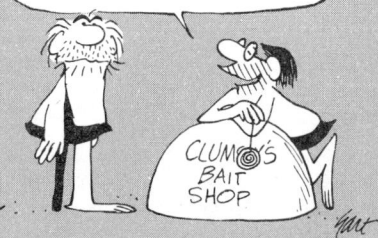

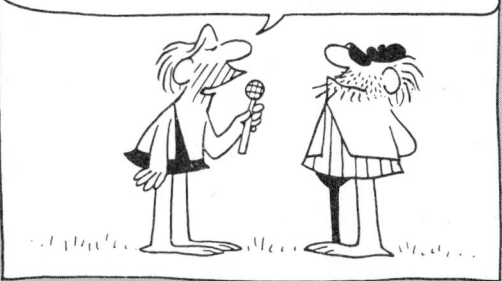

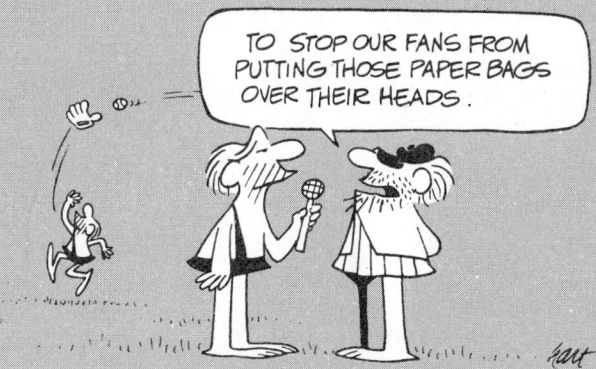

WHAT HAPPENED?
PLASTIC SURGERY.
...THEY LOWERED MY EARS.
WOULDN'T IT HAVE BEEN CHEAPER TO GET A HAIRCUT?
hart

...YOU CAN MAKE MY BAD LEG LOOK LIKE THE GOOD ONE?
GUARANTEED!
DR. PETER
PLASTIC SURGEON
...THEN THE SUCKER PULLS OUT THIS CAN OF PLASTIC SPRAY PAINT....
hart

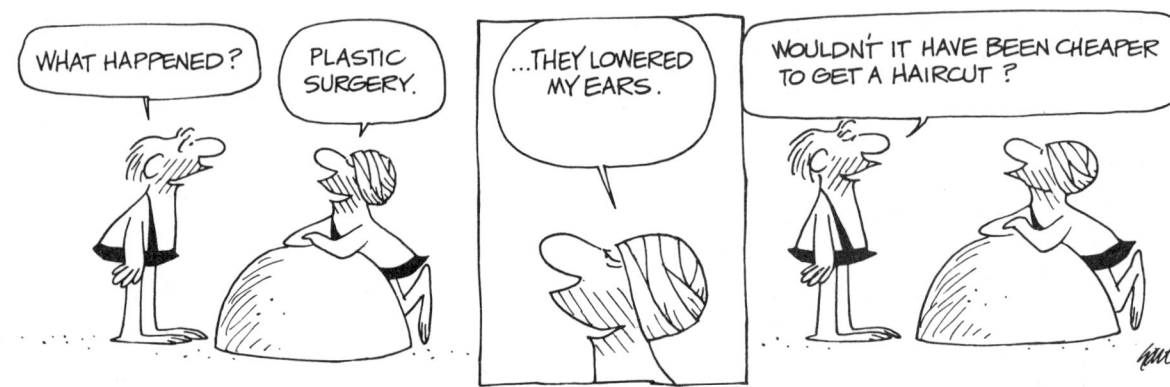

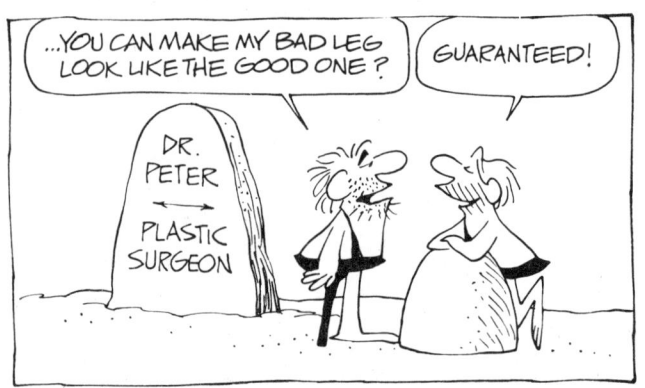

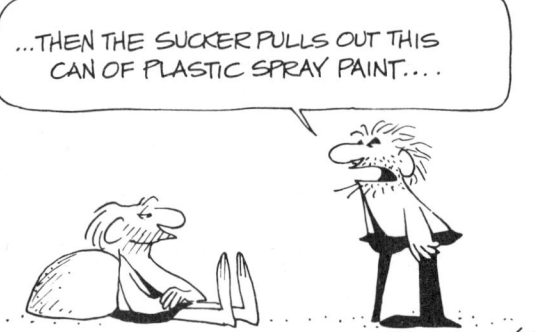

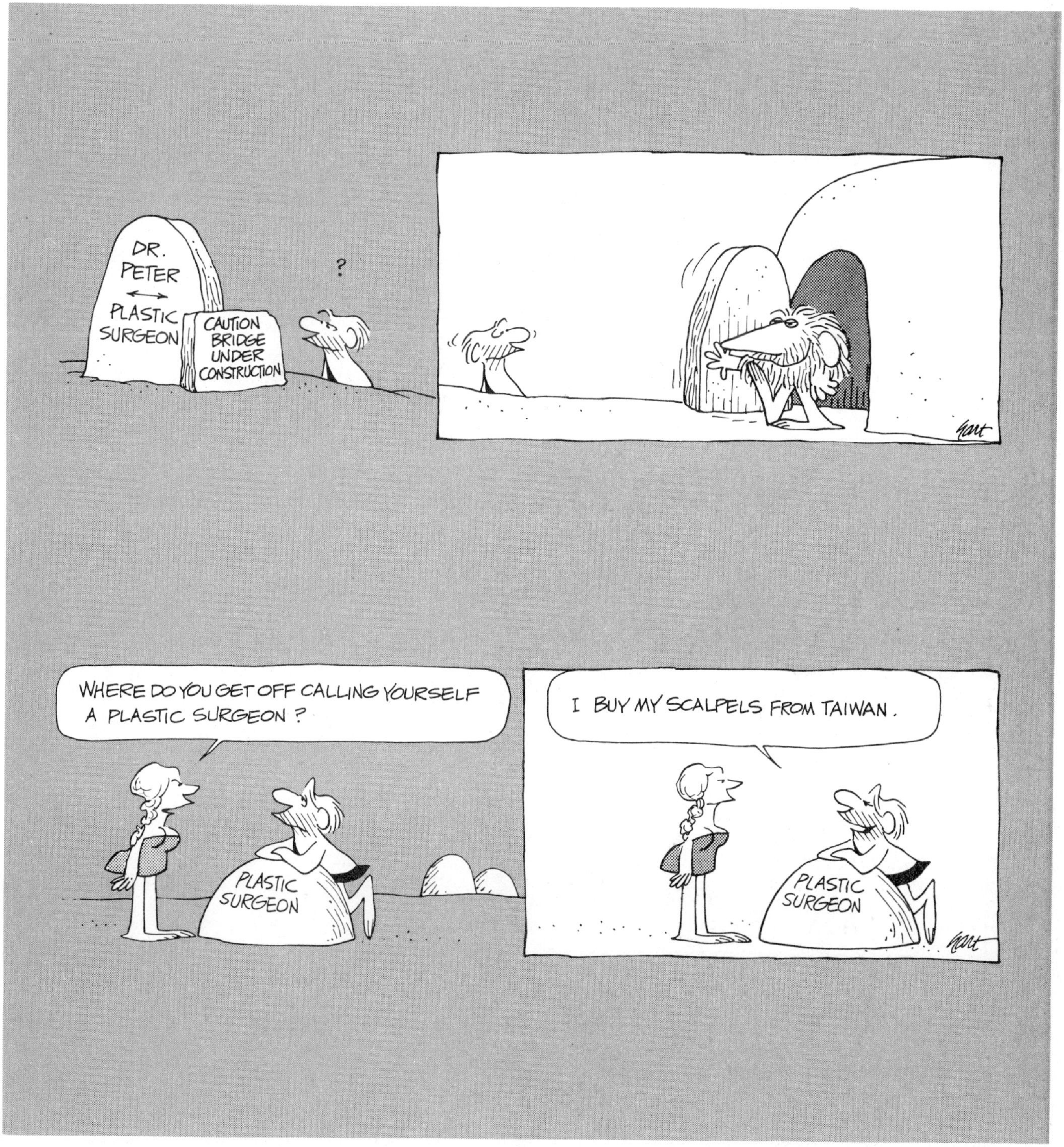
DR. PETER ↔ PLASTIC SURGEON
CAUTION BRIDGE UNDER CONSTRUCTION
?
WHERE DO YOU GET OFF CALLING YOURSELF A PLASTIC SURGEON ?
PLASTIC SURGEON
I BUY MY SCALPELS FROM TAIWAN .
PLASTIC SURGEON

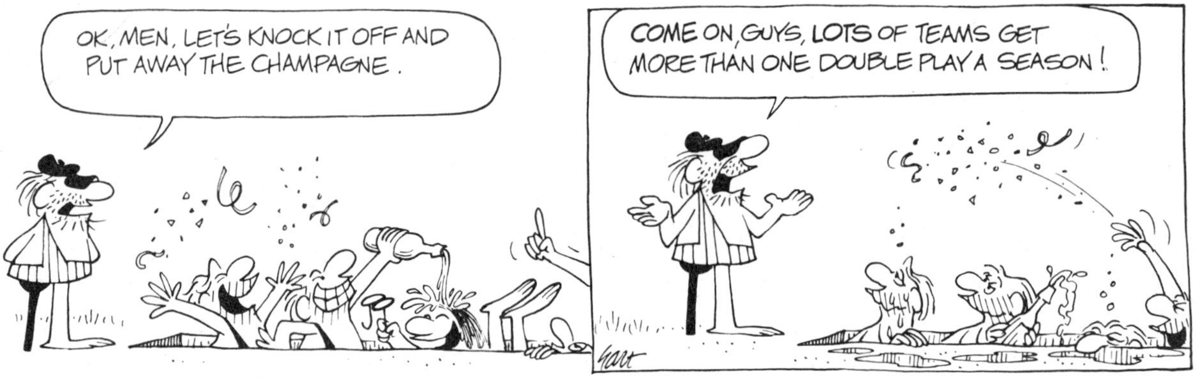
OK, MEN, LET'S KNOCK IT OFF AND PUT AWAY THE CHAMPAGNE.
COME ON, GUYS, LOTS OF TEAMS GET MORE THAN ONE DOUBLE PLAY A SEASON!

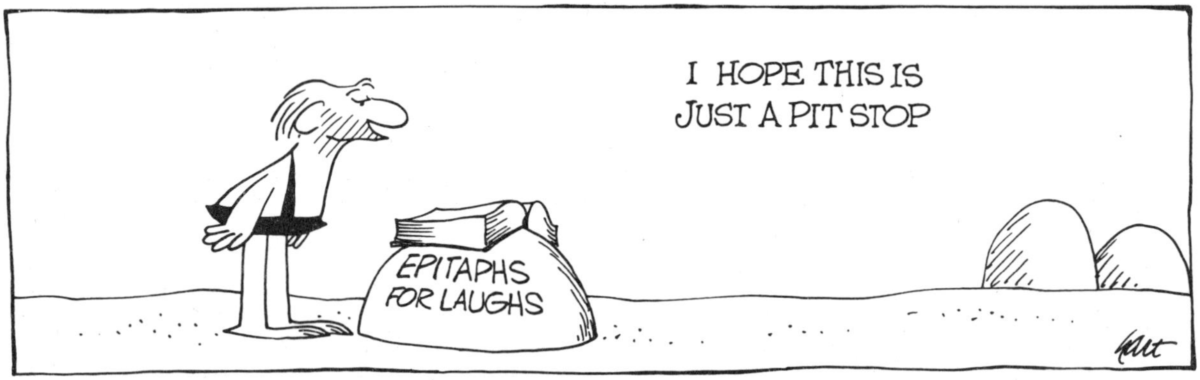
I HOPE THIS IS JUST A PIT STOP
EPITAPHS FOR LAUGHS